Pra

The Wounds That Bind Us

"It is impossible to put down this book. The story of Kelley Shinn's often dangerous but always thrilling and adventurous life will leave you breathless and awed. The courage, compassion, and joy with which Shinn lives her life is inspiring. She is the person every parent would want to see their child grow to be, the mother every kid wishes they had."

—Jessica Anya Blau, author of *Mary Jane*

"This memoir of single motherhood, disability, and an unlikely off-road adventure around the world delivers just what I'm looking for in my reading these days: courage. That, and fine writing, unforgettable characters, suspense, humor, tenderness, and a profound yet humble sense of moral purpose. Kelley Shinn is a marvel, and her book, despite its pain, makes a better world feel possible."

—Belle Boggs, author of *The Art of Waiting: On Fertility, Medicine, and Motherhood*

"*The Wounds That Bind Us* offers perennial relevance in a fresh literary manner. Kelley Shinn invites the reader, the voyeur, the accidental tourist into a world that is a brilliant jewel box of precise, complex, and beautiful turns, with language that bites and soothes the wound in the same stroke. These personal narratives, written with a deliberate genius of craft, usher an arresting memoir that lifts heavy veils and becomes bountiful succor for the parched truths we share."

—Jaki Shelton Green, North Carolina Poet Laureate

"A beautiful book about how the things we love are torn away from us and about the ways we hold on. Shinn is an anatomist of velocity. Thrilling."

—Thomas Beller, author of *J.D. Salinger: The Escape Artist*

The Wounds That Bind Us

KELLEY SHINN

WEST VIRGINIA UNIVERSITY PRESS
MORGANTOWN

ISBN 978-1-952271-86-1 (paperback) / 978-1-952271-87-8 (ebook)

Library of Congress Control Number: 2022049954

Book and cover design by Than Saffel / WVU Press

Portions of this book appeared previously in the following publications: "Airy Nothings," *Fourth Genre: Explorations in Nonfiction* 17, no. 2 (2015): 85–93; "Ebb and Flow," *Cold Mountain Review* (Fall 2012); "I Know Something about Running," *Bayou Magazine* 55 (2011); "Taking Heart," *Blood Orange Review* 6, no. 1 (2011)

For Celie,
the whole universe

I

....

Spring, 2001

"BlanK-it?"

The sound of jets overhead attempts to mute her voice. But I don't need to hear a word from those cherub lips. I see the need in the gloss of her eyes, in the oft-pruned thumb making its way to her mouth.

She was a thumb-sucker in the womb according to multiple ultrasounds.

The blanket came afterward, as did her pronunciation of it, accenting the *k* so hard that it sounded like two words, as if an incantation in which she could blank anything unpleasant from existence. The blanket was a chenille and silk patchwork number that I'd bought at some posh baby boutique when I still thought having a baby was going to be a glorified step-up from dressing up the Cabbage Patch doll I adored as a kid.

"Where's her blanket?" I ask her father.

"Yeah, that," J starts. "It may have gone into the trash."

I shoulder up two carry-ons and take our daughter, Celie,

by the hand. Airports, emergency rooms . . . you have to be on time. J scurries alongside us as we enter JFK.

"What the hell does that mean?" I ask him.

"Well, it may have been on the tray at breakfast, and it may have inadvertently gone into the trash. There were a lot of plates and napkins piled up—they must have camouflaged it. It *was* just a scrap."

I feel an extra dose of heat rising in my head, but all I can do that is beneficial is repurpose the anger into intent. Celie and I are boarding that plane. We are starting over.

BlanK-it is the twin to her thumb, à la Linus Van Pelt in the old Peanuts comic strips, but I tell myself that we have enough resources between the two of us to get her through this plane ride without her blanket that she has doted on since shortly after birth, despite the fact that I am an anxious flyer, and she quit comfort-breastfeeding three months earlier.

"It's called worn thin with love. Did you at least look for it?" I press J. He does not answer. In my head, I say— *You did this on purpose, you passive-aggressive asshole.* It is par for course for J. I was two months pregnant when the all-his-life, safety-first guy decided he wanted to start jumping off mountains with a kite strapped to his back. When I confronted him about my concern that his midlife crisis might leave our child fatherless, he purchased a multi-thousand-dollar, top-of-the-line paraglider and had it delivered to his mother's house instead of ours. We split up about a year later, less because of the paraglider and more because of J's overt affection for the paragliding instructor.

A year after we drifted apart, a wind shear slammed J

and his expensive glider into the side of a mountain. He was lucky to only have some bones replaced with metal rods.

When we arrive at security, Celie and her father are briefly separated from me because I set off the body scanner, like I always do. Both of my legs are prosthetic, have been that way for a near decade at this point, since I lost them to a rare form of bacterial meningitis and sepsis in high school. J's internal rods are a little over a year old, but they go either undetected or unquestioned.

A guard takes a wand and runs it down alongside my body. The wand beeps at just below the knee, and I glance over toward Celie, grateful she isn't old enough to know what is happening with this display of suspicion and wondering if her father is embarrassed by it. I pull up a pant leg and show the guard one fake leg, ask him if he wants me to remove it. Like every guard before him, he gives a hasty no, and sends me on my way. In college, I used to hide marijuana in a little hole I drilled in the bottom of the prosthetic socket. One little intelligence chip would have been just as easy to hide. *One little intelligence chip sold to Russia and I could retire for life,* I think, *and the guards would be so overwhelmed by the concept of mortality in someone so young, they'd never even think to look for it.*

When we hit the auto-walk, Celie and I quickly gain distance from her father. We are moving forward. We maintain a lead until we arrive at the final gate. It is a quick goodbye. J throws one arm of his weight around Celie's neck and it wraps like a strand of DNA all the way around her belly and onto her lower back. His eyes gloss. Mine, too. J and I kiss each other on the cheek, and I want to slap him and make love to him at the same time. And because Celie is the physical representation of our union, our real-and-lingering though divided love, her eyes swell with the weight of tears, too, but not for long, because she is only three years old, and she has never been on an airplane before.

We hand over our boarding passes, walk down the corridor, and do not look back.

The takeoff startles us both. Celie's mouth is working hard on her thumb, and when I see her reach instinctively for the blanket she loved to a scrap and that her father threw in the hotel lobby trash can this morning, I quickly put my hand in its place. It takes longer for love and need to wear down flesh and bones.

Celie presses her face against the window. I can barely breathe. I do not like to fly, though I've flown probably fifty times. I especially do not care for ascents and descents because I know they are the most dangerous part of the flight, and the last flight I took a few years earlier ended with an emergency landing in which one passenger broke an arm and the child sitting next to me vomited on my lap. Plus, my prosthetic legs are like conductors of metallic energy, and it's as if I can feel every judder of the massive nut-and-bolt operation flying through the sky, and I know how far we have to fall if something goes awry.

Once we are steady in the air, and as long as there isn't any insane turbulence, I can assuage myself with falsehoods of infallible optimism and a baby bottle of wine. This flight is no different, except that it is the first one I've taken with my child.

The plane steadies and starts out over the Atlantic—Celie remains in quiet awe. The seatbelt sign goes off, and I ask for the bottle of wine. The stewardess asks if the young lady would like a Shirley Temple. Celie's never had the ginger ale and grenadine mocktail before. I've been careful not to inundate my child's body with sugar, unlike my mother who gives her junk food on every visit as if to defy me, but I've come to understand that the saccharine tokens my mother feeds her are representative of her knowledge of bestowing love. I say yes.

This is the beginning of a grand adventure, after all.

I can understand why J's mother and my mother think I've lost my mind. Probably a few others do as well, but they are too polite to say anything. It's not every day that a single mother in her late twenties, without legs, decides to drive around the world visiting former war zones in a Land Rover with her young daughter in tow.

My off-roading buddies don't think me a lick of crazy. I delved into that world just before Celie turned a year. I was living in the Appalachian region of Virginia at the time, and a friend took me for a mountain excursion in an old Land Rover. I was hooked from the moment we got stuck in a mud hole and had to use a winch to get out. The scent of mountain clay mixed with lilacs abloom was heady.

Just weeks before my legs were amputated I'd been offered a college scholarship for cross-country and track. I'd started running regularly when I was nine, mostly away from my mother's ire. It wasn't long before I realized that

I was not only fast enough to keep my mother at bay, but I could go a long distance before I was spent, and I began to cherish dawn runs on the trails in the metropolitan parks near my childhood home. I knew every root and dip of those trails, knew where and when the blackberries would show up, knew when to pick up my speed and jump up to clutch a sassafras leaf. I'd suck the stem for the last mile or so before I went home to get ready for school.

After my legs were cut just under the knees, I thought all of that joy was lost, that is until I found that I could still roam through the glories of the forest with a diesel engine. Who knew that a four-wheel-drive vehicle could be a satisfactory replacement for flesh, bone, and blood?

One off-road excursion in the mountains led me to buying 4×4 magazines, and soon after, a used Land Rover. Then I started competing at off-roading rallies. And I was good. Same as in a plane, I can feel the articulations of the vehicle through my prosthetic legs, only I'm not afraid so long as the wheels are on the ground—or at least most of them. I got to know that transmission so well, that I could change gears without using the clutch—just by the vibrations I felt through my leg.

My father, a mechanic, rigged a car seat with a heavy-duty belting system so that Celie could go off-roading with me. Four-wheel drive lulled her to sleep every time. The minute I transferred the vehicle into gear, BlanK-it and thumb would also engage, and she was out in moments. I could be climbing a boulder, crossing through a riverbed, or cutting a pass at a forty-degree angle, and that baby girl would snore soundly, but the minute I turned off the ignition, her eyes would open, and she'd smile widely at me in the rearview mirror as if she'd just woken from an epic dream.

When Celie was nearing two, I packed her in the Land Rover and spent four months driving across the country from Virginia to California and back, trying to find myself again after the pain of leaving J, trying to remember my own strength. Celie and I spent evenings camping under the stars, next to the Land Rover, which I'd named Athena. We hit all the known off-roading locales north and south of Route 66.

One night, near Moab, where the desert terrain had no artificial lighting, the stars were so thick and illuminated that they looked like a celestial city. That's the night I started pointing out the constellations to Celie. They were all so easy to see out there—the Big Dipper, Orion, Cassiopeia, Andromeda, the bull, bears, ram and swan, the lyre.

Celie was tireless that evening after having slept a lot of the day while I traversed rock bridges and cliffs. She wanted to know the story of everything in the heavens. She wanted to write her own versions, too. Just before she finally nodded off that evening, she declared that "Cassiopeia and Andromeda are the Mama and Baby Girl of the night sky. Orion is their hunter who protects them and brings them food. Mostly, they play music on the lyre while their friend the swan dances."

That was the same night I had the dream in which Zeus came to me with lightning bolt in hand and told me that I was going to drive around the world. My paternal grandmother was Greek, and I was a classical studies major in college—so it has been ingrained in me to never question Zeus. Plus, I'd read in the 4×4 mags about folks who'd traveled the globe in Land Rovers and got as energized by those stories as I used to get by reading the stories of that fierce orphan Pippi Longstocking who I discovered right about the time I started to run.

Pippi was fabulous, had an endless supply of witty remarks, but my favorite, which I wrote at the top of every new journal I started as a kid was "Don't let them get you down. Be naughty and wild and wonderful." By the time dawn broke the next morning, I was envisioning myself with Pippi-like braids in my hair, standing at the edge of the Parthenon, Celie's hand in one of mine, and a machete in the other—ready to take on the world.

Almost a year later, and Celie and I are now on a plane to England, where we will live for a year before we travel the globe. I got a gig as an off-road instructor with a Land Rover crew, and instead of getting paid, I'm going to learn from the people I read about in the magazines about how to be successful at transglobal travel.

See, I have not lost my mind.

The Shirley Temple is a hit, but not as much as the paper parasol that comes resting on the edge of the plastic cup. Celie twirls it delightedly between her hands, then pauses to stare at the diminutive floral designs with an obvious appreciation for the care and detail that has gone into something so tiny. The wine is not such a hit. It's warm and slightly sour, but it will do the trick.

I can tell by the fidgeting of her feet that Celie is about to hit sugar buzz status. I grab a bag from the overhead compartment and retrieve her colored pencils and paper pad.

"What should I draw?" she asks.

"Draw the umbrella," I tell her. "Draw whatever you see."

She loves to draw. Her stick figure limbs began to flesh out and curve before she turned two. She'll spend hours illustrating a scene and recounting it back to me, and it always surprises me how accurate the drawings are with the story she's imagined. Her brows furrow, she chooses her color, and hits the paper. I return to hitting the baby bottle of wine.

J's mother is from Germany, so we refer to her as Oma. Oma hasn't been keen on me from the start. Oma and J's father are both preachers, and I was fresh off a divorce when I met J. I lived in a fancy house in Appalachia then, near the college I attended, and Oma thought I took the man I married for his money and was afraid I was out to do the same with J, but that couldn't have been farther from the truth.

I was married for less than a year, and six months of that was spent in legal separation. I hit some profound potholes on the looking-for-love road after having my nubile body carved up to save my life, some of which I couldn't get out of without a metaphorical winch.

At nineteen, I won a three-year lawsuit against the hospital where I was initially misdiagnosed, which gave me some financial independence that I never would have had as a working-class girl from Akron, Ohio. Because I had been a promising young runner, there were a lot of stories about me in the media during the three years of legal wrangling. The man I married was twenty years my senior, had been married more than once, had declared bankruptcy a year earlier, and had read all about me before we met. And since I wasn't yet convinced anyone would love me physically after I'd had my legs cut off and large portions of my body scarred, it didn't take me long to fall for his steady affection—and to excitedly declare to my family that a man I barely knew wanted me to be his wife.

Somehow, the world I grew up in, but to which I did not naturally ascribe, thought you were worthier of love and respect if a man took you to be his wife. Before my legs were cut off, when I was still in Pippi-mode, I felt an aversion to the "took" part, and I had zero knowledge yet of the woman-as-property origins of marriage, of disproportionate benefits given to men for scoring a wife.

After the amputations, specifically after I overheard a preacher at my bedside say that I had a beautiful face and that some godly man would find it in his heart to choose me as a wife, marriage almost seemed a challenge. That was before I healed from the physical trauma and the changes of puberty filled my blood and the desire to join flesh became a pulsating constant—then I thought of that preacher's comment in a way that was less of a challenge, but more of a sorrow. Would it be that difficult to find someone who wanted to touch me and explore the excitement of springtime with me? Did I have to wait for a godly man when some of the godliest men I revered in the church of my youth, including that preacher, turned out to be adulterers and perverts?

The man I married only referenced god at his AA meetings. And one day, mere months after we were married at the ocean's edge, a policeman showed up at the front door of the fancy house I'd bought for us to live in happily ever after, declaring that my prince was way behind in child support on a child I did not know existed. We argued. He hit me. I walked away. I realize that if he had held the purse strings, I may not have been so easily able to make such a choice, but if he had held the purse strings, he'd never have pursued me anyhow. In the end, I had to pay a considerable chunk of money to the conman I married—the conman who punched me in the back down a set of stairs—just to be rid of him, even with a prenup. That was the first time I had the notion that I was living in a world eager to conform me to something other than my naughty, wild, and wonderful self. Zeus, Christ, and all of those that claim to speak the words of gods began to become questionable.

I was a bit jaded by the time I met J, but he was so lovely and kind and funny it was hard to ignore him. I was trying to focus on college, but he made it hard. He came from old wealth, so I wasn't wary of his intentions. We simply and truly fell in love, and we knew how to laugh. How can you not fall in love with a man who takes an empty tampon tube from your bathroom cupboard, fiddles with it for a few moments, and then plays the German national anthem on it for you?

If the fact that I was a sullied divorcée wasn't bad enough, J's mother wasn't real keen on my disability. Though I was unaware of it then, the Americans with Disabilities Act was passed into law the exact same month I became disabled. The legal rights and hopes of differently abled humans to be considered equal was and still is an uphill battle. When J and I told his parents at lunch one day that we'd decided to move in together, Oma spoke of me in the third person even though I was sitting across from her. "J, have you truly considered all of this? Do you not understand that she will one day require you to take care of her physically?"

And when a year later, we discovered we were pregnant, we called Oma on the speaker phone at my mother's house to announce the good news. My mother was present and thrilled about the prospect of a first grandchild. Plus, she loved J. After J told his mother, there was a pause. He asked if she had heard him. "Yes, and I wish I hadn't," she replied. "I consider it a tragedy that this woman will be the mother of your child." If my mother could have punched his mother right in the nose, right through the phone line, she would have done so.

Needless to say, my working-class, high school–dropout mother did not get on well with J's well-educated and cultured mother, especially after that biting comment. But one thing they both agreed on is that there should be no more dilly-dallying. J and I had to get married before the baby arrived. Certainly, we did not want our child to be a "bastard."

Technically, a bastard is a child born to unwed parents, but orphans and bastards all belong to the same ilk historically in that they were considered a stain/burden on society at large. When Astrid Lindgren created Pippi Longstocking and Xavier Roberts created the Cabbage Patch Kid, I like to think they were part of the forces working to disprove that stereotype—not so much because I found myself pregnant and unwed, but because I was also both an orphan and a bastard.

I spent nearly the first year of my life in an orphanage. I used to make up stories about my parents endlessly as a child, much like Pippi Longstocking did—which is why, as a child, I felt as if that redheaded, misunderstood, nine-year-old spoke directly to my heart. I slept with those tales under my pillow. The pages of that book were as threadbare as BlanK-it would one day be.

Although I've never met her, I do know that my biological mother was a young teenager—one of the 1.5 million unwed mothers who "went away" in the decades between WWII and Roe v. Wade. She spent time in a home for unwed mothers, and like all of the young women in those homes, she was forced into a situation of relinquishment through shame and a lack of resources. To be unwed and pregnant in that era was considered a psychological issue, one that would render the mother an incapable parent. Although I was borne from a legacy of abandonment and shame, and afterward used as a commodity, I chose to see myself as someone with a kind, if impish, heart, someone, like everyone, with their own particular gift to offer the world. I had all the hope of the young who haven't been tarnished, and I held on to that like BlanK-it, too.

Following my long illness and recovery, a doctor said

that it was unlikely I would ever be able to bear children, yet there I was, confirmed to be knocked up by a pee test at a doctor's office. I'd never really thought of motherhood, though I did dote on that childhood Cabbage Patch doll with a longing I can only explain as affirmation. Finding out that I was going to have a baby gave me a sense of fulfillment I had not yet known—to be able to love and nurture a being in the best way I knew how, and the chance to know a being that was related to me by blood, to have what everyone around me referred to as "family." My adoptive family did their best to include me, to try and make me feel like part of the fold, but they were just as quick to throw out an adage like "blood is thicker than water," which reminded me that I would always be adrift.

And while I learned to drift well in the natural world, finding my own strength in the unknown jungles and seas, I felt like the child growing inside me was a boat that could take me to the shore of belonging. But to the acting grandmothers of my impending child, I checked all the boxes of the larger cultural voice for an unfit mother: Disabled. Check. Immoral. Check. Bastard. Check.

In one of the tales of Pippi, she walks by a beauty store. There is a sign in the window that reads *Do you suffer from freckles?* She marches into the store and tells the woman behind the counter *"No."* The woman, not understanding her, asks her to explain.

"No, I don't suffer from freckles," said Pippi.

The lady finally understood. Then she happened to glance at Pippi and exclaimed: "But dear child, your whole face is covered in freckles!"

"That's right," said Pippi. "But they don't bother me. I like them! Good morning to you!"

I was rather like Pippi being oblivious to the concept that her society had deemed freckles something of which to be ashamed. As much as I may have desired to please both J's mother and my own, I wasn't going to, so I turned away to create a new path, one that involved driving around the world with their granddaughter. In essence, I was saying that I did not and would not suffer from being a disabled, immoral bastard. I like who I am, freckles and all. Good day to you both.

When I was seven months pregnant, my extended family went on a vacation to the beach. I was getting quite big in the belly by then, but it didn't stop me from feeling the estrogen-inspired gloriousness of mothers-to-be. I wore a bikini at the beach every day. One day, a man spent a lot of the afternoon pretending not to stare at me. I imagined myself, with my pin-leg prosthetics, like the turkey float in the Macy's Thanksgiving Day Parade, floating above it all, grand.

J went for a run on the beach every morning. One night, he asked if I wanted to go walk with him on the beach when we woke up. The weight of the pregnancy was making it difficult for me to go long distances without more pain than normal on my stumps. I didn't want him to sacrifice his run for me. We'd brought my old wheelchair, which I rarely used, and J said he'd push me on the firm sand near the water's edge while he jogged.

I wore a linen dress, and the ocean air was so delightful,

and J carried my wheelchair out to the shoreline, and when we got to the firmest sand I sat down, and he began to run. My hair blew back on his belly and every now and again, I'd throw my neck back to feel the sun on my face and he'd bend down and kiss my forehead. Then suddenly, he stopped.

"Is it too hard to push me?" I asked J. "We aren't too far out yet, I can walk back," I offered.

Then he came around in front of me, knelt down into the sand on one knee, presented a diamond ring, and asked to marry me. It was such a stunning proposal, I couldn't say no, but I had a caveat. I'd been attending a woman's college for nearly two years at that point. I'd been learning a lot about the history of women. And though I'd been bitten and felt a bit twice-shy, I mostly just refused to be a shotgun bride. I told J that yes, I would marry him, but only after our child was born. That did not go over well with our mothers.

When Celie was born, we both nearly died from complications. I labored for fifty-two hours. She was a large baby, breech, and the umbilical cord was wrapped snugly around her neck. Although I'd hired a doula and a midwife and wanted so much to have my firstborn in the bathtub at home, we ended up at the hospital with an emergency caesarean.

When all the crises were averted, they wheeled me to a room where J's parents and my parents and grandmother were all waiting to meet Celie. When the nurse laid our daughter in my arms, none of the pain that preceded her birth—not the physical labor or the emotional turmoil from the family—mattered one bit; she was the perfect manifestation of anything I had ever learned about gods or love. She was the precious breath of life.

J leaned over us, cradling us both in his arms. His parents leaned in around him on one side of the hospital bed, while my elders leaned in on the other. There was a gentle silence, but then J started weeping. His mother stroked his back and asked him if he was okay. And J said, "Yes, I am. It's just that . . . it's just that . . . isn't she the most beautiful bastard you've ever seen?"

I have never loved him more than in that moment.

Celie wants another Shirley Temple, but I don't give in this time. Instead, I ask her to tell me the story of her drawing. The umbrella is obvious, the tiny flowers meticulously colored in, but there are dots and lines next to it that I can't make out, an elongated W, a squiggle that looks like a Mandarin character, another that looks like a butterfly missing an antenna.

"The umbrella is darling, but I'm not sure what these other things are, floating around it," I say. She looks at me cockeyed, as if it should all be obvious.

"I'll give you a clue, Mama," she says, pointing out the window.

I look out the window and see that the sun has gone down, that the moonlight is reflecting all the way below us to the ocean.

"Is it the wing of the plane?" I ask.

"No, Mama. One more guess. Look out the window again. Push your face close." I lean over her, arching my spine so I don't smash her, and do as I am told. And then, I see it all.

"It's Mama and her Baby Girl, isn't it?"

"Yes, and their friend, the swan," she says with a contented look on her face. "Mama? How did Mama and her Baby Girl get all the way up into the sky?"

Cassiopeia was the queen of an African nation, I tell her, and she was so beautiful it was hard not to stare at her, as was her daughter, Andromeda. One day, Cassiopeia bragged about it, saying that they were more beautiful than the nymph daughters of one of the sea gods, who were also known for their beauty. The nymph daughters didn't like that one bit and went and told their dad, and he went and told the main sea god, Poseidon. Poseidon was so angry that a mortal would dare think themselves better than a god that he decided to punish them by putting them in the night sky for eternity.

"Mama, is it bad to think you're beautiful?"

"No, Celie, not at all. But you shouldn't compare your beauty to others. You shouldn't say you're more beautiful than someone else."

"But it's okay to say you're beautiful?" she asks.

"Yes, it's okay to say you're beautiful, and sweet girl, you are . . ."

I kiss her forehead and pull her close to me. She reaches for BlanK-it like a phantom limb, then settles for my hand. The sugar buzz is wearing off, and the day has been long and full. She sucks her thumb, tucks her head between my armpit and breast and begins to settle in for the night. The plane lights lower, and I slip my prosthetics off for the rest of the seven-plus hour flight—unlike my legs, my daughter is an extension of me that I cannot bear the thought of removing.

I do not tell her that the story, passed down the historical human line, mostly recorded by men, is that Poseidon tried to punish Cassiopeia by threatening to flood her homeland of Ethiopia. That after consulting an oracle, Cassiopeia and her husband, King Cepheus, learned that the only way they could appease the god of the sea was to sacrifice their daughter to a sea monster by binding her naked to a rocky coast. That Perseus, a son of Zeus, on his way back from beheading Medusa (a woman who was also beautiful, seduced by Poseidon, and then punished for it) saw Andromeda bound to the rocky outcrop, saw the sea monster approaching the fair and lovely maiden, killed the beast, and took Andromeda for his wife. That Poseidon, unhappy that Cassiopeia got a happy ending, banished her to the stars, bound to an upside-down chair meant to torture her for eternity—all because she had a moment of feeling extra about herself and her daughter's beauty.

If the gods of mythology can be seen as the quintessence of humanity, then hubris by the gods is far worse than that of mortals.

At this point in the evolution of time and space, my daughter's vessel walls are just forming. I'm going to fill her with all the delight and joy in the known world that I can, believing that it will help her build a better barricade against all the forces that will attempt to drain her of all that fills her with the fiery light of life. She has only just been borne from the chaotic, organic cabbage patch of humanity, is only beginning to form the naughty, wild, and wonderful layers of her essence.

One day, when they try to chip away at her sturdy walls, I will tell her the whole story, even the part where Mama and Baby Girl's friend, the swan, was the animal Zeus chose to embody in order to seduce yet another gorgeous, mortal woman, knowing that she wouldn't have him in his true form. That he was so delighted with the success of his trickery and seduction that he threw a swan up there in the night sky, too, to remember his conquest.

I'll tell Celie that the joke is on the supposed gods, because humans are like stars on Earth—some shine brighter than others, but they all come together to make up this grand, celestial city. And just like stars, we are filled with ever-burning, searing fire that must run its course. You can't torture a star any more than its mere existence does.

What I'll tell my daughter is that because *they*—the ubiquitous, angry *they*—were so overwhelmed by women who were aware of their light and power, and who chose to let it shine as naturally and brightly as possible, they tried to bury them alive, deep in the cosmos, but all they did was turn them into eternal lodestars that humankind will always need to help find their way through the dark.

II

....

FIRST, we buy a map.

We buy a map because it is the only way to know where we are and where we're going, assuming the map is a true representation of such things.

Ptolemy created the first maps using latitude and longitude. He coined the term *geography*—the drawing of the world. He utilized complex theories to create the maps, intended not so much to lead a traveler from point A to B, but to be able to project more accurate horoscopes. Ptolemy believed that the place someone was born directly correlated with their divination. He ended up creating a science to support a pseudoscience.

The earliest maps were created mostly by religious orders with funding from wealthy patrons. They marked two things on their disproportionate, illustrated maps— the kingdoms owned by the man funding the creation of the map, and religious symbols.

The kingdoms were often exaggerated in size, akin to

the amplification of penis proportions that often occurs in male circles. The symbols were marks of deity versus the unknown—an ark presumed to be Noah's in Armenia; the home of the prophet, Muhammed, in Arabia; headless men, presumed to be savage, in lands that had not yet been conquered, like Africa.

In the beginning, a map was a guide to show humanity the way to the kingdom of heaven, funded by the greediest bullies on the block.

Celie and I buy a world map in London at Stanfords—the world's largest map store. We buy a 3'×5' laminated map and a Sharpie that I will use to show her over the course of the next year the lands we will be visiting. Unlike Ptolemy, I do not intend to predict the future, only to give my daughter a visual of the world outside of our own.

I also buy an updated copy of *Lloyd's List*, a registry of all things shipping that dates back to the late 1700s. Even though I do not have my entire transglobal route figured out yet, I know that I will need to ship my Land Rover to and from some locations, and *Lloyd's List* will provide me with all of the possibilities. A marine I know through the off-roading community introduced me to *Lloyd's List*, and it's why we flew out of New York, because a week before our flight, I put Athena, our Land Rover, on a ship headed to England. I also buy Celie a new journal with a world map on the cover, so she can feel every bit the world traveler she's about to become. I pay for our purchases and head outside to hail a taxi so that we can head to the Port of Tilbury to pick up Athena.

Celie holds on to her new journal like a preacher might hold on to the Bible, like an explorer might hold on to a map. I've got both carry-ons on one shoulder, and the laminated map sticking out of one of them. It's Covent Garden, central London, and it's frenzied. I set the bags down between my legs, holding tightly on to Celie's hand, and I raise my arm to flag a taxi. My arm feels like a sinker. The time difference is hitting. It's eleven in the morning, but my body feels like the sun hasn't risen yet. A hundred taxis stream by us before one finally stops, and as if to make up for all the ones that passed us by, the driver is kind enough to offer assistance with loading my precious cargo, but I do it all myself. He seems a bit dismayed when I hand him the address of the freight company—it's a good way away, but I promise him I'll make it worth the day. He makes a call on his radio and speaks in a foreign language that I cannot place.

When he hangs up, he's smiling, and in perfect English, the driver asks if the young lady can have a sweet, and here I go, obliging her sugar intake again. Plus, it's been some time since breakfast and I only have a pack of saltines in our bags. Celie knocks back the Cadbury egg slowly, like she's just discovered that England may be the greatest place on Earth, like if she made a map according to her idea of heaven, there would be a Cadbury egg drawn right in the middle of London. She won't share a bite with me. She lays her head back against the seat, staring out at the skyscrapers, the hodgepodge of passersby, her eyes getting wider and wider. Then, the sugar buzz begins.

She sits up straight, her legs start kicking, and she tells the taxi driver, "We are going to pick up Athena."

"And just who is Athena? Is that your nan?" the driver replies.

"No Athena is not a nan. What's a nan?" she asks.

"Ah . . . ," he says, registering her confusion, "in England, a nan is a form of grandmother. So, Athena is not your grandmother?"

"No, my grandmothers are in America. I have three of them. I have Grandma, Oma, and Grandnanny," she offers.

"Well, see there, a Grandnanny is a form of nan—so you do have a nan, after all."

Celie scrunches her nose, not liking being bested. She retorts, "Well, Athena is not a Nan! Athena is our chariot!"

"Your chariot, eh? Does she come with horses?"

"No," Celie replies matter-of-factly. "She comes with four-wheel drive."

The driver looks at me through the rearview mirror, smiles with only the eyes that I can see, and says, "You've got quite a lively one there, don't you?"

"At times, yes," I reply, reaching into a bag to get her colored pencils. I'm thinking of Art Linkletter and *Kids Say the Darndest Things*. I'm thinking that I hope a drawing utensil and her new journal are enough of an outlet to channel her saccharine-laced energy, because I'm also thinking for the first time that if she continues to explain to the driver what our purpose is, he may well think I am as crazy as her nans do.

Turns out, Celie isn't the only lively one. Maybe I am giddy from exhaustion, but when the taxi driver asks me what kind of four-wheel-drive chariot I'm off to pick up, I spend the rest of the hourlong cab ride telling him the whole story—how I lost my legs, fell in love with off-roading, decided to drive around the world. I also tell him that even though I now have a small degree of financial comfort, that I wasn't born into money—I tell him how one time after I lost my legs, I crawled down the stairs one night to get a glass of water and I overheard my parents in the dining room trying to figure out what bills they could get by without paying that month. My hospitals bills were astronomical, I tell him, and my father's a mechanic for Goodyear, who'd been laid off several times in the years before I got sick because the tire products started being made overseas because it was cheaper, and the company was putting long-term employees, like my father, through the wringer. I tell him that I crawled into the dining room and told my parents that when I grew up, I'd become a doctor so that they would never have to worry about paying bills again. And I told him that my dad responded by saying, "I don't care if you pump gas for a living, I just want you to be happy."

That's probably a large part of why I'm doing what I'm doing, I tell the taxi-man, because it does make me happy. But I can't just drive around the world in a Land Rover like some leisure-driven trust-fund baby—I had to have a reason that benefited more than just me. So, I tell him how I went to college for a few years, and before I dropped out to take on this expedition, I attended a lecture on landmines. There were all these slides of women and children with amputations. And there was one image, of a young girl in a rice paddy, with her prosthetics starting just below the knees like mine, and at the top of the image were the words *To Know That We Are Not Alone*. It hit me right then and there, I tell this first of many strangers, that I was going to drive around the world to bring to light the plight of landmine survivors worldwide.

After the lecture in college, I found the nerve to write an email to Landmine Survivors Network (LSN) head-quarters in Washington, DC, and ask them if I could meet with them for a possible collaboration. Princess Diana had worked in conjunction with the organization before her un-timely passing—she died the day my grandmother hosted Celie's baby shower.

When LSN agreed to hear me out, I bought a suit, put together a PowerPoint presentation, and drove to the na-tion's capital where I nervously but assuredly told them that I would spend a year in England training and finalizing plans before I'd go, but that I thought it would be possi-ble to raise funds with a story like mine—a young woman, a single mother with no legs, driving around the world to benefit others who have lost their limbs to landmines.

"And they said yes?" the driver asks me.

They didn't say yes right away. In fact, I think they thought for a moment that I was crazy. I drove back home a little more deflated with each inch of fading sun. But the next morning, I got a follow-up email asking me what it was exactly that I wanted from them—that they could not sponsor me financially for the trip. I was so re-lieved to hear that. I emailed them right back and said I didn't want a dime from them. I'd pay for everything. All

I wanted was permission to put their logo on my truck, a letter from them to help me with border crossings, and for them to agree to let me visit their five networks world-wide—Bosnia, Ethiopia, Mozambique, Vietnam, and El Salvador. They emailed again. We could definitely work something out.

"And, well, almost a year later, here we are," I finish, as we are closing in on Tilbury. "Do *you* think I'm crazy?"

The taxi driver doesn't answer. The traffic is thicker nearer the port. He weaves in and out of amblers and engines with concentration and ease, then begins speaking to someone again on his radio in the other language I can't comprehend. Heat rises in my chest and cheeks.

"I'm not sure I know exactly where you should drop me off," I say, returning to the business at hand, hoping I wouldn't have to walk too far to find Athena, hoping he hasn't written me off as insane.

He doesn't answer again, just keeps weaving, tapping his fingers on the wheel when the traffic comes to a standstill. His radio pipes up once more—he sounds happy in the thick fricatives of his private communication, and suddenly, he veers hard to the right through tall metal gates, well away from the main thoroughfare. There are cargo containers and crates as far as the eye can see, but no more traffic.

A seed in my gut fast forwards into a ripe nervousness. I've said too much. Maybe this man thinks I have a satchel full of money and Celie and I are going to be found dead in one of these containers weeks from now. Sweat builds at my hairline, though I've been chilly the whole ride. In my head, I apologize to Celie's nans, her father. I run my hand through my daughter's hair and she looks up at me, eyes wide and curious as to the reason for such sudden affection. Her first two journal pages are full to the corners with skyscrapers, a taxi, a Cadbury egg. She looks out the window past me, and screams.

"Look Mama, it's Athena!"

Sure enough, there is Athena, in all of her bronze-green glory, though she looks much smaller in the context of this port, the larger comings and goings of the world. Celie jumps out of the cab as soon as it stops and hugs the corner grille as if Athena is a long-lost family member. She walks around the vehicle, patting each tire, saying "feels good!" after each pat. She puts her fist in the air and shouts, "Yay, Athena!" Then she sits on the running board and warms her back against the sun-kissed body of the truck.

I watch her, feeling each of her emotions in the same nostalgic way. The taxi driver is watching her, too, a broad smile pasted on his face. I don't think he's going to kill us anymore.

Another taxi pulls up beside ours, and both drivers get out of their cars and embrace, speak again, in the words that are their own. I set the carry-ons on the ground next to Athena and Celie and walk over to pay our driver.

Our driver introduces me to the other one. They are brothers. They are brothers from Bosnia and Herzegovina whose family fled to London almost nine years earlier, when the siege of Sarajevo was just beginning. They aren't much younger than me. I can't find the right words, so I just say that I'm sorry.

I offer our driver twice the fare, but he refuses to take any of it. "I don't think you are crazy," he says, "I think you are brave, and I wish you both the best of luck. I hope to hear one day that you brought some joy to our homeland." He kneels down in front of Celie and hands her another Cadbury egg. Then the brothers drive away, honking their horns and waving until they blend into the quotidian mayhem.

All of our belongings traveled across the ocean, inside of Athena, so our reunion is more than just the satisfaction of having our steadfast wheels back with us. Heavy-duty box upon box was slammed inside of her—off-roading gear, toolkits, camping equipment, clothing, medicines and first aid, and one heavy-duty box that was filled with all of Celie's tools for creation—paper, paints, pencils, glues, scissors, spirographs. She wants it now, but the truck is jammed, so much so, that neither of us can put our seats back an inch.

"We've got three hours to drive until we get to our new home," I tell her. Home is one side of a duplex I've rented in the midlands for the year. "Your journal and colored pencils will have to do until we get there."

"Where are the midlands?" Celie asks.

"In the middle of England," I tell her, pointing out England on the front of her journal cover.

"I'm going to draw a map of our new home," she says, unwrapping the Cadbury egg with a grin.

"Can I have a bite of this one?" I ask her. She stuffs the whole thing into her mouth.

I'm looking at a map to figure out how to get out of the

city; I'm reminding myself to drive on the left. *Right, Left, Right, Left . . .* my brain is a drill sergeant trying to regroup a fatigued unit that doesn't want to engage in battle anymore, it just wants to go home. I realize I am at home right now, in this dockyard, with my daughter. We aren't going to war, nor to a kingdom, nor are we on the road to salvation; we are going for a drive to a place where we can rest. We have a map, and if we don't like where it takes us, we'll draw a new one, and home will be wherever we are on the page.

The sun is long fallen by the time we find the duplex I've rented, sight unseen, on a dead-end road in a tiny village. Traveling the English motorways isn't nearly as straight and speedy as an American highway. I stopped at the first grocery store I could find once we got out of the city. I bought milk and Weetabix and three cans of baked beans because my stumps were aching from the travel and rest was becoming a requirement instead of a desire.

I leave Athena's lights on and find the key under the mat on the left side of the duplex, just where the landlord said she'd leave it. Celie wakes from a short nap as I walk back to the truck to retrieve her. She takes in her surroundings, smiles when she spots a pink bicycle with sparkly streamers coming out of the handles, just at the edge of Athena's headlights. "There must be a kid next door," she says, her eyes glistening at the prospect of a friend.

"We'll find out in the morning," I say, lifting her out of the seat; she nuzzles her face into my neck. I want nothing more than to lie on a sofa, holding her just like this, and to fall asleep for a day, or forever in this moment. The door opens to a kitchen. I find a light switch, then another. There is no sofa, no furniture at all. I head upstairs where there are two bedrooms, but no beds. It's almost eleven at night. How long have I been awake now?

I grab the scant groceries from the truck and ask Celie if she wants cereal or baked beans. She chooses beans. Luckily, there is a microwave and a coffee mug, and some silverware to be located. Celie has never used a microwave before—I don't like them, but I pop open the can tab, dump half the can into the coffee mug and show her how to use it. She loves to push buttons. She is her mother's daughter. I put the other half of the can in the fridge and leave her on the countertop to eat lukewarm beans.

Outside, I can see her tiny body through the kitchen window. She's playing with the strings of a window shade between bites of beans. I turn off Athena's lights, and a fog washes over me, a cool wet haze. It is quiet, save for a symphony of night bugs. I find the flashlight under the driver's seat, unlock the padlock on the back door of the vehicle. Luckily, I only have to take a half-dozen boxes out before I locate the one I'm looking for—one with camping equipment, a blow-up mattress, and a lantern, because the lights upstairs don't seem to work.

Celie wants to blow the mattress up, so I let her. She shrieks with delight as it quickly swells, like a life raft in the middle of an ocean. She places our carry-on bags, one on either side of the bed—hers nearer the window, even though we can both only see the sky out of it from an air mattress on the floor.

"Did you get enough to eat, dear one?" I ask her.

"Yes, Mama," she says, rummaging through her bag. "Where's my toothbrush?"

"In the outer pocket," I say, then I go downstairs to wash out the bean mug, so she has something to swish with when she's done. Tomorrow, I think, I'll find the box with the camping kitchenware, and the one with all of her art supplies. I'll find our bearings. At least in the box with the mattress, there's a sheet, and one towel.

On the way back upstairs, a prosthetic leg starts to slide off. They've been on too long, the prosthetics—my stumps probably look like Celie's thumb after she's sucked it until it's shriveled like a raisin—parched of air, the moisture sucked out. I ease it back on, step slow, force the anaerobic seal into existence long enough to get me up the stairs safely to Celie.

She's turned on the lantern. There's a welcoming glow in the barren room. Our new home is cozy. She's laid out the sheet evenly across the mattress. The bags look like weights on either side, keeping us from drifting. Our home for this rest is a lifeboat, like an island in the midlands of an island that's a country on a map.

Celie pulls out the laminated map from Stanfords and unrolls it across the bottom half of the mattress. I roll onto my side, slip off my legs and the gel liners that keep my skin-grafted stumps from coming apart at the seams. I sop up the moisture with the towel.

"Mama, they smell," she says, pinching her nose shut.

"I know. I'm sorry," I say. I roll back off the island, crawl over, and crack the window to clear the room of any evidence of rot. I crawl to the bathroom, adjacent to our spot on the map. There's no soap, so I run my raw body under the faucet until the hot water grows too hot to bear.

Celie is ready for her first geography lesson when I return. She is on her knees, poring over the multicolored continents. I am also on my knees, ready to put her to bed with continents. In North America, I tell her, outlining the boundaries on the map as I speak, is everything you know—of animals, forests, deserts, dads, and nans.

Now you're in Europe, I say, demarcating her unknown. Here we are now, in England, where there are Cadbury eggs and Bosnian taxi drivers turned kind from trauma, and much more that we have yet to explore.

I end the night with Africa, because it's right in the center of the map, like an elongated, melting heart, and I can fill her with visions of the Serengeti—giraffes, and lions, and elephants, and villages that sing the long nights into short ones.

There's so much more to tell her, but Mama has to sleep for now.

Okay? Okay.

One good thing about the world, I say, is that it all sleeps under the same stars. She nuzzles into my neck again. I run my hand through her hair and down her back, pull her body close, sweep the sheet over our bodies, turn the lantern out.

The sun can only light half of the globe at a time, and it's our turn on the dark side.

"Love you to the moon and back, Mama," she says, giggling, pointing at the sliver of moon out the window.

"I love you the whole universe," I say.

The sunlight blinds.

For a moment, I have no idea where I am. I use my hands to feel what's around me—rubber filled with air, a make-shift bed, our life raft, our island—England.

I sit up, ready to declare another day of adventure, and I must immediately lie back down. I am fevered as fuck, sick to the bones.

Celie walks in the room with a mug full of beans.

"Mama, you're a sleepy head," she says.

"Did you microwave those yourself?" I ask.

"Yes, because you're a sleepy head."

"I'm afraid I need to sleep again," I tell her. "Mama is sick."

"Are you bad sick, Mama?"

A year ago, we were at our home in Roanoke, Virginia. J's sister was visiting with her daughter. Celie and her cousin were on the floor playing with blocks. I was gathering a small meal. Celie asked her aunt to take her legs off and get on the floor with them, so they could all build a castle together. J's sister told her that her legs didn't come off. Celie rolled her eyes, and said, "Oh Auntie, all mamas' legs come off."

Later that night I had to explain to her that most mamas' legs do not come off, which brought on the questions. "Why do your legs come off, Mama?"

"Because they're pretend legs," I say on the fly. It's not like there's a manual I can read to tell my kid why her mom has legs that come off. I'm winging it, because all I have left are my wings.

"But pretend means seeing something that isn't really there. I can see your fake legs. Why do you have fake legs, Mama?"

"Well, honey, because a long time ago, I had a bad sick in my body, and they had to take my real legs off in order to save the rest of me."

She went silent for several moments, and then concern for her own survival bubbled to the surface. "Will I get the bad sick?"

"You have a better chance of getting a pet unicorn," I told her. Her face lit up with the thought.

"What happens if you get the bad sick again?" she asked, the unicorn not entertaining her mind long enough for me to change the conversation.

"I have a better chance of getting a pet unicorn, too." I told her. "Then, we'll have to build a fence to keep our pet unicorns in together."

"Mama, don't be silly. Unicorns can fly."

"It's not the bad sick," I tell my daughter, knowing that the bad sick started just like this, like a flu.

"Do you want some beans?" she asks, sitting her bum next to my shoulder on the air mattress so that the whole bed billows, and pain shoots through every bit I have left of me.

"No, baby, I just want to sleep a little while longer."

I don't wake until early evening, the air mattress soaked with the temporary break of a fever. Celie isn't in the bedroom, but the empty bean mug is on the floor. I take it and crawl to the bathroom, fill it up in the sink, and drink. My body is as parched as my stumps were the night before. I feel so weak that I lay my head against the cool toilet seat for a while in order to gain enough strength to crawl back to the island.

Celie comes up the stairs, sees me half-naked on the floor of the bathroom and says, "Mama, are you sure it's not the bad sick?"

"I'm sure it's not the bad sick," I say, unsure. "It's going to take a couple of days for me to feel better, that's all."

"When you feel better can we get a Cadbury egg and my art box?" she asks.

"When I feel better, you can have whatever you want," I say. I muster up the strength to crawl back in the bedroom. I ask her to fill up the mug with water and bring it to me. She's a good girl. Maybe she deserves a better Mama, I think. What if this is the bad sick? I don't have a cell phone yet. I don't even know the British equivalent of 911. What if something happens to me in this empty place, and she ends up wandering the streets of this dead-end village?

I try to stop myself, but the thoughts cascade—the voices of a society desperate to tame nature, the voices of my own family. Will they say that I should have known better because I've experienced the bad sick before? Will they say I should have never left the United States as a single mother with a child? Will they say I should never have had a child because I have a disability? You bet they will. But the truth of the matter is that anything can happen to any mother with their child at any time, in any place—that's nature, it can't be tamed. And right now, nature is telling me to sleep, so I do.

I have no idea what time it is, or how many days I've lain here on this mattress that now resembles a life raft with water seeping into it. Overwhelming heat occasionally sears my brain, my insides, then a break, the fever washing out of me like a slow leak. I wake because I'm shivering. I wake because I feel something on my hand.

Celie is alight in the glow of the lantern, drawing on my hand with the Sharpie pen. I pull away and see that she's traced the skin graft on my right hand. It's one of my favorite scars, heart-shaped, like instead of wearing my heart on my sleeve, I wear it on my hand.

"Celie," I say, "please don't draw on your Mama with permanent ink." But there's no logic in that. A Sharpie eventually washes off, unlike a tattoo, unlike the permanence of the scar itself.

"I'm sorry, Mama," she says, her mouth forming a pout, eyes filling with tears.

"It's okay, baby. It's not a big deal. It isn't really permanent. It will wash off in a few days."

"Mama, when will you be better?" Celie asks, one tear escaping over the dam of her chubby cheek.

"Probably tomorrow," I say. I hope.

"Will you open the milk for me tomorrow?"

Then a tear falls down my cheek instantaneously. "I'll open the milk for you now. Can you bring it upstairs?"

Celie runs downstairs, and I feel like the worst mother in the world. I roll over and see the bean mug with a dry Weetabix biscuit in it, a bite taken out of one edge. More tears fall down my face, and they burn. She arrives with the milk carton. "Can I eat with milk up here even though there's carpet?" she asks.

"You can eat wherever you want, right beside me is better. I don't care if you spill it because we don't cry over spilled milk, do we?"

She grins. "No, we don't," she says. I watch her fill her gullet with the biscuit that's now gone to mush. She doesn't even have sugar for it, and nary a complaint. I'm going to buy her all the Cadbury eggs, I think. Watching her eat, I have a pang of hunger—a good sign. But I can't ask her to share any of her scant provisions. I remember the saltines in the carry-on and roll over to retrieve them. They're smashed into bits, and delicious. When Celie finishes her cereal, I pour a bit more milk in the mug and drink it.

"Tomorrow, baby, I promise, Mama will be better."

"Mama," she says with pause, waiting for me to respond.

"Yes, sweet one," I urge her to continue.

"I'm sorry I drew on your hand. But Mama, you have Africa on your hand, from the bad sick scars, and I wanted to make a map of you."

How do mothers deal with all the attempts a heart makes at leaping into the throat, floating outside of the chest, exploding into ether from the love of the innocence that pours out from their children?

Of course, I have Africa on my hand.

"The United States is on your thigh, but you woke up before I could trace it."

"Do you think we could find all the countries on my scars, Celie?"

"You have a lot of scars, Mama."

"Yes, I do, baby." A whole map of them.

I ask her to run the milk carton back downstairs and into the fridge before nightfall since she's scared to leave the bedroom after dark. Before we go to bed, I have enough energy to play a game with her, one that doesn't require me to move much.

We make shadow creatures on the ceiling with our hands and the lantern—she narrates something fantastical that I'm only half listening to because I still feel pretty delirious. We make cats and birds, a giraffe and a unicorn. Celie is smiling, happy, cozied up with me on the air mattress. I fall asleep before her. I cannot stay awake. The last thing I see is her bird shadow flying over me, saying, "Everything will be better tomorrow."

There are voices coming up the stairs. The sun is cooking me through the window. I pull the sheet to cover myself before the intruders find me half-bodied, half-naked, a mess. Celie isn't next to me. My heart begins to thump so hard I can see it pulsating on my chest. I want to cry out for her, but I'm afraid. Maybe she's hiding from whoever is in the house and if I call out for her, they will find her, too.

I close my eyes briefly as whoever is coming approaches the top steps and is about to round the corner. When my eyes open, I see Celie, standing next to a unicorn.

I blink to see if the image washes away. I blink to make sure it's real. It's another girl child, blonde like Celie, but ruddy, and stockier, too, with a unicorn bike helmet on her head.

"Mama, this is Leia. She is my friend, and she gave me some smarties."

"Smarties?" I query, because it's the only thing I can think to utter.

"They are sweeties," the unicorn child answers. "Candy-coated chocolate sweeties."

"Did you get a pet unicorn, Celie?" I ask, still unsure of what's happening.

The unicorn child answers. "I'm not a unicorn. I'm a girl named Leia. This is my unicorn bike helmet, and I live next door."

My mouth is so dry, I think of cartoons in my childhood where characters run head long into a body of water in the desert only to have their heads smack sand. Oasis. Mirage. Unicorns.

A hurricane of long red curls appears behind my daughter and Leia, the unicorn child. It pauses long enough to shout in a friendly manner. "Girls, get downstairs now, or this is the end of sweets for you both. I've work to do."

The daughter and the unicorn child disappear. The ruby-headed whirling dervish remains but grows more still. I pull my body into fetal position, embarrassed, overwhelmed.

"I'm Jane. I'm your neighbor. I hope you don't mind. I saw your daughter through the window, and she let me in. She says you're sick. You've the flu. The eye can see that. We'll get you better soon."

"I'm thirsty," is all I can manage to say.

"Of course, you are," Jane answers, stepping past me,

opening the window wide. "Give me a few minutes. Every-thing is going to be okay."

Jane returns with her arms full—a laundry basket, a large sack. She runs back downstairs and comes up with a tray. "Can you sit up?" she asks.

I rise up slowly. My head is throbbing, but the fever feels as if it's run the full course.

"Atta girl," Jane says. She gets on her knees next to the mattress, hands me a glass with a straw. "Let's start with this."

Ginger ale like manna—I could drink a gallon.

"Sip it slowly now," Jane says. "Or it might come right back up." Then, she holds a bowl of oyster crackers in front of me. I eat one, pause, and then I down several. "You're going to be at it in no time," Jane says.

"Thank you," I say. "I think the fever has finally broken for good." I lie back down, resting on my elbow, still weary. It took more of an effort than I thought to sit up and receive sustenance. I look at Jane. Her hair is fiery, halfway down her back, pulled back from her face with a plastic head-band. She's wearing a bright blue tracksuit that matches her eyes. She has a broad smile, big teeth, and as many freckles as the sky has stars. Even though I feel as if I've known her forever, I ask, "I'm sorry, but who are you?"

"I'm Jane, your landlord. Well, technically I'm just your neighbor. My fiancée, Michael, owns this duplex even though I do all the upkeep. We live on the other side. And Leia is our daughter, she's two years older than Celie.

Michael has an older son, too, from another woman, but he doesn't visit too often."

It sounds strange to hear my daughter's name come so casually from this woman's mouth, and yet it doesn't. "I'm sorry for being a burden before we've even properly met. I hope Celie hasn't given you any trouble," I say, wanting to fall asleep.

"Are you kidding? Your daughter is darling, took me forever to get her to open the door for me. I have a key but didn't want to frighten her. And now she's entertaining my Leia, which is the best thing ever because Leia is a pain in my arse, just like her dad. What about Celie's dad? You married?"

"No, I'm not married. We left Celie's dad behind in America," I say.

"Better off that way," Jane replies. "I wish I could put Michael on a plane somewhere with a one-way ticket. I'd have been here to help you a lot sooner if it hadn't been for him. I knew it was odd that you hadn't left the house since you arrived, no lights, no movement. He told me to mind my own, but I'm not good at that. Better yet, I'd like to leave him here and have him pay for me to go somewhere. I'd go to Disney World. Have you been?"

"I went as a small kid, but I don't remember much." I don't tell her that I'm not a fan of Disney World, nor amusement parks in general—expensive illusions aren't my fancy.

"Celie says you're going to drive around the world. That's amazing. I watched a program on the BBC once about a tribe in Africa. They were like the only tribe that had no fighting between them. The experts decided the reason they didn't fight was because there was a river that ran through the village, and the men lived on one side of the river and the women and children lived on the other. There was a drawbridge, but it didn't stay down all the time because the water would get high and break it, so instead, on special occasions, they'd lower it out over the river to visit. Michael and I would get along a lot better if there were a river between us. Do you get along better with Celie's dad now that you've got a whole ocean between you?"

A slight titter comes out my mouth, but I'm too exhausted to respond in full.

"I'm sorry," she says, "we'll have time to catch up once you've recovered. I'm going to draw you a bath. I saw only one towel in there. I've brought some more, and soap and shampoo and salts. That should make you feel worlds better. Let that ginger ale soak up and I'll have the bath ready shortly."

I close my eyes, feeling grateful for angels, unicorns. I fall asleep almost immediately, but I wake up just as quickly, because Jane is back in the bedroom. "You can sleep soon, but go in there and soak, will you? I'm going to get some supper in the girls, and then I'll be back to check on you, okay?"

"Okay," I say. "Thank you," I say. And I watch her red mane disappear into the hall and down the stairs.

The bathroom smells like lavender. The mirror is fogged from the bath steam. There are fresh towels and a fuzzy rug and clean pajamas set in a pile. I feel puny, humbled. I cry a little. I take off the tank top and underwear I've been wearing for several days and set them aside, crawl over the tub wall and slowly lower my bone-weary body into the water. I cry a little more when I see the fresh bar of soap on the side of the tub. I wet the soap and run it all over my limbs, my torso, then I try to scrub the ink of Africa off of my hand. The outline pales, but it isn't ready to come off just yet—it wants to remind me of peaceful tribes with rivers running through them, about women helping women with the rearing of children, about men who respect boundaries.

There's a knock on the door.

"Mama, can I come in?"

"Yes, Celie."

She opens the bathroom door; behind her I catch a glimpse of Jane coming up the steps with a vacuum cleaner in hand. "Mama, Leia is my best friend. If she and her dad put the training wheels back on her bicycle, can I try to ride it please?"

"I guess so, but please be careful," I say.

"She's going to let me use her unicorn helmet. I'll be okay, I promise," she says. She sits on the toilet seat next to the tub and pulls out a packet of candies from her pocket. "Want some?" she asks.

"No, I'm okay. You eat them."

"Try one, Mama," she insists, jumping off the toilet seat, and leaning over the tub to place one in my mouth.

The chocolate melts quickly on my tongue. It tastes as good as the fact that she finally has enough of something to share. "Mama," she says, as she grabs onto the door preparing to leave, "I'm glad you're feeling better."

"Me too. I love you."

"I love you to the moon and back," she says.

"The whole universe," I say as she shuts the door behind her. Then I submerge my head under the water and baptize myself in the gift of this moment.

The bedroom has been thoroughly cleaned. There are parallel stripes on the carpet from the vacuum cleaner. There are fresh sheets and a blanket and pillows on the air mattress. There are pajamas for Celie. There's a bottle of water and another glass of ginger ale on the tray, a bowl of oyster crackers, a bottle of lotion. The carry-ons are neatly lined against the wall, no longer anchoring each side of the bed, and the laminated map is stuck to the wall with thumbtacks. Our life raft is steady. The water has calmed.

The sky is darkening. I apply the lotion all over my body, rubbing it gently into each scar, each country etched upon me. My body is a map that Celie thinks has been sanctioned by the bad sick, by the greed of things that only know consumption. She doesn't know that all of these scars aren't from a single airborne pathogen—the invisible untamed nature.

She doesn't yet know about the visible savageries—that humans are as capable of such cruelties, too. She doesn't know that the slight, faded scar under my right eye is from the ring on a man's finger who backhanded me after taking my virginity by rape in an abandoned parking lot. She doesn't know that over eighty percent of women with disabilities are sexually assaulted in their lifetimes. She doesn't know that if I had been born only a generation before, she may have never been born because the entire globe participated in the forced sterilization of disabled women and women of color.

She doesn't know that the crisscross scars all over my thighs and knees are from my adoptive mother, her beloved grandma. She doesn't know that so many women before us were never given a healthy outlet for the abuse they received, the entrapment they felt in a world where they couldn't have control of their own lives—that they were expected to live in silence and false shame, and that sometimes, it all burst out of these women in a rage against their own, perpetuating the cycle of pain. She doesn't know of the years that my mother grabbed whatever was nearby—belts, coat hangers, sticks—and tried to subdue her adopted daughter's feral independence, my refusal to be tamed.

And I still refuse it, because you can't tame nature. This map on my body isn't made by kingdoms that have conquered me. No, these lines are from the kingdoms to which I would not submit, even as they carved my flesh and tried to drain my lifeblood. They took my legs and I got up and walked away.

This map on my body leads to salvation, and it's all I have to offer my daughter that matters—living proof that there is abiding joy in resisting the whims of cruelty. This map, my body, my life, is her key to freedom, a map for her to draw on, a way for her to extend the route of compassion—the ability to live and let live.

III

....

IN the middle of a limestone quarry, bobbling in a sham of a pond, a Buckingham Blue Land Rover is a mere ten inches from total submersion. Three men are standing on the roof.

On the bank, a small crowd is trying not to snicker out loud, as if fearing their own dose of schadenfreude. The owner of the Land Rover Defender, a man named Liam, his bald head red in the cold air, laughs and beats his chest, as if sinking his vehicle is the greatest thing that has ever happened to him. As his fists smack his chest, the truck totters and sinks several more inches: the prospect of swimming in the nippy water doesn't seem to faze him in the least. He kicks up his legs, dancing like a foolhardy gnome. The two men with him up on the roof beg him to stop.

I'm standing dry on the bank, with a grin growing wider as the antics play out. It hurts to smile this wide. Late spring in England, I am learning, amounts to cracked lips and a constant salty burn. The murky water ripples out from the rich blue island of the roof as Liam continues his jig. Some of the crowd laugh with him. One man calls him a twat.

I grab a recovery rope from the back of my truck and set it in the cab. I start the truck in second gear and head down a gravel decline toward the mouth of the pond. My new boss, Vince, is standing there, and I realize I haven't yet considered the pecking order. I am an American, the only woman on the crew, and I've only been working as an off-road instructor for them for about six weeks. So far, the only things this crew seems to respect about me are my truck and my boobs.

"Your intentions?" Vince says to me, as I climb out of the cab. His other three instructors, who I'll call Mick, Mack, and Bob, stand in a triangle behind him with their arms crossed like thugs.

"Well, Vince, I thought I'd fasten the rope to the winch end and walk it out along the bank, toss it to them best I can, let them fasten the hook, and then we can just winch them out."

"And how do you imagine they are going to fasten the winch hook?" His cell phone starts ringing. He looks at the screen and ignores it.

"Well, one of them is going to have to get in the water, sir."

"Ah, but they are clients."

"Yes sir, clients who didn't pay attention to the instructions."

"Kelley girl," as Vince has taken to calling me, "why don't you walk the winch out to them? You'll only have to hold your breath for a few moments to fasten the winch."

Vince walks closer, adding, "After all, your legs won't get cold."

"With all due respect, Vince," I say loudly, smiling reluctantly, "they are Mack's clients, not mine."

Another client, a well-regarded businessman and father of a bunch of young boys speaks up. "Enough of that nonsense. Mack, I have extra clothes that will fit you and a towel to dry off." Vince shoots Mack an eye roll, and the matter seems resolved. Mack grudgingly takes hold of the released winch hook and starts out into the rainwater sludge. A few people in the crowd applaud. I sit on the engine hood and watch, avoiding any eye contact with Vince.

A kink in the chain sets Mack tumbling, and he falls on all fours only a few meters in. He loosens the kink and swims out to the truck, dives under the water three times before he secures the winch. Once Mack sullenly waddles back out from the mire, the three men on the roof lie down and hold on. I hit the winch switch and within minutes, Liam opens his doors over dry land, and the last of the water rushes out with a roar. A man begins to take bets on whether or not they will be able to start the truck again. Vince demands a percentage of the profit, and twice that if they don't manage to succeed.

Liam walks over to me then, a crooked smirk on his face. "So, are you still going out with me tonight?"

"How are you going to get anywhere tonight?" I say, nodding my head toward his vehicle.

"Oh, I'll get her started. No problem. We'll just dry out the spark plugs, and away we'll go." He puts on a lame,

Hollywood Western affectation and adds, "Wild horses couldn't keep me from taking you out tonight."

I tell him to be quiet, afraid that Vince might hear him, or anyone else for that matter.

"Are you ashamed of me?" Liam asks.

"Well, you happen to be a client, for one thing. And you did just sink your truck."

"You're taking the piss out of me, aren't you? At least you look beautiful while you're doing it. Now, to Blue—" Liam says, galloping toward his Defender. He turns back toward me once more. "You don't happen to have a dry towel, do you?" I'd already grabbed one from the back of the truck and I throw it at him.

A crowd of eager men hover over the bonnet. I sip coffee and watch from a distance. Men are hunched, headfirst, over the engine of Liam's blue beast. The Land Rover reminds me of Polyphemus, the Cyclops, with a mouthful of men, the grille a grin underneath all of those men's legs hanging out over its engine jaws. I grin, thinking that an ancient Greek monster could solve my problems of potential romance. Liam's head surfaces momentarily above the crowd. He looks over toward me with his thumb up. Vince walks over then and says, "Watch out for that one, Kelley girl. He'd shag a frog if it stood still long enough."

I bite my lip. I taste blood. The quarry goes quiet but for the sound of the bonnet creaking shut. A bitter wind brushes the side of my head. "That'll do it!" Liam exclaims, wiping his hands dry on the towel that I'd given him. I watch, hopeful, as Vince's comment festers. Liam turns the ignition and giddy-up, it chugs and then purrs. Money starts changing hands.

I met Liam two Sundays ago, when the quarry was open for a fee to off-road enthusiasts, and instruction was available, though seldom desired. Celie was enrolled in preschool now, but Jane kept her on Sundays so I could train. On that particular Sunday afternoon, a young punk arrived with his father. The son's Land Rover was merely a shell, with a home-rigged, welded snorkel, steel plating, and a roll cage. He was about seventeen, and therefore fearless. The boy's father would just stand to the side, as his offspring blasted that engine up a sixty-degree-angled hard mud slope.

Once, the boy made it over the top. He was shaking after his first several attempts. During every failed attempt, his steel plates held up between the ground and the differentials and the engine. But I wondered, as he teetered several times on the edge of flipping backward, if his roll cage would be able to handle it. He would always quit gunning it after an airborne upright that brought him back down on two slick, back wheels, and then he'd shift his body like a jackhammer in the cab, trying to put the weight to the front.

A crowd gathered, as a crowd would, every time this boy started his act of half-witted bravado. That Sunday, while good citizens were at church, I was in the middle of a testosterone circus. The boy revved his engine. I stood among Vince, Liam, and his buddy, Chris. I winced as the boy's truck was upright, the front tires clutching air. "They've all signed the release forms, right Kelley girl?" Vince asked me, taking his black leather driving gloves off, and folding them gently, like some bulbous-nosed, James Bond wannabe.

I didn't answer. Liam spoke then, saying, "Kelley, is that your name?"

"Uh-huh," I replied, without looking at him.

"That's quite a kitted-up truck you've got there, Kelley. What have you done to it?"

"Six-inch suspension lift, steel under-plating, hand-crafted, heavy-duty tie rods, stainless steel exhaust, front and rear air lockers, 8,000-pound winch, steel winch house and bumper, bullet-proof window stickers, and a modified interior, too," I replied, my eyes never wavering from the mud shooting off the back wheels of the boy's truck.

"As I was saying," Liam kidded me, "that's quite a kitted-up truck." I took a breath, turned my eyes to a limestone boulder just behind Liam, and on the way there, quite unintentionally, noticed the bulge in his jeans. I grew embarrassed, further so when I found myself trying to get another glance. Stick to Land Rovers, I thought. The boy on the slope gunned his engine for another try.

"Her name is Athena," I told Liam. "She's got an internal roll cage, built-in GPS and compass, SAT phone capability, and I fit inside comfortably to sleep." I paused. "I'm going to drive her around the world."

"Ambitious, eh?" Liam said.

Vince rolled his eyes.

The boy's wheels were grinding against mud and stone. He was beyond showing off, gassing the engine until the truck looked like a spooked mustang on hind legs.

"Life is short," I said.

"Yeah, but all that kit is worthless if you can't drive it, woman," Liam said. His friend, lighting a cigarette, laughed out loud, like an obnoxious seagull.

"Come on, then," I replied. I jumped in Athena's cab and started the engine. Liam followed suit in his Defender, and Chris, his bemused, flask-wielding friend, positioned himself into Liam's passenger seat. I led them down a hill to a deep trench, slowed, slipped the transmission into neutral, and transferred the differentials. Then I pulled the handbrake, got out, and motioned for Liam and Chris to join me.

I took a shovel out from the equipment rack in the back of my truck and walked toward the near three-foot trench ahead. Two other trucks had joined us. "Can you cross this trench?" I asked Liam.

"As long as I got me a mate with a winch," he joked. The small group of men that had followed started laughing.

"The only way to cross a trench like this is to dig parallel tracks at forty-five-degree angles. You've got to give your wheels somewhere to go. And when you drive through it, forget speed, slow and steady, or you're stuck. Drive in at the angle. You only want one wheel in at a time. At a point, you will be on two opposing wheels at a thirty-five-degree angle; this is the time to give a small, controlled kick, but don't gun it."

None of the men snickered at what I was saying, nor did they help me shovel. Nobody wanted to get stuck in front of a woman. They were quiet, waiting to see how high I'd set the bar. No matter how many times I have crossed deep trenches successfully, I still grow nervous each time. "When you're not nervous anymore, that's when you should be," Vince had said to me the first day on the job. I got in the cab, and noticed that Vince, the fearless boy, and his father were coming down to join us.

I took a deep breath, lurched and bobbed as I crossed through to the other side, though not without a ribbing from Vince for giving the engine a hair too much gun. Liam gave me a thumbs up, said "that looks easy enough," and then he cursed for show when I had to winch him out moments later.

After several trucks passed through the trench challenge, everyone dispersed, each man wanting a different obstacle in the quarry to test his limits—that's why we were there, after all. Liam motioned for me to follow him through the back mud run, a mile of mazes, some partially wooded, all muddy dips and peaks, long gullies that required a steady gas, a bow wave always in front—the same technique, that in failing, sank Liam's Defender two weeks later.

When Liam cut to the left, I took a parallel track, slightly longer, but I knew it well, and gunned it. I was going beyond protocol, racing him like that. As an instructor, overzealous fun was supposed to be done on our own time, but how could I resist a small challenge, hidden from Vince by the geography of the course? I confess that as a tomboy, a part of me loved being in the middle of all that male bravado—the swaggering, the swearing, the scratching of balls.

Once in the Blue Ridge Mountains of Virginia, at one of my first road rallies, we went for a night run to a steep hill. The race had ended earlier, and I'd gotten fourth place and pissed off most of the men. I was the only woman in the competition. So that night, after many had had a beer or two by the fire, we went to show off our kit some more. It was a steep hill, deep in the woods, quite muddy. Halfway up, the hill plateaued slightly, and then there was a short, steep jaunt up the rest of the way. You couldn't slow down on the plateau or you'd get stuck in the mud pit. You had to know your route and maintain a steady gun on the engine, but it was hard to know your path in the dark of the night, even with a roof rack full of high beams.

I didn't drive that night. I rode shotgun with a man who didn't like the fact that I was trying to navigate for him one bit. He paused as we edged onto the plateau and asked me if I wanted to drive the rest of the way. But it was too late. He slowed on the plateau, rolled right into the mud pit, gunned it to get out, but only sank more. Pissed, he told me to get out and run the winch up the hill and secure it to a steady tree. Pissed, I started up the muddy hill with the winch. Soon, I was out of the high beam light and still had a way to go before I crested the hill. I was going to have to secure the winch to a tree in the dark. And then, I took a step into an unseen mud hole, and when I went to step out of it, my prosthetic leg stayed behind. I was down on my knees in the mud and the dark. I tried to pull my leg out of the mud, but the suction was too strong, so I secured the winch around the socket just as the man yelled out to ask if I had finished securing it. He didn't ask me to what I had secured it. I told him to let her rip. The cable went taut, then suddenly my prosthetic burst out of the mud on the side of the hill and within seconds I heard a crack, and then lots of cursing. My leg smashed right into the window of the man's truck, shattering it. That was the last time they picked on me.

I heard Liam's engine working hard. I knew he thought he had me beat, but I swerved Athena at a hard left, and cut him off right at the end of his path. I tried not to grin to the point of boasting. Chris had the flask to his mouth like a baby bottle and when Liam slammed the brakes, the liquor went all over his face and down his chest, and he immediately coddled his teeth and lips with his hands. Liam leaned out the window, mud spots all over his bald head. He pointed at me and just started laughing. I wasn't quite sure what to do next; a moment of euphoria and a hormone rush swept over me, and if Vince hadn't honked his horn to gather everyone for a lunch break at the pub, I may have risked my job with more tomfoolery.

Shepherd's pie in the pub, and afterward a bet on a game of billiards—if I lost, I gave Liam my phone number. If I won, I'd decide whether to give him the correct phone number. He was charming with a sense of British, middle-class humility and humor. He was both crass and a gentleman. And the chemistry was undeniable, albeit for me it was primarily physical. He won by five balls. I gave him the correct phone number, and we made a date.

Now, with his Defender started again after submersion, and the evening still to come, it would be completely dismissive to back out. The only side of me that wants to back out is the one fond of self-preservation. I am here in

England on a mission. I am preparing to drive around the world and visit landmine survivors with my daughter at the end of a year. The last thing I need is to get involved with someone that I cannot, or will not, see filling all of my days.

After the quarry I return home, and Leia and Celie help me wash the truck, as I have to do every day after work. Mostly they just hose each other down. There are three hours before I have to leave to meet Liam, and everything but me is in perfect order. I haven't been on a date in probably a year. And as if she senses my nervousness, Jane comes out the door, all giddy.

It's been a couple of months since Jane and I met over my pseudo-deathbed, and we've become fast friends, like sisters. She helped us find used furniture to fill the rooms. She cleans houses for a living, so I give her money and she does our laundry and cleans our side of the duplex weekly.

Celie and I also eat dinner several nights a week with Jane, Leia, and Michael—Jane insists on it, so I pay her extra for groceries, too. Plus, her Yorkshire pudding is to die for. We watch *Pop Idol* every week while we eat on television trays in their side of the duplex. Jane and Michael fight like Edith and Archie Bunker from *All in the Family*. One night a week, we all go to the local pub and shoot pool. Jane takes hours to get ready for those few hours at the pub, practically uses a whole can of hairspray for one night out at the local. We all have a beer or two, unwind from the week, and laugh while the girls eat french fries and run amok. They feel like family.

"Are you ready for your date?" Jane asks me, walking into the yard. The girls have gone inside.

"No. I don't want to go."

"Oh, but you've got to go. You're not obliged to sleep with the bloke, especially if he's a total wanker. But you probably could use some sex, and besides, our girls are really looking forward to their first sleepover."

"Knock it off, Jane. I'm not going to sleep with the man on the first date."

"Are you telling me that you've never done that before?"

"I'm not telling you anything."

"What are you going to wear?"

"My work clothes. That's all I've got." My work clothes consist of jeans, earth-toned button-ups, and a Barbour oil-skin that I received when I took the Land Rover job.

"I was afraid of that. So, I've brought you a few things. Let's go inside and make some tea."

Jane chases the girls out of my living room and tells them to go bother Michael.

"But we're drawing," Leia protests. Celie just keeps drawing.

"Tell your dad I said you could have some sweeties," Jane says, and both the girls drop everything and run out the door. Jane starts a kettle on the stove and throws a gro-cery bag on the table. Lacy undergarments edge out of the bag as it lands.

"You've got to be kidding me. Jane, I can't do this. I hear Pan playing his lute," I say, half in earnest.

"And after we get you dressed, you need to remember to

stop at the chemist and buy yourself some protection, just in case."

"You're incorrigible, Jane."

"Well, I don't know what that means, so I'll take it as a compliment." Jane continues to fuss, pours tea. "Don't you want to be in love, get married, make a home with somebody?"

"Add the white picket fence," I say, "and they call it the American dream."

"Yes, don't you want that?" Jane asks.

"I had it—the whole nine yards of white picket fence, and I'll tell you what, Jane. It doesn't make you happy. I had a regular appointment at the local salon, a closet full of designer clothing, and a shoe collection to rival Imelda Marcos, only I didn't have any damn feet. We went to wine auctions, galas—we had money and the illusion of clout it bought, but it's not happiness—not even close. I'm lucky though—most folks spend half their lives saving enough money to buy that dream. Their life is half over before they realize it's an illusion. I figured it out at twenty-five."

"Okay, but I just want to go to Disney World," Jane says.

I settle on conventional black lace—bikini underwear, a natural, mesh-cup bra—if it gets to that point, none of it will be on long anyway. I know that much about myself. I will not, however, let her convince me to wear anything revealing on the outer layers. I no longer own anything risqué to begin with; a couple of low-buttoning shirts barely reveal the beginning slope of cleavage. My three pairs of Levi's are at varying stages of degradation, and the only footwear I have now is a pair of Redwing boots, cinnamon leather with thick, black rubber soles.

My father bought the boots for me with a whole pay-check when I was fifteen years old and went to Ireland to do missionary and construction work at an orphanage. The leather on the inside of the boot, more than a decade later now, still retains the smell of my sweaty flesh-and-bone foot.

I look down at the bra and feel a tingle inside that I've tried to suppress for some time now. I have been trying to take this mission seriously, which is as hard to do as it is to sometimes say with a straight face. I have managed to avoid all serious manner of flirtation. Liam, however, I am unable to resist, even if he looks like a runt pirate.

"Jane, I hate this."

"Hate what, dear?" She pinches the teabags over the cups, then hands a cup to me.

"First, you like someone, whether you're looking to like someone or not, more often when you're not. Then, you suddenly have an excessive amount of physical chemistry. And then, just as you're about to get all romantic, you have to pause and explain, *Oh, by the way, if we have sex, my legs are prosthetic and may fall off.*"

Jane laughs, then says, "Surely, you've encountered this before?"

"Yes, of course, but it varies, you know? In one way, it's a quick test to determine whether someone's decent or not, but sometimes, when the chemistry is hot, you don't want them to be indecent, nor—decent or not—do you want them to hurt your feelings."

Jane rolls her arms up in the folds of her extra-large Mickey Mouse sweatshirt and sits across from me. "Are you sure he doesn't already know?"

"Not unless Vince told him, but what reason would he have to do that?"

"Well, if the bloke is bothered by it, then he isn't worth a petticoat. And that's that. I think all women feel that way about their bodies, pins or no pins." Jane stands up again. She's not good at sitting still. "Go fetch me the jeans you're going to wear. They'll need pressed. You want to look your best."

My new cell phone rings on the sink. Jane answers it. Her eyes grow wide. "My name is Jane . . . and who is this . . . well hello, Kelley's mother. I'm her neighbor and we love having her here. Hold the line." She cups the receiver with her hand. "Give me the jeans. I'll be back in a flash."

I pass the jeans to Jane in exchange for the phone. "Shit," I say, taking the phone. "Well, hello there," I greet my mom.

"Hello there? That's the best you got?"

"Come on now, relax. How are you and Pops?"

"Worried sick, but you know that. You haven't called since you got off of the plane over two months ago. For god's sake, you're in a foreign country."

"It's England, mom," I reply. Has it really been eight weeks since we stepped off of that plane?

"It's still foreign. It's across the ocean. And you have my only grandchild."

"I left a message for you last month. The job is great. Celie loves her new school. She's starting to pick up a

British accent—she called me 'Mum' the other day. And I have a date tonight." I bite my lip. I should have left that last part off.

"A date? What about your child?"

"She's going to stay with our neighbor. Jane is the sweetest woman, and she has a daughter just a bit older than Celie."

"You hardly know these people, and you're going to leave my granddaughter with them?"

Then there's silence across the ocean on the long, strange lines of telephone communication, another awkward moment between my mother and me in a line of them that has stretched out our whole lives together.

"They're really lovely people."

I start to say that they saved my life, but I stop myself this time.

"How do you know they're not kidnappers, or perverts?" My mom can't stop herself.

"I don't know, but I trust my instincts. I wish you would trust me, too. You know, I should probably go now. I'll call again soon," I say.

"Don't hang up," she says, but I hit the end button before she sounds the *p* in up.

I take a sip of tea, shake off the self-doubt starting to creep in and head up to the bedroom to try on the undergarments. They fit better than I expect.

Jane rounds the corner soon after, a huge, excited smile on her face. "Here's your jeans." They are still hot, hardened with a perfect crease. The concept of pressed jeans is foreign to me. It makes me smile. I push my mother, and the thought of all I've left behind, to the back of my mind.

"I've brought one of my blouses for you, too." Jane says, holding up an orange, sequined, scoop-neck blouse.

I start laughing. "It's so Las Vegas. Do I look Las Vegas to you?"

Jane looks hurt. Her shoulders slump and a few of her turmeric-hued curls drape over them.

"I'm only trying to help. I thought the color would be good on you. I just want you to have a nice time."

"I'm sorry," I say. "I'll try it on, Jane." Maybe this gaudy shirt will turn Liam off of me, I think, and I'll be okay with that. Maybe he'll be fine with the fact that I have no legs, but the orange-sequined shirt will be a deal breaker.

I'm meeting Liam in the city center of Leicester. It's halfway for both of us. It's just under an hour's drive, and on Jane's insistence, I book a hotel there so that I won't have to drive back if I have a drink—so I'll have some autonomy. I check into the hotel, throw my bag in the room, and start walking toward the pub where I agreed to meet Liam. I am already ten minutes late because I had to kiss Celie just one more time, ten more times, before I left.

There's a cold rain falling down on the road as I walk, and a coppery smell, leftovers from a day of merchants— a sweet, candy-like scent mixed with human sweat wafts up from the cobblestones. It's a pretty, old town center and I'm tempted to walk and wax poetic (alone and safe) when I look up and spot the pub.

Liam is sitting at the bar, sipping a Guinness. He's sitting right under a bar light, so when I spot him it's like out of a movie where everyone else in the room fades and the human of your dreams is suddenly revealed. I sidle up next to him and order a pint of John Smith before I even greet him. I start to take my coat off and he stands up and assists me, then hangs it on a peg under the bar.

"You got caught in the rain," he says, sitting back on the barstool and taking me in—my damp hair, the raindrops on my collarbone—his eyes widen. I wonder if it's the shirt. "I'm glad you came," he says, taking a sip of his beer to hide the fact that his eyes are darting toward my cleavage.

"Did you think I wouldn't?" I ask.

"You never know about these things. Besides that—you are the talk of the town; didn't know if you'd have time for the likes of me," he said.

"What's that supposed to mean?" I half-shout. The pub is crowded.

"It's not every day that an American bird like you shows up in a quarry driving a truck like that, telling everyone she's going to drive around the world."

"I'm just the new girl in town. They'll get over it," I say, feeling a tad of heat in my cheeks.

Liam grins, and leans in close to me. In the quarry, he had this bad-boy, rugged look with a little wool cap, and now he is wearing this big-collared, '80s, diagonally striped shirt, that, incidentally, has alternating lines that compliment my orange sequins. It looks like something his mother might have bought for him for Christmas.

We talk on, smooth as the bitter ale. We share a safe exchange—his father is a pub owner; Liam's loved Land Rovers since he was a child. He drives a lorry for a living, considers himself a simple man.

As the general knowledge is complete, I ask him how well he knows Vince.

"Land Rover Vince? From the quarry?" he asks.

"I don't know another Vince," I say.

"I don't know him all that well. I mean, I've read about him—he's in the Land Rover magazines advertising all the safaris he takes rich, bored people on, but I've only been to about half a dozen of his open quarry days, and we've only just had some banter. I don't take myself nearly as seriously as he takes himself, though. Why do you ask?"

"Because he told me to watch out for you," I say, cutting to the heart of the matter. "He seemed to think you're a ladies' man," I add.

"What?!" Liam replies. "Try as I might, I'm nothing of the sort. I was in a decade-long relationship until about a year ago, and you're the first girl to get my attention since, to be honest with you. Vince is probably jealous that a single woman at the quarry isn't fawning over him."

"But he's married, isn't he?" I ask.

"Yeah, that's what I hear. I saw her once at a rally. Who wears high heels and miniskirts to a Land Rover rally? Vince's wife, that's who," he says.

"Is she nice?" I ask.

"No one knows, no one I know in the Rover circles has spoken to her. They've only been married a couple of years. Vince told everyone he was off-roading through Russia when he met her, that she was translator for the expedition. Six months later, she showed up and moved into his house, hardly ever comes out from what I hear."

"Why doesn't that surprise me?" I say, disheartened.

I order my third pint when a random redhead named Jolene butts in between us to order a drink. She's sloppy drunk, but cute and says, "You wanna know why I'm out with my girlfriends tonight? You really wanna know?"

"Sure do," I say. I'm buzzed enough to be interested in several things.

Jolene orders her drink, looks me in the eye, with her back to Liam, practically sitting in his lap.

"Because he is an asshole, and he cheated on me. He cheated on *me*. But I'm gonna rise above it, I am."

I'm happy to have a distraction from the intense heat I feel with Liam. So, I engage Jolene. "Honey," I say, "you deserve to have a good time tonight. You deserve to have a good time every night."

"Yes, Love, you're absolutely right. I intend for that very thing you just said." Jolene takes a full-fisted swig out of my pint glass. "You know, I just wanna tell you something before I go. You're a beautiful woman," she slurs, leaving the *t* out of beautiful. "Can I buy you a pint?"

I consent, and her red hair swishes along the bar top. She orders me another pint and wanders away. The bartender asks if I want it in the hole, since I'd already ordered my third. I nod my assent. Liam's hand appears out of nowhere on the small of my back and electrifies my spine. I freeze and then I thaw. "Liam, there's something I want to tell you."

"Go on then, speak up."

I sit upright on the stool and lean back away from him. He cocks his head for a second, leans in toward me, and says, "I'm all ears," which is true. His ears stand out from the side of his bald head like bracket mushrooms on a tree.

Buzzed as I am, getting beyond my limit, I still hesitate. I don't think he'll reject me, but I don't want him to turn out to be a shallow prick either—I like him. So, I get all nervous and switch back to shop talk instead. "You know, I really get a kick out of the fact that it's my job to tell men what to do all day."

"I imagine that is satisfying," Liam says.

"I'm only going to be here about nine more months."

"Off around the world then, is it?"

"Yep. First real stop is in Bosnia and Herzegovina."

Suddenly, Jolene is back and throws her arms around Liam and me both, puts her head between us in a huddle, as if she's about to discuss a game strategy. "That slag is here," she says in a loud whisper.

"Which slag?" I ask.

"The one that slept with what's-his-face, and she's with some other bloke!"

I giggle, but add, "That's terrible."

"Dance with me," Jolene commands. She stands upright, extends her arm toward mine. I smile politely and decline her offer. She starts dancing around me, then close to me. The music is as bad as her dancing, but two drunken left feet don't matter when you've got an hourglass figure and delightful confidence. I hold her at arm's length, lean in toward Liam, and whisper in his ear, "Do you know about my legs?"

"What about them?" He whispers back.

Jolene leans over my shoulder and gets right in my face. "Please come dance with me." Then, she plucks a hair from a ring on her finger.

"All right, Jolene. I'll dance with you. You start. I'll be there in a minute. I need to talk to Liam here briefly," I say.

Winking at me several times on her way to the dance floor, Jolene departs. I watch the way her hair bounces on her one exposed shoulder.

Then I look back at Liam. "They are prosthetic," I say.

"Oh, okay," Liam says, averting his gaze from me to the floor for a moment, and then back to me. He cocks his elbow on the bar, places his chin in the web between forefinger and thumb. "So, how does that work exactly?"

"That's a long story. The short of it is that you figure it out as you go."

"I thought that maybe one day you wore a knee brace. Sometimes your leg seemed a bit stiff, that's all. Both of them, you say?"

"Yes, both of them—about four inches below the knee," I say, looking him straight in the face now.

"Well, may I ask what happened to you?"

"I'll give you the short version: Meningitis. Misdiagnosed. Sixteen."

"This is back in America?"

"Yes, in Ohio."

"Is that near Kansas?"

"No," I reply, laughing.

"What? No one on this side of the pond knows American geography outside of New York, California, and Florida," Liam responds, defending himself unnecessarily.

"It's near Lake Erie."

"That's a Great Lake, right?"

"Yes," I say, smiling so widely that I can feel my chapped skin again, "it's a Great Lake."

"Well then," Liam starts and pauses, then grows quiet as if his mind needs to absorb loss and land. Suddenly, he gazes hard into my eyes.

"Well then," I say, "I have to dance now."

Jolene grabs me on the dance floor, pulls our bodies close. Her forearms rest on my shoulders. I clasp my hands atop her lower back. Our breasts rub against each other during each sway. She puts her head on my shoulder. Her hair smells like smoke and jasmine. It is a heady scent, and I am already intoxicated.

Liam comes to the dance floor, tries to cut in between us, in jest. We all begin to gyrate to some Euro-pop club music. I position Jolene between me and Liam, but he keeps coming straight for me. I know he wants to bed me. A woman knows these things. What I don't yet know is that Liam and I will continue to spend time together for the rest of the year I am in England, and when I leave, it will make me sad, but it will break his heart.

I am dizzy in the best sense of the word. I have had too much to drink. Jolene is perfect eye candy—well on her way to drunken bliss, sexy as all get-out—it's her chest, it's the metal studs on her belt, it's the way she laughs—as if she's nothing else to lose. The music is pulsing in all my parts.

While we dance I decide that I will tell Liam that this will be a temporary fling. Why shouldn't I have a good time on the way out, as long as he is willing and well-informed? Why am I even assuming that we will have sex? Why and how am I so delightedly bold? And why *delightedly*? I dance toward a table, sit down, and fan myself with a coaster.

Liam dances with Jolene a moment more, then politely excuses himself, and joins me at the table. I suggest that we pay the tab and depart for the night. I leave the destination open. I insist on paying my half of the bill, and Liam accepts the offer. We slip out on Jolene. I blow her a kiss that she never sees.

I tuck my arm inside of Liam's as we head out into the still drizzling night. The cobblestones are slick and the way the streetlights reflect on them makes the stones look like a thousand eyes in the dark. I am not walking in a straight line.

A man appears out of a nearby group of them—a taller, balder version of Liam. He says, "I'll be damned if it isn't my brother, Liam."

Liam gives him a hug, and says, "This is the American bird I was telling you about."

And the man says, "She's legless."

I'm shocked by the comment. The man is now a blurred tower of farm jacket and an earring. I feel like vomiting, so I start to walk away. I can't remember if I said goodbye—I am as terrible about goodbyes in person as I am on the phone. I just hang up when I think the conversation is finished. When Liam catches up with me, I'd forgotten the man altogether for the time being.

"Come on, let's get you home," he says.

"I'm not going home. I'm going to a hotel room. Are you coming with me?"

"I can certainly do that."

"You'll take advantage of a half-lit young woman?"

"And she'll take advantage of a half-lit old man?"

I forget about everything then.

As we walk into the hotel lobby, the hard physicality of being drunk is gone; perhaps it was the walk in the rain, the understanding, but euphoria is now setting in. We wait for the elevator. I smile dumbly at the man behind the desk. I wave to a random woman.

There is a mirror in the ceiling of the elevator. I wave at Liam in the reflection. He grabs me by the hips and attempts to kiss my neck. I pull away, giggling. I hold on to the railing for a moment, rub my cheek against the velvet interior of the elevator, and lunge for him, throwing my arms up under his. When we look up into the mirror, all I can see is Jane's orange-sequined blouse and his diamond stripes, and I burst out laughing.

The doors pull open. As I rush out, Liam cups my ribcage from behind, whirls me around in the hallway and kisses me hard. I indulge him, all the way to the door of the room, opening it with the key behind my back as he presses himself against me. The moment in the quarry flashes through my mind—the bulge in his pants. I was right. He presses up against me, and I feel him all the way up to my belly button.

The room is as gaudy as our clothes—plush velvet curtains held back by gold-dipped, leaf-tipped brackets. The carpet is dark maroon with a thin, swirly design, matching leaves in gold. There is a minibar, a whirlpool bath, and a big bed upon which Liam lays flat on his back while I kneel over him and kiss him, eventually fondling that denim-covered bulge. He slips the orange-sequined shirt off over my arms and head, throws it to the side.

Then I briefly remember who I am and roll off of him, step back from the bed. "Where are you going?" he asks.

"Bathroom. Be right back," I speak in fragments. I am fragmented.

I shut the door and start warm water in the bath. I take my legs off one at a time and wash my stumps with soap under the water. I take a hand towel and wash between my legs, under my arms, neck and face. The residue of the pub washes down the drain. I am too drunk to be nervous.

I dry off and slip on a robe hanging from a hook in the bathroom. I do not tie it before I walk back out to the bedroom.

Liam is under the covers now, his hands behind his head. His head is redder than the rest of his pale body. He is bare-chested now, save a couple of gold chains around his neck. He has a tattoo of a hand flipping the bird on his shoulder—the British version, the backward peace sign.

"Look at you," I say.

"Look at me what?"

"Your tattoo, your chains . . ."

"What about them?"

"You're like a mix of American redneck and rapper," I say. "They've got more in common than you think."

Liam shakes his head, grabs my arm and wrestles me to the bed, disrobing me in the process, taking off the last vestige of my bravado. "And what are you?" he asks.

"Kelley," I say. "Nothing more." And before I can add nothing less, his lips are covering mine.

The first round is both sloppy and exciting. Round two, he pulls my loose prosthetics off and lays them at the end of the bed without saying a word. Round three, and enough to call it a round four, are nothing short of primal longing. The fifth round just plain hurts.

Eventually, we sleep, and in what feels like twenty minutes, the sun starts pouring in through the window. I pull my face off of Liam's arm where my mouth has been propped open in a sneer. I wipe it with the blanket. I look at Liam, his skin foreign in both sunlight and sobriety. I smack him in the chest.

"Bloody hell, woman," he says, wiping the sleep from his eyes.

"How did he know?" I demand. The smell of beer on my breath disgusts me.

"How did who know what? What time is it?"

"Last night—how did your brother or whoever he was know that I was legless, when you had just told me that you didn't know."

Liam rolls over on his pillow and starts laughing. I punch him in the arm. He starts laughing harder.

"In jolly old England, my dear, to be legless means you're drunk." Then he laughs some more.

"Oh god," I groan. My head aches. I throw my head into the pillow, roll over, and press my backside into him. Orange sequins in a pile on the floor shine golden in the late morning sun. It's as cheap and lovely as it gets.

IV

....

The capital of Ohio? Columbus.
The capital of Pennsylvania? Harrisburg.
The capital of New York? Albany.

For months on end, Celie and I spend all our late nights and early mornings with the map. We begin with American states, move on to Canada, and now she's memorized almost four continents worth of capitals.

The rapeseed field across the road from the duplex has been shorn for a season of hibernation, marking the passage of time—we are halfway through our year in England.

I print out a world map with only lines, no words, and test Celie—she aces it every time. We muse about what each boundary holds. A capital, I tell her, is like a heart—the place from which lifeblood flows. In Ohio she recalls feeding ducks at a lake, but grandma and grandpa, my parents, are the capital of Ohio to her. She hasn't been to Pennsylvania, so I tell her about the Liberty Bell, a sign of freedom. In New York, she recalls only the Statue of

Liberty, her first plane ride—and though she doesn't say it, perhaps, it also represents saying goodbye to her dad.

In Brazil, the capital is Brasilia, and we talk about the rainforest, coffee. The capital of Australia is Canberra, land of kangaroos and koalas. Moscow is the capital of Russia. We talk about *matryoshkas*—Russian dolls, of which Celie has a set that her Oma has given to her. With each demarcation on the map, I give her an image beyond a name to help the lands stick in memory. I know they are simple images, with which I give equally uncomplicated explanations—Celie's just shy of four, after all.

I tell her that people in different countries are like ice cream, which she loves—they all have different flavors, but the same basic ingredients. She will discover soon enough how complex it all is, much more like a nesting doll than a scoop of ice cream, with layers upon layers of experiences shaping the way each of us fit inside our borders.

At the quarry this week, we've been hired to train some folks that are preparing for a global road rally. Vince explains that this rally, in particular, is cross-continental, and that the participants will be driving some of the most glamorous vehicles along some of the most scenic roads in the world. In one portion they will be driving Land Rovers, as there will be some off-roading involved. So, they've hired our crew to teach them a little beyond the basics. "These are high-caliber clients," Vince says. "Don't embarrass me."

Vince has been a little shorter than normal with me since I returned some equipment to his home last week. He wasn't there. I met his wife, Olena—the translator he'd met on the Russian expedition—only her English, I found, was quite limited. At first, she was a bit sheepish talking with me, wouldn't open the door, but then I saw a child behind her, a young girl. "Is that your daughter?" I asked. She nodded proudly. "I have a daughter, too." I told her.

I ended up staying for over an hour, having tea and biscuits in Vince's kitchen. Olena's daughter was maybe ten and had been in school for a little over a year. Her English was much better than her mother's. She translated some, but mostly she just wanted to go play music in her room. Olena confessed that she was lonely. She wanted to get a license to do hair but said Vince didn't approve. She hardly left the house—just cleaned and cooked while dressed to the nines.

I suspect she wasn't a translator, but a mail order bride. She insisted she was happy. She conveyed that Vince was kind and generous to take in her and her daughter both—that the schools in England were much better for her daughter. And Vince never hit her, she said, so she had no reason to complain.

It was suddenly clear why Vince had a hard time dealing with the likes of me.

And then, Vince came home. He smiled when he saw us at the table, almost looked happy to see her with company, but he rushed me out the door pretty quickly after that. I showed him where I'd put the equipment and instead of goodbye, he said, "Kelley girl, don't get any ideas."

I cleaned and lubed up the Land Rover extra for this day, even waxed my boots. Vince is assigning a client to each of us—but of course I am going to be last. He assigns Mack to an older, sophisticated-looking gentleman in head-to-toe Barbour, but the man says, "I think I'd prefer the young woman to instruct me, if that isn't a problem."

"She's new," Vince says, "American, with the expected sass, to boot."

"I'm fine with that," says the client.

Vince doesn't look me in the eye as he introduces me to Sir Terence English, and I don't care one bit. I'm delighted by small victories.

"Shall we begin?" I open the driver's side door for Sir Terence.

"I should be opening the door for you," he says. "All the way from America just to teach off-roading?"

"No, this is just a pit stop," I say, buckling my seat belt in the passenger seat.

Between explanations of differentials and failed hill climbs, Sir Terence elicits all the details of my impending journey, which I've now officially titled *Expedition Athena*—even had a little business card made up with a tiny Land Rover on it and a byline that reads: *A Transglobal Journey Driven by Compassion.*

I also tell him about an upcoming ten-day expedition to Morocco in another month that Vince has invited me to go on as a support vehicle, which will provide me with some desert and dune driving experience before I cross the Sahara in full. I'm a bit embarrassed by the attention, but he shows a keen interest and keeps asking questions. I try to divert him as we head down to cross the trench.

"I'm not supposed to ask you questions," I say, "but don't you have to do something fancy or important to become a knighted Sir?"

"There are so many important things that people do in this world," he replies.

"So, what important thing did you do?" I ask.

"I performed the first successful heart transplant in England," he says, matter-of-factly.

"That's nothing to sneeze at," I say. "Did you actually meet the Queen? Did you kneel down, and did she tap your shoulders with a sword?"

"It is always good to be acknowledged for your work," he replied. I felt a bit naive, so I changed the subject.

"Sounds like you earned a jaunt around the world," I say.

"Perhaps, but this is quite unlike the adventure that awaits you. Everything on my trip is prepared in advance for me. All I have to do is show up and drive a pretty stretch."

"It's still brave—maybe not as brave as taking the heart out of a man and sticking it inside another," I say.

"The heart is a robust, resilient organ—and speaking of robust, I rather think you're the brave one here," he says. "Now, let's cross this trench, shall we?" And we do.

The afternoon goes as well as the morning and the conversation turns from off-roading to medicine. Sir Terence is curious about the loss of my legs and after I answer every detailed question in the medical jargon I've learned along the way, he says, "You're quite lucky to be alive, you know?" I tell him that if I had a pound for every doctor who has ever told me that, I could probably afford to go on the road rally with him. He chuckles at that.

At the end of our day together, I feel a little dispirited that this will be the last time I get to enjoy the company of Sir Terence. I tell him what an honor and a pleasure it has been to work with him and wish him well on his rally. As if he can sense my thoughts, he says, "You're not saying goodbye, are you? I rather hope we'll stay in touch. I have some connections at the BBC and when it gets closer to the time of your departure, I'm sure they'd love to give you a bit of publicity." He asks for my contact info, and I hand him one of my new cards. In return, he hands me one of his, and all I can think is that I'm not doing too bad for a legless, working-class orphan from Akron, Ohio.

The capital of Saudi Arabia? Riyadh.
The capital of Iran? Tehran.
The capital of Iraq? Baghdad.

A week after I meet Sir Terence, I'm working on logistics at the duplex. I have a long table in the middle of the living room covered with books, papers, a laptop, and all over the wall in front of me are sticky notes that Jane gave to Celie. Celie has spent a full week illustrating each sticky note with the outlines of countries she's been learning. Inside the perimeters are symbols of the concepts I've given her to associate with each one.

It's a quarter until two in England, fifteen minutes before America opens for business. I'm waiting to call so I can have some money transferred because I have found the Land Rover that we are going to drive around the world. Our Athena is small, has almost two hundred thousand miles on her, and has been through a lot—I'm wary about taking her around the globe. Plus, I've found the right truck for the job.

In 1998 to coincide with the fiftieth anniversary of Land Rover, the company built eight Land Rover Defender Wolfs. Normally light military vehicles, these were the first of their kind ever built for civilian use. Land Rover built them to celebrate their anniversary in style—by having the decorated expeditionist Sir Ranulph Fiennes and a crew drive them around the globe.

Among many achievements, Sir Ranulph was the first man to cross the Antarctic by foot. He was a decorated British legend and, like most legends, had a reputation for being difficult. The Wolf models were painted gold for the special occasion and were quickly referred to as Goldilocks. Rumor was that they cost almost two hundred thousand dollars each to manufacture. The Wolfs were planned to the most minute detail for the expedition. They were even made to transport power to specialized catamarans that would carry them across certain straits and fjords.

At the last minute, the expedition was canceled. Rumor, again, had it that Fiennes demanded more money than originally agreed upon, and when Land Rover didn't concede, the effort disintegrated, and the eight Wolfs were eventually sold to private collectors for half their worth or less. Two years after the fiftieth anniversary, a year before

I arrived in England, Sir Ranulph attempted to walk solo and unsupported to the North Pole—a feat he did not finish due to frostbite. Infamously, he cut the tips of his own fingers off with a saw because of the pain. In Land Rover circles, most likely still bitter about the broken anniversary deal, rumor was that he had to cut part of his frostbitten penis off, too.

A year after Sir Ranulph lost some bits, I am introduced to a wealthy Land Rover enthusiast who has a small museum on his estate that houses some of the rarest Land Rovers. I tell him my story, and he agrees to sell me one of the eight Wolfs for so much less than it is worth that it feels like charity.

I stare at the wall while I wait to call America for money. Celie's added some new sticky notes. I spot Iran, with a robed man holding a paper and a quill. Iran is famous for poets, I've told her, such as Rumi and Hafez. Inside Iraq, there's a bottle of perfume because I once read about Yaqub Al-Kindi, considered the father of perfume due to his novel-at-the-time distillation skills. The heart of Saudi Arabia is Islam, a religion that considers the divinity of Christianity a polytheistic sin, since God in Islam is the whole totality of the universe, everything and anything comes from the one God. Inside the sticky note that is Saudi Arabia, Celie has drawn a heart that's bursting out of the borders.

I notice that the three new sticky countries are aligned similarly to where they would be on the map, then I stand up to get a better look and realize that my daughter hasn't been placing the notes randomly at all—she's been making an accurate map on the wall of sticky countries and their symbols. A breeze through the window sends them all a flutter, as if they have a pulse, as if they are a hundred-and-growing hearts beating on the wall, a map of the bodies of the whole human family, in sync.

I call America at nine-on-the-dot to have the money transferred for the new Athena. I know the secretary pretty well, so we start the usual small talk about weather, family—then suddenly, she seems to drop off the call.

"Hello," I say into the receiver. "Are you still there?"

"Yes, I'm sorry. It's just . . . have you seen the news? A plane has crashed into the World Trade Center."

I finish the call quickly and hurry over to Jane's side of the duplex since I don't own a television. She makes us tea, and we spend the rest of the day, with the rest of the world, helplessly watching as one plane after the other crashes into both towers of the World Trade Center, the Pentagon, a field in Pennsylvania. Four in all. Four chambers in a heart.

It pains us to look on as bodies and flames descend from windows, as the buildings collapse inside of themselves, as people desperately flee from the gaping wounds and others heroically run toward them. We watch as the smoke and debris billow over into neighborhood after neighborhood, as the spirits of nearly three thousand rise into the ether before they blow out to sea, settle back to the ground.

America, the glitzy infant of the globe, both beloved and despised for its childish stubbornness, selfishness, and showiness has just been mortally wounded in unfathomable tragedy. I can barely breathe. Jane is weeping. The heart of the whole world map, the capital of human spirit, is broken, just like that.

The days to come are filled with languish—a numbness that makes a spirit both desperate for joy and fearful that it will never be able to know joy again. In England, every window is filled with an American flag. The days pass with the unfurling stories of the dead, rising anger at terrorists who have long been terrorized themselves, a fear of retaliation from all sides.

Several weeks later, I'm gearing up for the ten-day Moroccan expedition. I spend every free minute I have with Celie because with the travel to and from Morocco, we'll be separated for two weeks—the longest we've ever been apart. Celie's young teacher from the day school, with whom Celie has a tight bond, has agreed to stay in the duplex with her while I'm gone, and between her and Jane and Leia, I've little to worry about—though I do.

The day before I depart, we do everything and anything Celie wants—we walk around a nearby lake, we make princess crowns out of paper, we go to see the horses that live down the road. We eat pasta and cheese for dinner and ice cream for dessert. After dinner, we study our map. I introduce her to the countries that will be between us starting tomorrow.

The capital of France is Paris. Bread and wine, something for each of us.
The capital of Spain is Madrid. Siestas, I tell her, are naps. Again, something for us both.

The capital of Morocco is Rabat. Rugs come to mind. Magic carpets, she prefers.

I take the Sharpie pen and connect the three countries on the map. Celie begins to add them to her sticky country collection. "Mama," she says, while drawing contentedly, "will you bring me back some bread from France?"

"No, I cannot, because even though France will be between us, I'm not actually going there. I'm taking a ferry from England to Spain, and besides the bread would be moldy by the time I got it home." She looks disappointed. After the month we've all had the last thing in the world I want to do is disappoint her. "When you and I set out on Expedition Athena in the spring—France will be the first country we go to—and you can pick out your own bread, okay?" That brings a smile.

We brush our teeth and cuddle into bed, turn on the light for a last game of shadow theater. Celie places her hand flat and ripples it through the air. On the wall it looks like a floating tilde.

"You make an airplane, Mama." I cross my hands, and though the shadow looks more like a bird, I soar up and across the wall toward her tilde. "No, Mama, don't fly up, fly straight across." So, I do, and suddenly the tilde comes rippling toward the plane at high speed until it stubs my finger.

"Ouch," I say. "That hurt. Why did you do that?"

"I didn't mean to hurt you, Mama, but the magic carpet keeps the airplane from flying into buildings."

My heart skips a beat, feels lodged in my throat.

"Mama, there won't be any airplanes with bad guys when you're driving through the desert, right?"

"No, baby," I say, scooping her body up against mine, her back against my chest. "Mama promises to be safe. And besides, there are magic carpets in the desert."

I turn off the lamp and let the starlight in. We lie there for several minutes, our hearts both beating rapidly, one against the other. Finally, I feel hers slowing, so mine slows, too.

"Mama?" she whispers.

"Yes, Celie?"

"I love you to the moon and back."

"The whole universe," I say. Then I hear the thumb lock into the mouth for comfort, and she's asleep within moments, but sleep doesn't come that easy for me.

I take a ferry from England overnight to the port of Bilbao in northern Spain. From there, I have two days to get two clients and their Rovers across the country—650 miles. Vince has already shipped his and the rest of the crew's Land Rovers to Algeciras, in southern Spain. Some of the clients chose that option, too. They will fly in early and spend a day or two at the southern beaches, meeting us in Algeciras, where we will all catch a ferry to Morocco.

Liam and Chris have forked up the money to go, and I'm glad for familiar company. There is only one other client making the cross-country drive with us—he has his wife and two teenagers with him, and after conferring with them on the ferry, we decide to spend the first day mostly driving. We set up camp for the night at the base of the

Andalusian mountains, but it's nearing dark by the time we get there, and everyone is too grumpy to commingle, so we set up our tents and fold in for the night. I hear Liam and Chris, their tent near mine, getting sloshed, talking about how stupid they were not to pay extra and spend a day or two at the beach. I'm hoping the other clients aren't as disappointed in the lack of fun, but we don't have a lot of time. Just as I'm about to fall asleep, I hear the zipper on my tent. I grab the flashlight under my pillow only to see Liam's bald head poking through the top of the door flap.

"Want some company?"

"No," I say. "Chris gets cold at night. Go away."

He looks a little dismayed, but I can't help it. I'm responsible for more than just him. We've been spending less and less time together since 9/11. Partly because he spoke of marriage, and he's only met Celie once so far, and briefly. She doesn't know we're dating because I have a six-month rule, as in I have to be seeing someone for six months before I will introduce them to my child in any serious manner.

I was excited when I heard Liam was going on this trip, until I heard that Chris was coming, too. Those two are often better behaved alone. The other reason I've been putting him off is because he's been hinting about going on the expedition with Celie and me, and even though the idea of a man there to protect us is tempting—especially the more I learn—I know that a man on the expedition will ruin the whole point.

When our ragtag crew gets to Algeciras, Vince is there,

looking sharp and well-rested, with a buxom blonde at his side—not Olena.

"What took you so long?" he asks.

We are plenty on time, but I get the sense he knew it wouldn't be a leisurely trip and that's why he put me in charge—to take care of the clients who couldn't afford the extra expense. I'm tired and mad, but I bite my tongue when Vince hands me a newspaper and calls on the entire group—about thirty-five folks—to gather around. I look down at the headline and bite my tongue harder.

While I was sleeping cold in my tent the night before, America started bombing Afghanistan in retaliation for 9/11. Vince discusses the latest events with the clients and crew, and then asks if anyone feels uncomfortable continuing from here—after all, the world could erupt in war any moment, and we are about to enter a Muslim country. The family of four are the first to raise their hands. Liam and Chris are next. When no one else raises a hand, Vince pulls me aside and tells me that I need to make sure they get back to England in one piece.

"They've signed waivers," I say. "I still want to go."

Vince is motioning the new buxom blonde to tell her he'll be right with her.

"Who's she?" I ask.

"She's a photographer I met recently. I decided last minute to bring her along, to document the expedition." I roll my eyes. "Look, Kelley girl, I know you were looking forward to this, but you're the only American in the group. I think we'd be safer without you."

I raise my voice a bit, to try to tamper the surging tears

with anger. "Do you think that if we crest a dune, and the jihad starts coming toward us on horses with automatic weapons, I'm going to step out of my Land Rover and announce that I'm American?"

Vince takes an ugly tone with me, then softens it, then offers to pay for my return trip, then walks away as if I've never existed, off to the buxom blonde who I imagine doesn't know how to operate a disposable camera.

The family of four opts to find their own way home. Chris and Liam get giddy about the prospect of beaches, but we decide to go spend the night nearby at the Rock of Gibraltar. Once I'm alone in Athena driving ahead of Liam and Chris, the ugly cry begins. There's not a name I don't call Vince or Liam or Chris. I wish I'd never left my daughter. I wish I'd just taken her to France for a week to get all the bread she could ever want.

The Rock of Gibraltar is a big rock. There's no place to swim. There's a large town center with a beer garden, and Chris and Liam head straight for it. I have a beer with them to attempt to calm my nerves. There are monkeys everywhere—Barbary macaques—and signs all over town warn visitors not to feed them.

I watch the monkeys scoping the perimeter of tourists, waiting for them to get loose enough from alcohol to throw caution to the wind, to throw them a french fry. Chris and Liam go on and on about Málaga. Vince told them about a white sand beach there that couldn't be missed. Liam brings up the fact that I don't need to be back for my daughter for a week and a half, and we should take advantage of the time. I'm so angry I'm not speaking. The beer isn't helping much, nor is the fact that before I finish the first one, the boys have already ordered a third.

I excuse myself to go find us a room for the night. The boys would be happy to get drunk and sleep in their truck, but I want a bed and a bath. I throw my travel bag over my head and walk down a side street—a monkey follows. He darts along the corridor, sniffing this, investigating that, but always keeping pace with me. I'm amused by him. I find a visitor kiosk, grab a map, and sit down on some steps to rest and pick out a hotel. My stomach starts growling and I remember that I've a sandwich left in my travel bag, and I reach in the bag to get it. Cue the monkey.

He now resembles a dog, with huge, sad eyes begging to be fed, as if he's starving and I am the only thing between him and death. With total disregard, I break off a piece of the sandwich and toss it to him. He's not a small monkey. His face is pink, his coat yellow-gray, and I watch as he greedily gobbles up the bite. Then suddenly, he jumps toward me. I stand up quickly, toss the sandwich in my bag, but he's gregarious, pulls at my pant leg. I mildly kick him to the side, thinking I should be kicking myself, and head to a nearby hotel, the monkey trailing behind.

There are only two rooms available. One room has a balcony with a large bed, and one room is small with a single bed. I deliberately give the woman Chris and Liam's names for the tiny room and book the large one for myself. Outside my room, I set my bag down, open the door with the key, and walk in to open the balcony doors. It's a lovely view, and I look forward to sleeping with the breezes lapping off the strait of Gibraltar. When I go to retrieve my bag, the monkey is on top of it, attempting to open it and get the rest of my sandwich. I shoo him, afraid of getting bit, and he shoos right back, swatting my prosthetic leg just enough so I lose suction between my stump and the socket. It's too sudden for me to gain control, and I tumble over the steps into the grass. It's a hard enough fall that I need to be still for a moment and assess that everything still works, that nothing is broken.

A stranger nearby comes to check on me just as the macaque dashes away with a prize—my leg. Someone else darts after the monkey. The stranger checking on me helps me hop into the room. The lady at the front desk has been called and tells me they'll do their best to find my leg and hope the monkey doesn't take it to a nest in the crags.

"Well if you do find it," I say. "I'll be right here. I'm not going anywhere."

It's a desperate attempt at humor, but when she smiles and shuts the door behind her, and I'm alone, I ugly cry for the second time today. There's nothing like complete vulnerability. I don't know how I'm going to get home to Celie. I question myself for ever having left America. I cry for a long time in the bed, not sure what to do, and then I notice the sun setting over the water outside. I feel the breezes I had so looked forward to, and I fall asleep.

I wake up in a pitch-dark room to a streetlight blinding me, a silhouette in the door. I'm not sure what's happening, and my heart starts beating against my ribcage. Then I remember my leg—and now there's an intruder—maybe it's best that I die, I think. The light in the room comes on, and there is Liam, holding my prosthetic leg. I'm so relieved I start laughing.

He's wobbling toward me, obviously drunk, and I don't care one bit. "Love," he slurs, "it was the strangest thing. Chris and I are down there enjoying the beer and the atmosphere, and all of a sudden, the crowd starts roaring, like a wave, from one table to another. And there it was, a monkey carrying your leg. And Love, I'd know your leg anywhere. It was quite a show, Chris and I chasing after this fellow, but I got it! And I found you, too! Can I stay in here? There's no room in that tiny bed with Chris."

Liam passes out on the bed next to me within moments, snoring like a beast, still holding my leg like a trophy. Sleep doesn't find me that easy, but at least I'm not legless.

Málaga, I find, does have a beautiful beach—it's also a nude beach, and now I know why Vince told the boys about it, and why the boys wouldn't let it go. I swim for an hour and excuse myself back to a hotel to eat something. Chris and Liam stay out there so long they come back looking like overripe tomatoes, stinking like beer.

Liam helps himself to my leftovers, and afterward I tell him I'm going back to England early. He's disappointed, begs me to stay longer, tells me that no one out there had prettier breasts than me—as if that's going to change my mind. I miss my daughter, and with the world in such tension, I can't have fun even if I wanted to, anyway. I am unable to disconnect myself from the tragedies of a body of which I am a part.

Liam and Chris decide to follow me back home, but we can't leave Málaga the next day because they are both covered in blisters and pain. We take two days after that in the high roads of the Andalusian mountains, and though the scenery is magnificent, the company has done me in. I want to go home, to my heart, to Celie.

When I arrive back to the duplex, the village is shrouded in darkness, except for the stars and the moon. I turn the key, listen to the engine rattle down, and wish my overwhelmed body and mind could rattle down as easily. I think of the map, Celie's magic carpet stubbing my finger, airplanes crashing into buildings, the cruelty of humanity, and I feel the old seed of self-doubt. I wonder if I should call the whole thing off, go back to America, to college, live within my prescribed boundaries.

Celie's young teacher meets me at the door, hugs me, tells me everything went fine. She goes home to sleep in her own bed, and I head up to the bedroom where I see my daughter's mop of blonde curls on the pillow, in the moonlight. I sit at the edge of the bed and take in her fresh beauty—she seems to have grown an inch.

I don't want to imagine the cruelties of the world ever befalling her. I don't know when I should tell her the truth about such things. I don't know if I'm doing the right thing in this world at all, but I slip off my clothes and legs, and curl up behind her, my chest to her back, and I lie there until our heartbeats sync.

The heart is a robust and resilient organ. The heart of one waning body can restart another. What might happen,

I wonder, if all the hearts are in sync, fluttering in the tempo of the breeze like the sticky countries on the wall—finding enough joy in the music of the shared beats that for a time, the whole world remembers the simplicity of happiness and sets out to create a brand new chart, a map without borders, a map of homes—not kingdoms conquered—where salvation lies in kindness, a giant global heart so full of compassion that it stretches to the moon and back, the whole universe.

V

....

WHEN I first meet Poppy, it's a bitter cold morning, early spring, and I am sitting inside of Athena II. This truck is a gem—a man's man's paradise—and now it's ours.

The heater rattles inside the cab, where Phil and I sit, waiting for Poppy to arrive. Even with the heater on, our breath materializes in the air. Phil specializes in Land Rover modifications and has helped me kit out this vehicle over the last few months. Poppy is a photojournalist and has been assigned to do a story on Athena II and the expedition for a Land Rover magazine.

Poppy pulls up in a Daihatsu, a tiny but mightily modified 4×4. She opens the driver-side door, steps out, and the first thing I notice is the length of her leg. It goes on forever, and I wonder how it ever fit in the wheel well of the Daihatsu. Then all six-foot-plus-some inches of Poppy makes her way out, and I notice the kitschy mauve leg warmers, the rugged, coffee-hued boots, the black-velvet quilt jacket—the matching hat with a magenta flower tucked into the brim. The scene reminds me of a cartoon where people just keep exiting a small vehicle, even though there's no possible way to have ever fit them all inside.

She slings a huge camera around her neck, tucks a notebook under her arm, and walks toward us. We step out of the pseudo-warmth of the truck to meet her. She brushes a limp, dark curl of hair away from her face and holds out her free hand to Phil.

"So sorry I'm late—the traffic was bloody hellish. I'm Poppy. You must be Phil. How do you do?" Poppy's voice is deep and raspy, but high-pitched, like a prepubescent boy.

"Fine, thank you," Phil says.

"And you must be Kelley—the woman with this stupendously crazy idea."

"There have been more stupendous, crazier ideas," I say, feeling defensive, imagining my Land Rover anthropomorphizing and eating Poppy's Daihatsu.

Truth is, I feel like Alice after she drank the *Drink Me*. It's too late to turn back now, and as the days go by, I find that I'm winging it on equal parts thrill and fear, giving back tit for tat at the tea party.

Poppy says, "Yes, but it's not every day that a woman decides to go solo, or excuse me, with a child, from London to Sarajevo to South Africa, all the way to Ecuador—a woman who is, pardon me—a double amputee—and an American, to boot." She pauses, assessing my face for a response. I go stoic, stay silent. She shifts gears, "But you've picked the right beast for the job."

A beast indeed, Athena II is a gorgeous piece of machinery encased in a hollow steel roll cage that's able to withstand 9,000 pounds of pressure—a drastic increase in the chances of survival should one roll down a mountainside. She has twin diesel tanks that could cover six hundred miles and outside cubbies that can hold four more jerry cans for an extra twenty gallons of diesel—enough to cross the Sahara and get slightly off track. Phil installed an internal roll cage, too, a winch capable of a 12,000-pound pull, a refrigerator, and more. We can fit the two years' worth of supplies we need to live inside and on top of that truck.

We're all staring at the truck when Poppy breaks the silence. "The sun won't be up forever. Phil, lock the diffs and drive it up on the embankment over there. Turn the wheels toward me, please." I quickly volunteer to ride shotgun in my own truck.

"She's a character," I say to Phil, as he positions the wheels according to Poppy's direction.

"Indeed," Phil says, his chin stiff, "she is that."

Picture Phil in a green Barbour jacket, a rifle cocked under his arm in a gold-framed painting, and at his side, two sturdy, auburn-haired setters, a pheasant in the distance. He is proper with a capital *P* and has the most immaculate and efficiently run garage I have ever seen.

He pulls the handbrake up, turns off the ignition. I ask him to turn it back on for warmth. Poppy darts about the truck, snapping away. She's got a good dose of masculinity, and yet her gestures are effeminate. I wonder if she's a lesbian.

We drive back the short distance to Phil's garage for the interview. Poppy plops herself behind Phil's desk, in his comfy chair, in his office, and begins to take out recording equipment from her bag. Phil and I sit on the other side of his desk.

Poppy asks for coffee and Phil jumps up to get it. I notice his absence immediately because Poppy starts in on me as soon as the door shuts. "First, we'll have the off-the-record interview, assuming that is kosher with you," she asks. She removes her hat, starts pressing the pads of her fingertips into her scalp, a meager attempt to revive limp, thin hair. She removes her scarf, flinging it into the wind-less office like a starlet. "So, why are you really doing all of this? I mean, there is the obvious story of you losing your legs to meningitis at sixteen. That must have been just awful."

"Yes—" I begin to speak, but she continues.

"Anyhow, I figure that explains the charity side of things, your desire to meet with landmine survivors. But let me see if I have this correct—you are proposing to circle the globe, while visiting some rather dangerous locations, in nine months' time—and all of this with your little girl? Is that correct?" Poppy speaks rapidly, taking sharp, deep breaths where pauses beg to be.

"Yes," I interject. "That's the tentative plan. I could do it all in nine months, but I'm allowing two years to accommodate any inconveniences. I've been planning this for a year and a half with the help of some experienced folks and have no intention of knowingly placing my daughter or myself in any danger." I pause, get lost in a brief thought of danger, and add, "Some of my family thinks I've lost my mind."

"I'll bet they do." Poppy pauses and smirks, then says,

"So, how much are you getting paid? Obviously, there is money to be made with a story like this."

"I'm not making a profit," I say.

"I find that hard to believe," she replies.

"Well, I've had a few things donated—like a GPS system, some off-roading equipment—all in exchange for advertisement on the truck. But that's it."

Poppy snickers, her upper lip curling in a way that suggests appetite. She cocks her head down, peers at me, grins widely, and gives me a half-wink. I admire her bravado.

"Really?" she says, leaning as close to me as the desk between us will allow.

"Really," I say, leaning back in the chair and crossing my arms.

Phil comes back, not a moment too soon, with a large personal thermos held tightly to his chest. His secretary follows with a small tin tray of coffee, two Styrofoam cups, a bowl of cream and sugar. She sets the tray on a stack of backlog magazines at the corner of Phil's desk. She takes a step back, exhales into a wide, nervous smile while gazing upon Poppy, and clasps her hands together in front of her plump waist. Then she near-curtsies and leaves.

"Phil, would you mind? A touch of cream and two cubes," Poppy says.

Phil turns his head toward me without looking me in the eye and asks how I like my coffee.

"Strong and black," I say.

"How do you like the silver?" Phil asks Poppy, as he prepares the coffee.

"On the Wolf?" Poppy asks. Phil nods.

"Well, I'm sure someone like you would find it blas-phemy to have one of the historical Goldilocks Wolfs painted silver, but I'm sure she has her reasons."

"Thank you," I say. "Phil definitely took issue with it, but I had it repainted because I feel that if I come blazing into any threatening scene with a shiny, gold, rare Land Rover, then I might as well as paint 'Rape me, Kill me, Steal my truck' on the windshield."

Poppy grins. "Seems a good reason to me," she says.

Phil knows he's lost and moves on. "We've done a lot of work to that Rover."

"Splendid work," I add, and then we start talking shop—roof racks, spare tires, jerry cans. Poppy likes a truck the way that I like a truck, and we delve into a rapid-fire conversation. Phil's head veers back and forth as if he's at Wimbledon.

"Rear lockers?" Poppy asks.

"Yes, and stainless steel underbody plates," I add.

"Rock sliders?"

"Yes, for those pesky boulder crossings."

"A lift kit?"

"Not overkill, but yes."

"I saw the snorkel—impressive."

"Thank you."

"Favorite tire?"

"BFGoodrich All-Terrain."

"Excellent choice. Kinetic ropes with the winch, tree bands?"

"They come in handy."

"CB, Sat phone, GPS?"

"Hell, I put in a ten-disc CD changer and had a solid steel box welded just to protect it. If all hell breaks loose and you're going to die, you ought to have good music in the background."

"Yes!" Poppy exclaims.

Phil jumps in like a comma, a needed pause. "Would anyone like more coffee?"

Poppy and I both say yes, take deep breaths, and sit back in our chairs. I have absolutely no sexual attraction toward her, but the spirited conversation has me aroused. Land Rover enthusiasts in Britain often refer to themselves as "randy lovers," and there's a reason. After a day of winching through mud pits, river crossings, or resolving situations in which one must instinctively reach for the gearshift through a mixture of water and red clay mud, your adrenaline is charged. Steam rising from the engine when the hose hits it after a long day, clumps of clay and stone washing out from the skeletal underbody, the way that truck ticks down gently after going hard at it—the machine has its charm.

"How about press coverage?" Poppy interrupts my thoughts, just as I start shifting in my chair.

"I am getting a bit," I say. "It's good for the cause."

"I'd love to cross the Sahara with you. That would make a phenomenal follow-up article. Maybe meet you in various locations. What do you think?"

"That's something to consider," I say, feeling heady.

Poppy, in two hours, has gone from a brief amusement to a potential travel partner. And perhaps because my head is all askew, I throw in, "If you want, you could meet me

at the cliffs of Dover and do a departure story. There's a
lovely restored farmhouse hotel with a Roman spa there
where I plan to stay the night before," I say, before I can
stop myself. "I figure a night of luxury is acceptable before
I go sleep in a truck for the next two years."

Poppy places one hand over her firm, large bosom and
the other over her mouth. "I'm flattered," she says, fanning
herself for show, "and I humbly accept." Then she reaches
over the desk and shakes my hand.

Sir Terence English kept in touch and kept his word, and in
mid-spring, a BBC crew arrives at the duplex. Everyone but
Celie is excited—we've done a few interviews with local
outlets already and she doesn't like the attention. Leia is
outside bragging to the crew as they unload.

"She knows every country on the map, and their capitals!" Leia garbles, her mouth filled with sweeties.

The cameraman goads her. "She knows all that at the
age of four, you say?"

"Why yes, she does, and she's my best friend," Leia says.

"So, tell me, what do you know?" the cameraman
replies.

"I know you don't believe me, but I'm telling the truth.
You'll see."

Leia runs inside and tells Celie about her interaction with
the cameraman. Celie is not impressed, especially when the
cameraman comes inside, sees the map, and starts testing
her in a chastising tone. Celie clutches her colored pencil
tightly and falls into a drawing, trying to will the man
away with lines. He quickly points to three countries then

stands in front of the map to hide it. She side-glances from across the room as he points but doesn't give in. She simply gets up and walks outside to play with Leia.

We finish the interview more quickly than the time it took the crew to set up for it, and when the cameraman is back outside repacking his equipment, Celie pulls up to him on Leia's bike, unicorn helmet on her head, and says, "Bogotá, Colombia. Lomé, Togo. Ulaanbaatar, Mongolia. You could have picked harder ones."

Leia crosses her arms and cocks her head. "I told you so," she says.

"You could probably read them from across the room. Still impressive, though. But I didn't point to Togo," says the cameraman.

"Well, they're all close together there, now aren't they?" Celie says. "So then, it was probably either Accra, Ghana, or Porto-Novo, Benin. Did you know that voodoo started in Benin?"

The cameraman now looks impressed and asks Celie if she'll say that again for the camera. She shakes her head. She suffers no fools. Then Leia bites into a hunk of licorice, and says, "I think you better go now before we practice some voodoo on you!"

As their van pulls out of the driveway, Leia high fives Celie, shouting "Girls Rule!" Celie slaps her hand and shouts it back.

Michael comes outside and hands me and Jane each a cold beer.

"I'll drink to that," Jane says.

"To what?" Michael asks.

"Just drink your beer and shut up," Jane says. Then we pop the tabs and chug.

A month later, Celie is tucked into the passenger side of our new Athena with paper, colored pencils, and a bag of sweeties from Jane. As she and I pull out of the driveway, everyone is in tears—even Michael. As the three of them grow small in the rearview mirror my heart grows heavy. Leia chases behind us as fast as her legs can pedal on her bike, the unicorn horn waving to and fro like a magic wand, as if it can will us back. Celie sees her in the mirror and begs me to slow down. I slow a tad, but I'm not sure I can prolong this goodbye much longer. Celie unbuckles her seatbelt as the dust blows around Leia. She gets on her knees, sticks her head out the window and waves to Leia, and Leia shouts, "To the moon and back, Celie! To the moon and back!"

And Celie shouts back, "The whole universe!"

There is nothing more to be said, and Celie and I barely speak the whole way to Dover.

Poppy is inside the lobby, wearing tight capri jeans with her hair pulled back in a tiny, curled ponytail. She is more gangly without the winter layers she was wearing at our first interview. When she sees us, she walks over, shakes Celie's hand and strikes up a conversation with her while I check in and arrange for an evening babysitter.

When I return to them, an album falls from Poppy's lap. I bend over and retrieve it and hand it to her. Our hands brush against each other, and I feel a sudden unease. I was more comfortable with Poppy when we were surrounded by the smell of diesel. In this fancy place, there are proper ladies whose haircuts probably cost more than my clothing, who not only know how to pronounce *pâté de foie gras* but know exactly what's in it.

The lobby walls are thick oak, with benches and book-shelves built into them. The cushions, vermilion velvet. The bar is stocked with fine amber, the glass polished to a perfect translucence. I feel a pang of nostalgia, wishing I was sitting on Jane's side of the duplex, about to tear into dinner with a cold can of beer.

"Maybe it isn't the right time, but your daughter seems to like them," Poppy says, handing me the album. I want to crash for half an hour after the four-hour drive, spend some quiet time with Celie before Poppy and I have dinner in the dining room where no children are allowed, but I take the album out of politeness, sit down, and open it.

Inside the pages are a series of modeling photographs. Poppy is into cosplay; her alter ego, Lara Croft. In the pho-tographs, she has donned various tailored outfits, repli-cas of the costumes worn by Angelina Jolie in the *Lara Croft: Tomb Raider* film. She has clothes for Siberia to Cambodia and anywhere in between, including a cat suit. In the photos, there is a lot of crouching action, artillery, and often in the background, her kitted-up Daihatsu.

I am not sure how to respond, so I opt for practical. They are photographs of high quality, and I tell Poppy just that. She shyly thanks me. It is a striking paradox, the way she ordered Phil around in his own office, and the way, in this lobby, she nervously curls her hair around her finger while I look at the album.

Celie isn't about to let me have a nap when we get back to our room. She's excited by the posh surroundings. She pulls furniture together, makes herself an "office," and tells me that I must write down what she says—"word for word"— a letter to Leia, that we must put it in the post before we leave in the morning. I tell her to draw the pictures for the letter first, but her energy level far exceeds paper and colored pencils.

There's an indoor pool in an old stately barn, and I take Celie for a swim to wear her out. In the locker room afterward, she covers herself in the potions provided, makes a robe out of a plush towel since the robes on the wall don't fit her. Let her enjoy it, I think to myself. We won't be this comfortable forever. By the time I get her back to the room and bathed, the hotel sitter has arrived with a special dinner tray for Celie. I've lost track of time. I've got five minutes to get to the main building where I told Poppy I'd meet her at the bar before dinner, my cargo pants are dotted with chlorine water, and the armpits of my shirt are showing sweat. I've only time to change one, so I go with a shirt.

I didn't realize there was a dress code in the dining hall, and they almost don't let Poppy and me in because of my cargo pants—my shirt is collared. Poppy, wearing all black and pearls, takes the maître d' to the front windows of the lobby and points out Athena, explains to him what I'm about to do, and tells him that I probably don't have anything but casual pants, but it's all for a good cause. He lets us eat.

With every course brought to the table, there is a glass of alcohol to complement, which would be fine if Poppy and I hadn't sipped a bourbon at the bar before dinner. By the third course, the waiter is beginning to sound like Charlie Brown's teacher.

"I won't eat this well again for some time," I say. "Come to think of it, I haven't eaten this well in some time."

"It's quite decadent," Poppy adds. "But well deserved. Are you nervous? I mean, you're actually taking off tomorrow."

"If I let myself think too much," I reply after a moment of staring out the window at my silver Armageddon-ready home on the other side, shining in a haze of fog and street lights. "There are moments when it becomes overwhelming, but providence has carried me this far, and I really believe in what I am about to do." I motion out the window, "And as you are aware, there's no better truck for the job."

"I meant to ask you, why the name Athena? I love it, by the way," Poppy says, staring at the truck through the glass and drizzling rain.

"My grandma is Greek. I grew up hearing stories of the gods and goddesses. I thought maybe if I paid tribute to Athena, she might protect me."

Poppy leans against the windowsill, runs a finger across her bottom lip. I wonder if the alcohol is starting to hit her, too. I shift in my seat.

Another course arrives, and I have to loosen my belt under the table. "Poppy, are you sure about crossing the

Sahara with us? It will take about three weeks, there are books you'd need to read, and well, it's a weighty commitment."

"I'm absolutely up for it," Poppy replies. She rambles on about logistics, chances of a lifetime, all the while her fingers are twirling her hair.

I swish my wine. I'm glad to have a buzz. The gravity of what is coming is starting to sink in, and I'm more nervous than I let on.

I glance around the dining hall to distract me from my thoughts, and perhaps I am a tad paranoid, but it appears that couple after couple are staring at us, sneering even. I look over at Poppy to see if she notices, and maybe it is the alcohol or simply the lighting, but Poppy looks bigger than life—as if she doesn't fit quite right inside her body. Her cheeks are flushed from the alcohol.

I've become so used to stares since I lost my legs that I rarely notice them anymore unless they are obnoxious. These stares are just that, but they aren't toward me. My legs are covered. Poppy is the anomaly. On second thought, maybe it's my cargo pants.

I look across the table as she occupies herself, lost in a gaze toward the window. The orbits around her eyes are cavernous, her forehead high, her hair thinning. Her broad shoulders arch over a long tangle of strong limbs that she struggles to hold close to her core. The thought comes to me that these other diners may think that we are some odd, lesbian couple. I decide to ask for the check when the waiter shows up with yet another tray.

On the tray is a tall, thin glass pitcher with a bulbous

base and an arched handle. I can see the carpet patterns, distorted through the vase and the clear liquid it holds.

"Grappa," the waiter says, "to aid your digestion."

He pours the alcohol into thin crystal shot glasses and gently sets a glass down in front of each of us, also, silver bowls of pear sorbet doused with liqueur, gooseberries, a sprig of mint.

After that, I don't much care what anyone thinks about anything. I feel good and drunk. "Let's, let us go sauna," I stammer loudly to Poppy. I admire her wit, and this may be the last adult conversation I partake in for some time. I just want to engage in more pleasure. I stand up and a well-coiffed woman at another table shakes her head at me in disdain. My pants are still unbuttoned. I button them quickly, then walk behind Poppy's chair, and gently pull it out for her.

Don't cargo pants deserve respect? And doesn't Poppy, in all her oddity, deserve the same respect, the same human kindness as anyone else? I think about the sympathetic artifice that often accompanies people staring at my prosthetics. It makes me sad to the think of the judgments people cast. I lead Poppy out of the dining hall, pushing her forward by placing my palm on the small of her back. I glare back at the woman, who quickly puts her well-coiffed head down and hides her mouth with a fancy napkin.

We walk outside. It is cold enough to smell like snow and bitter this close to the sea, even with a drunk on. The sign on the spa door says it's closed, but when I try the door it opens.

"That's not a no," Poppy says. We bump into one

another, trying to get through the door and out of the cold. We grab robes and towels from the vacant reception area and head to the locker room. Noise echoes off of the tile walls, even though we are trying to be quiet.

Poppy doesn't bother to get into a stall in the locker room. She whips off her bra and shirt almost simultaneously. I pretend not to notice, but I glance at her from a distance in the mirror anyway. Her tits are large, and because one of my first jobs was taking before and after photographs at a plastic surgeon's office, I know they are enhanced. I wonder for a moment if she'd undergone the boob job for her Lara Croft ambitions: the heroine has comic-strip-large breasts.

I also change in the open. I have little modesty anymore. She doesn't try to hide it when she glares at me. She walks by me slowly toward the shower, traces a scar on my shoulder on her way.

"Ouch," she says.

When I was in first grade, I had a crush on my teacher. Her name was Valentine, but she went by Val, and if handwriting could sing, hers did. She used to bring in velvety wallpaper samples to class and let us write books about our feelings; we'd make covers for our books out of the wallpaper. I dreamt about making valentines for Valentine out of those lush samples, but she was my teacher, and that seemed inappropriate—not the fact that I was a girlchild and she was a woman. I had a crush on who she was—her elegance, the way she wore a scarf around her neck, how good she smelled, how she was always ready to lead us through a new day. One day, I even dreamt about proposing to her, so we could live together and write books all day.

Almost two decades later, I was far more aware of judgment, in San Francisco visiting a distant cousin. He was the funniest at the family reunions, always making light of what could have been tension points for the family. So, when the adults in my family would wink and whisper that he was the "funny" one, I took them to mean that he could make everyone laugh about the burnt hotdogs we all had to eat because Grandpa had one too many beers on grill duty. I was a preteen when he graduated from college in West Virginia, and I remember driving down from Akron through the mountains to hear his senior recital. It was the first time I had ever heard opera outside of a Bugs Bunny cartoon, and his voice moved me in a way that nothing else on Earth had yet. So, when J and I broke up, and Celie and I headed west, we stayed with him in the Castro district and he introduced me to a whole new world out loud, not whispered the way it was in the conservative Midwest.

I loved the way that my cousin and his friends were overcoming projected shame to be themselves in the most colorful and witty way possible, though I wasn't wise enough to state it that way yet because I was still in the early days of discovering my own self after years of feeling judged and being unable to please the people in my life who were bound to morals other than my own.

I got my long hair shaved in California, which made Celie cry hard, as if I'd shorn off her own hair. I was shedding the old hurts, trying something new. One night, my cousin insisted that we leave Celie to dress up his roommate, his partner—she'd already been doing his makeup for days on end—and my cousin took me out to the clubs, all the while introducing me as his little dyke cousin. The clubs we went to were full of boys and although the dancing was cathartic and fun, there was nothing there I wanted, and I asked him to take me to a club for girls.

He dropped me off at a bar called Steel Magnolias. He wouldn't go in with me. He said he'd go home and make sure Celie was sound asleep and said that I should go and have a good time, San Fran style. I was nervous walking inside, so I headed straight for the only empty barstool I saw and ordered a drink for calm. I learned that night about butches, femmes, and bisexuals, but mostly I learned about the girl with whom I spent hours playing pool.

When she leaned over the table to take a shot, her chocolate brown eyes reminded me of the way Valentine used to lean over my desk, so focused on helping me with my handwriting, on being my best self. When someone came up and asked the pool girl how she identified, she snickered and said "French-Asian." We closed the bar down and walked the streets that were bathed in moonlight. When we sat at a garden bench to rest, lilac perfume filled the air, and when she ran her hand through my hair and laid her soft lips on mine, I opened up to her completely. It was a true expression of love we shared there in that hidden place; it was not a voracious hunger where there is a taker and a giver but a How can we each empty our vessels of unnecessary burden and refill them with flower petals so that when we are both gone from one another, our hearts will beat perfume into the dark streets?

Inside the sauna, the heat of the steam having increased the fermentation of the alcohol, I am starting to feel really drunk—not drunk to the point of being anesthetized, but just before.

"So, this is nice, huh?" I say to Poppy, sliding my back against the warm cedar. I find it hard to breathe.

"Bloody good. Now tell me something," Poppy replies, invisible in the steam. I feel like swooshing the steam away with my hands in order to see her. So, I do. She starts laughing in a high, hard cackle.

"What?" I ask.

"What, what?" Poppy answers.

"What did you want me to tell you?"

"I've forgotten," she says, then undoes the tuck of her towel and it slides down to drape the bench below her.

Though my vision is foggy, I know what just happened. I grow a little stiff, then loose again from the drink, then stiff again. I don't want Poppy to make a move on me. I don't want to do something I wouldn't consider sober, and while I like Poppy a whole lot, she doesn't make me dream of Eden like the girl who identified as French-Asian. Sexual chemistry is either there or it is not, and in this case, it is not.

"Let's talk Land Rovers," I say.

"Or randy lovers," she replies.

"What about them?"

"Have you got one?"

"Well, that's personal, isn't it?"

"We're drunk, naked, and in a sauna. Tell me, is that too personal?"

"I've had a lover for nearly the whole year I've been in England now."

"How does he or she feel about you leaving tomorrow?"

"He thinks it sucks."

"How do you feel about it?"

"I think I've got something really big to do, and though he is kind and the sex is good, I'm not in love with him enough to disrupt this dream. Or maybe, it's just that I need to do something I love by myself for once."

"Well, that's honest."

"What about you?" I ask.

"I was with someone for almost ten years, until recently. She was incredibly special to me, and I haven't recovered."

"Why did it end?" I ask.

"Well, I guess she didn't like who I really was."

"That's unfortunate."

"Yeah, I'm not so bad."

"I'm always keen on anyone who's as big of a Land Rover junkie as I am," I say, trying to make her feel better.

"Keen, hmm?"

"Keen, yes," I reply, forgetting that the British version of keen implies more of a longing. "I don't know about you, but I'm about to pass out in this heat. And I need to get some sleep. The ferry isn't going to wait on me in the morning."

I grab my towel at the fold to make sure it doesn't come undone and open the sauna door. The cool air rushes in like freedom. I bid Poppy a hasty goodnight, grab my clothes and rush out into the dark parking lot toward my room with nothing but my pins and a towel, where I run into the sneering woman from the dining hall whose jaw is now agape. "Glorious evening isn't it?" I greet her.

When the sitter opens the door, her jaw also falls momentarily agape, but she manages to put a finger to it to indicate quiet, that Celie's gone to sleep. We step outside and I pay her, and she tells me that Celie was fantastic and hands me a letter. Celie dictated the letter for Leia to the sitter, and the sitter has lovely handwriting.

Dear Leia,

> *You are my best friend, and we girls have to stick together always. I went swimming in a pool today, and it would have been much more fun with you. I promise to send you sweeties from all over the world. Thank you for sharing your bike and helmet with me this year.*

> *Love,*
> *Celie*

VI

....

CELIE has been singing a tune or three, all day. We've been
in traffic all morning, and I wonder when her patience will
grow thin. Athena is chugging up a small mountain road,
and Celie sings "She'll be coming 'round the mountain
when she comes . . ."

" . . . when she comes," I echo.

As we near the top of the low mountain, the sky clouds
over rapidly. We have arrived at the border of Germany
and the Czech Republic, on our way to Prague. As soon
as we cross the border, the clouds heave and break open
with rain. Another delay. I have a strict rule on this expedition—no driving after dark. I want to know our surroundings before the sun sets every day—I want us to be as safe
as possible.

As we descend the mountain, I notice wildly colorful
spots below on the side of the road, like gigantic poisonous
mushrooms. The rain mars visibility and the windshield
wipers on the Land Rover are going at full speed as we ap-
proach the first cluster of the mushrooms. One by one, the

giant mushrooms suddenly rise up, and it isn't until we are almost on top of them that I realize they are umbrellas, and underneath them, are scantily clad women trying to flag down oncoming drivers.

My heart breaks a little with each popping cluster, the thought of them crouching alongside this mountain road in the rain. They stretch on for miles, these members of the "oldest profession in the world"—the euphemism for prostitution coined by a man in a world where men learned early on that they could gain sexual favors by hoarding equity from women.

Slut, prostitute, whore, hussy, nympho, tart, and tramp. Loose, of ill repute, harlot, slag, and skank. I've heard these terms my whole life—some I've been called, and of some, I've grown fond. Reclaiming, they call it—the same as the way I've taken to the word *cripple* to describe myself. Cripple is the most appropriate word etymologically—it simply means someone who has difficulty walking. I find nothing wrong with that.

When I was young, though, these words frightened me. They were mentioned in conversations about young girls who gave their virginity away before marriage, especially if they were impregnated. The boys who impregnated them weren't called such names. We girls were given the interpretation that it was the boys' God-given nature to try to implant their seed, and that it was our imperative to avoid such a fate until we were sealed in holy matrimony, as if a flower can stop itself from blooming.

My biological mother was impregnated at fifteen and

was sent to a home for unwed mothers. My adoptive mother, I found out much later, was a shotgun bride—two months pregnant at her own wedding—then had four miscarriages before she was diagnosed with uterine growth retardation, which meant that the fetuses could only grow so big before her womb refused to stretch, and then the fetuses suffocated, aborted by nature.

Because of the miscarriage, my adoptive mother never had to cope with public shame—only her family knew of her indiscretion. Indeed, when she went on to adopt children a few years later, she was looked on by the community as a saint, but the unspoken shame sat inside her nonetheless, festered in her like the fetuses that never became babies.

The shame wasn't left on the women alone. Some men spent their whole lives wondering about the girls whose lives they ruined, the children out in the world who they might never know. And some men who took in shotgun brides, like my father, were considered soft for giving up on their own dreams by "honoring" the young women they impregnated with marriage. My father was the first kid in his whole family to go to college, but he stopped after one year because my mother's miscarriages were expensive. He went to work as a mechanic for the Goodyear tire factory, and never looked back. No matter which way you put it, the morals imposed on women by a society that interprets their communal God based on the narratives of men in different historical times have broken the lives and hearts of too many generations. Something's got to give, unless this is all we are.

When I was fourteen at a church camp, I fell to my knees at the altar of the God of my community, Jesus Christ. I was told that I had sinned (I sneaked out of the house more than once after dark. I hated my mom for a time because the hurt she bore ended up hurting me. And I used to smoke the butts of my grandpa's cigarettes when no one was looking.).

I had apparently sinned so badly that Christ had to die on the cross for me—a brutal, public death. There were musical chords meant to pluck the heart at the evening service— it was a passion play—a weepy affair. The adults around me that were revered as church leaders said it was all true— the cross, the nails, the heavenly mansions—and I felt like I did years later when I smoked my first joint, that the whole world was in on a secret that I was only just discovering.

I loved Jesus so much that it hurt, so much that it made my mom crazy when one day I denounced Guns N' Roses (who I adored, and she did not) and threw all of my "ungodly" belongings out my second-floor bedroom window. I loved Jesus so much that I started a Bible study at high school that only two other kids came to—once. I loved Jesus so much that I went on a teen mission trip to Ireland when I was fifteen and spent a summer mixing cement at an orphanage during the day and proselytizing to orphans in the evening.

When I lost my legs a year later, I was told it was God's plan. I was the miracle that the church prayed for when I survived against all odds. Shortly after I was discharged from nearly one hundred days in the hospital, the church hosted a southern gospel concert and raised money for my family. I was still emaciated and without prosthetics, in a wheelchair, when they paraded me down the aisle to give testimony on behalf of Jesus in between gospel bands. And that's when I said something akin to being grateful that God had allowed this loss. There was a catch in my throat as I listened to myself say those words that sounded like everything but love.

When I needed the church the most, there was silence—the truth of grief proved too great a burden for a Sunday-Wednesday social club. Dare I say that the Christ-minded interpretations I did receive weren't satisfying, didn't ring true, felt like Band-Aids on an amputation?

I had to come to terms with my new body and life on my own, especially when the leaders of the church became embroiled in their own scandals. One preacher was transitioned to another church in order to remove him from the so-called temptress that led him astray from his wife, while an older married deacon pursued my underage female cousin in secret, staying on with his gold chains and overbearing cologne in the walls of the holy sanctuary for many years to come.

I went for a year to a Quaker college that had offered me a running scholarship and still honored it after I lost my legs. The first day of the first semester, I fell heart first for the English professor, also a preacher, who taught me *The Canterbury Tales.*

I was thrilled to discover the affection was mutual, as if I'd found the godly man who would make me seem acceptable. It didn't seem odd to me, in all my desperation, that he would only meet me five miles from campus, that we had to be a secret, that the more physical we became, the more he prayed with me, and wept. After several months of secret dalliances, in which it didn't count as losing my virginity if his penis didn't enter me, he left on spring break to go to the previous university where he had taught, and when he returned, after kissing my lips raw for half an hour, he told me that he'd had a dream and God told him that he couldn't have me.

Two days later, I smoked a joint for the first time with a philosophy major. A week later, after I found out that the professor-preacher had gone back to the old university for the week to ask for the librarian's hand in marriage, who he had been dating for a decade unbeknownst to me, I lit up a second joint in the college chapel as an act of rebellion, minutes before the service began.

The president of the college was compassionate, and I was given the choice to drop out or be expelled. I chose the former. The English professor got married and eventually received tenure.

A few months later, I lost my virginity in a way that counted, by rape in the back parking lot of a bar. And for a few years after that, I said no to little—be it drugs or booze or sex. I gave myself away in shame once God told the godly man he could not have me—that I wasn't even worthy of the godly man. It didn't occur to me to think that the professor-preacher, over twenty years my elder, might have asked the Lord if he could have me before he ever laid his hands on my body, or my heart.

The rain picks up as we reach the bottom of the mountain. For an hour, I must ask Celie to be quiet so I can concentrate, the way my father used to do with me when he found himself in heavy traffic.

My father, who once drove an hour to change a tire in a snowstorm for the professor-preacher who stole my innocence when I was raw and delicate. My father, who cleaned up the blood and vomit on the porch when I crawled into the house after being raped, even though I hadn't lived at home for several months. My father, who never asked any questions, despite the laceration under my eye, the shiner. My earthly, but heavenly father, who always wanted me to spare the details that would break him, who would sweep me up after the ravaged world left me for dead. "Treat me like a mushroom," he'd say. "Keep me in the dark and feed me shit."

When I think of Jesus, I think of the "soft" man who gave up his dreams so he and his wife could adopt me—all she wanted was a family, a marriage, a white picket fence—the American dream that did not bring her happiness.

When I think of Jesus, I think of the man who couldn't come into my hospital room without bawling, so much so that my mother stayed the course—the man who eventually served his time playing Super Mario Brothers with me night after night while I recovered from having a third of my body and all of my dreams removed. The man who told me I could pump gas for a living as long as I was happy. My father saved me from everything he could, except my mother and myself. Just as he couldn't enter my hospital room and witness my suffering, he could never enter the rooms of my childhood either—the ones in which my mother spent her rage on my body, the rooms where I was taught that I ought to be full of shame, the rooms I've had to unlock myself from again and again.

I'm getting tired. It's nearly dark. I decide to stop at the first town we see. It's hard to see anything through the on-slaught of weepy skies, but then I see a sign, some light ahead.

I pull off the main road—into a tiny rundown town—and see a large building with a sign in German out front: *Frei Dusche mit Zimmer.* Free shower with room. Maybe it's a shower that operates by coins, I think. I pull up to the door because the rain is coming down in pellets now and what light is left is waning. I leave Celie in the car momen-tarily, to make sure there's a room. I peek my head in the door, so I can still see my daughter through the window.

A woman wearing a long red silk dress greets me. I'm relieved that she speaks some English. I ask her if she has a room available.

"For how long?" she asks.

"One night," I say, "with a child."

"We have no children," she says harshly.

"I have a child, my daughter," I say. "Do you not allow children?"

"No children," she says again.

"Is there another hotel? It's raining so hard and I can't see to drive, and we need a place to stay and rest until tomorrow."

"There is no hotel," she says. "Wait here."

She disappears for several minutes, and when she re-turns, she says that we can stay for one night only. When I ask her where to park, she comes outside with a large umbrella and guides me to the back of the building, where there's a fenced-in lot with barbed wire at the top of it, like a prison. She opens a gate, and I drive Athena II inside. She waits while Celie and I exit the vehicle with our overnight bags, then she locks the gate behind us and guides us back to the front entrance, sharing the umbrella.

"Are you hungry?" she asks Celie.

"Yes, I am," Celie says.

The lady cups one of Celie's chubby cheeks and says, "How can you be hungry when it is clear that your mother feeds you well?"

Once inside, she takes us to a large, plain dining room and seats us at a table. There are only two other customers, both men, sitting at individual tables, quietly eating.

"Do you like potatoes?" The lady asks Celie.

"Very much so," Celie answers, and the lady walks to the back of the room where there's a swinging door that leads to a kitchen.

The lady comes back out and sets a bowl of potato salad in front of Celie, then sits down next to her. Celie makes a face at me that I'm grateful the lady cannot see. We both hate mayonnaise. A bell on the door of the front lobby rings just then, and the lady rises to greet whoever is there. "Someone will be with you soon," she says.

"I don't want to eat this," Celie whispers. I don't blame her, but I also don't want to be rude. She won't even try it, so I do, and I still hate mayonnaise. I grab some napkins from a dispenser on the table and discreetly spit out the attempted bite. Then I take several more napkins and wad spoonful after spoonful into them until the bowl has one bite left and stick the whole mucky parcel in my overnight bag.

A young woman comes to the table just as I zip the bag. She doesn't look more than sixteen—the age at which I lost my legs—and she's wearing a miniskirt that is so tight she might as well not wear anything at all. She dotes on Celie, praises her appetite. Then she asks me if we'd like some pasta and a salad, to which I heartily agree. As she's walking back to the kitchen, she picks up the empty dishes of the other two patrons.

There's a man standing alone in the lobby. There's a stairwell beside him, and suddenly the lady with the red silk dress comes down the stairs with three women behind her. The women are all wearing robes. They have on heavy makeup, hair like movie stars. The lady introduces the three women to the man in the lobby, but he only takes the hand of one, and then they disappear back up the stairs. The lady with the red silk dress comes into the dining room and takes the other two patrons, one by one, back into the lobby, and they each follow one of the dolled-up women up the stairs, too. And it is only then that I realize I have rented a room for the night in a brothel.

My face gets hot. My chest builds with pressure, but there's nothing I can do except act calm. The young lady reappears and sets two bowls of pasta salad—again with mayonnaise—in front of me and Celie. In between us, she sets a plate full of radishes, carrots, and olives. I thank her, and I can hear the fear in my voice.

"More mayonnaise, Mama," Celie says. "I'll get more napkins."

Her sweet voice triggers me back to earth for a moment. She starts handing me wadded napkins full of pasta salad bites under the table.

"I'll take care of it," I say. "Eat some vegetables." She takes a carrot stick and shoves it in her mouth. Her faces scrunches in disdain. The veggies are pickled, and I realize it's going to be a long night. I bypass the wasted food in my bag and grab her a pen and some paper and ask her to draw, which luckily satisfies her.

The miniskirt girl comes in and out of the swinging kitchen door, cleaning up the tables where the men sat. With each swing, I can see other young girls working in the kitchen, washing dishes, stirring bowls, engaging in safe toil. I sneak bite after bite—not bitten—into the bag, while my head spins. The kitchen door keeps swinging, swishing, as if putting me in a trance. I don't know what to do.

The lady in the silk red dress comes back to the table, pulls up a chair next to me. "We took care to clean your room," she says.

"Thank you," I say.

Miniskirt girl comes out from the kitchen, walks up to the table and crouches down beside Celie.

We are surrounded.

"Would you like some ice cream?" miniskirt girl asks Celie. Celie's face lights up.

"Where are you traveling?" the lady in the red silk dress asks me. Miniskirt girl extends her hand to Celie. Celie climbs down off of her chair and takes the hand.

"Prague," I say, my heart pushing up into my throat.

Miniskirt girl is walking Celie toward the swinging

kitchen door. The lady in the red silk dress is talking, but I can no longer hear her. I'm starting to panic. I don't want to know what's behind that door. I don't want Celie out of my sight. I don't want her to disappear forever into the sad buildings that house young women who can eat only because they sell their bodies to strangers. I don't want them to snatch my daughter. I try to act calmly, but I know that if she comes anywhere near close to passing through that door, I'm going to make a scene. I'm going to jump up past the lady in the red silk dress and I'm going to take Celie from miniskirt girl even if the act fills the room, the evening, and all of our hearts with strife.

"Are the disability checks enough?" my attorney asked.

"I get almost four hundred a month," I answered without answering.

"Have you got money now?"

I had a five-dollar bill in my pocket that had to last me two more days. "I can pay for my part of the pizza," I said.

He shook his head, and then placed cash on top of the bill. He fingered through his wallet some more and handed me two hundred dollars in twenties.

"I can't take this," I said, though I wanted it desperately.

"Yes, you can, and you will. Consider it an advance until the lawsuit is over if you want."

I thanked him, remembering when he first looked me over in his top-floor, corner office, thinking he must have seen dollar signs flashing. I overheard him telling his paralegal that I was very attractive, well-spoken, and very scarred—the perfect plaintiff. Later that day, he would look at me with all seriousness and say, "Do you know just how wrongly you've been treated?" I answered no, trying to explain further that God works in mysterious ways, which may have been the last vestige of a juvenile devotion to the God of organized religion, but the attorney interrupted me and said, "With all due respect, we aren't talking about God here; we're talking about humans who neglected to do their jobs with due diligence and, as a result, took away your college aspirations. You stick with me, kid, and I'll have you running again."

The idea of the lawsuit being over and me not having to figure out how I was going to pay rent every month was impossible for me to grasp. Getting through the next moment was all that was ever on my mind. I was eighteen years old, and though I didn't tell the attorney, I had just been evicted from a condo in the downtown Akron projects because my roommates struggled to make the rent more than me.

"Do me a favor, will you?" my attorney asked. I figured I could agree to most anything for two hundred bucks. "How long has it been since you talked to your parents? Please give them a call, let them know you're okay, will you?"

It had been at least six weeks since I had called them—what would I have told them? That I'd been hired and fired from four menial jobs—that I was scared, injured, angry, homeless? And though I told the attorney okay, it would be several more months before I did.

That evening, I walked into the Lucky Gentleman's Cabaret with two hundred and five dollars in my pocket and a hell of a desire to spend half of it on marijuana that I would try and convince Rami, the owner, to sell me. When I was stoned, nothing hurt. Rami and I had met at a bar a month earlier, and when I lost my lease, he said I could stay with him until I found a new place. He told me to meet him in the parking lot at nine o'clock—closing time—but it was a half an hour early, and I walked right up to the door.

"I'm a friend of Rami's. He's expecting me," I said to the man at the door. He snickered but let me inside.

The Lucky Gentleman's Cabaret smelled like cherry car fresheners and cigarette smoke. Girls were dancing on the two-pole stage; one was wearing a red-sequined thong and matching pasties with tassels. The women were lit up by stage lights; their sweat was glistening, and their heavy cosmetics were shining like porcelain doll faces do. I couldn't move for a moment. I just stood and stared at the way their bodies flowed—all flawed and beautiful. I was shocked to feel an aching twinge of jealousy. Half a dozen men sat in comfortable chairs in the shadows. The lights flickered off a man's glasses one moment, and the next, red pasties jiggled in front of his face.

"What are you doing here? Rami wouldn't hire you. You're too skinny. And why are you limping?"

A redheaded woman was standing next to me. She was wearing a sheer, purple robe that hung just below her ass. Underneath, I could see her huge breasts, dark nipples, black underwear. She had on open-toe, black high heels and her toes were polished purple, too. Across her cheek, there was a long, pencil-thin scar.

I told her that I wasn't looking for a job, hoping there

was no judgment in my voice. I told her Rami was my friend. Cocking her head in disbelief, she asked me if I was his niece or something. She continued trying to put me off, telling me that he was in his office and that he didn't like to be disturbed unless it was an emergency. I told her again that he had asked me to meet him. She scratched her midriff and told me to scram. I held out, finally explaining that I was living with Rami. She didn't buy it. She told me to leave again.

"I'm not leaving," I said, with a strength that surprised me. I broke out in a sweat. This woman made me nervous, and at the same time I had the strangest desire to cling to her like a child to its mother, to lay my head upon her breasts and wrap my arms around her. I also desperately wanted some weed.

With a wicked smile on her face, she agreed to go let Rami know I was there.

If that was what playing with fire tasted like, then it tasted good—bitter and heady. I felt the music pulsing in my body. The girl with the red-sequined pasties was grinding up against a pole to the beat, the metal squeezed between her thighs, one arm holding on as if to the high ropes of a mast, the other hanging down behind her nearly to the floor. I wanted to be her.

Suddenly, Rami was grabbing me by the arm and dragging me back to his office. It was like a miniature warehouse, all cinder-blocked with fluorescent lighting, the polar opposite of the atmosphere on the other side of the door. Rami let me go and sat behind a desk that was covered in rolls from an adding machine; a television was mounted above the desk and was hooked up to rotating surveillance cameras. He was mad.

"I told you to wait outside."

I decided it wasn't a good time to bring up the weed.

As instructed, I sat quietly for about ten minutes, waiting for him to finish up calculations. I watched the transitional gray images of the parking lot—the bespectacled man getting into a Mercedes, the stage, the exit doors on the screen. Finally, Rami finished and began to lead me out of the club. The stage had gone dark, the music had been lowered, and the women were sitting at the bar. He handed them each an envelope, and the woman with the scar looked at me, said, "Hey, kid. Good luck out there."

At Rami's condo, he served me bread and cheese, a glass of wine, and then finally, he lit up a joint. He smoked half of it while cleaning up the kitchen, and then passed it to me. I took a long drag. I wanted to be out of my mind, and it only took a couple of hits for me to get there. When Rami sat next to me on his plush leather sofa, I tried to kiss him, but he pushed me away, laughing.

He wanted to talk.

"I don't want to talk," I said, unbuttoning my shirt, but not taking it off of my arms.

"Take it all the way off," he said.

I resisted, but Rami slid the blouse off of my shoulders and then he picked up my right arm, which is deeply gouged and covered in skin grafts that were taken from my thighs.

"This looks like a snake," he said, sliding his finger down from the ball of my shoulder to my elbow over the raised, red scars. "And this, a heart." He traced the back of my hand. "At least your breasts aren't scarred."

I told him that I am not scarred anywhere where it matters, wanting to focus him on sexual matters, anything but my scars.

"Will you show me your legs?"

"No."

"Come on, take your pants off."

And I did, though I'm not sure why. Somehow, it was a tremendous relief. I trembled, sliding the slacks down over my carved thighs, pausing as I sat down, naked. Then I took them all the way off.

He studied me like a corpse, not like a woman. He didn't touch me, just stared, as if not wanting to destroy evidence at a crime scene.

"It's strange," he started.

"What's strange?" I asked, suddenly wanting to be covered.

"The irony," he said, in a philosophical manner that I wouldn't normally associate with the owner of a strip joint, "of how beautiful you are. It's haunting, really."

I wanted to cry. Rami's words stung. How many times had I heard that sentiment while lying in the hospital? *She's such a beautiful girl!* The translation was easy and despicable. Would it have been any better if this happened to an "ugly" girl?

I tried to save face. I got on my knees and tried to sit on his lap, but he stopped me mid-stance. He stroked my breast, stood up, slapped my ass and walked out of the room. He returned with blankets and a pillow.

"Don't you want to have sex with me?" I asked.

With all of those women working for him, he could have sex anytime he wanted it, I imagined—with full-bodied women. After making up a bed on the sofa, he took me by the hand and said that he knew all about me—that he read the papers, that he was sorry for what had happened to me, and that he wanted to help. He told me that I made him feel more honorable than he was, and that he was selfish that way. And so, with nothing to lose, I asked Rami to sell me a hundred dollars' worth of marijuana.

"No, I'm not selling you any drugs," he said. "You're far too innocent for all of this." He covered me with a blanket, and walked back to his bedroom, shutting the door.

I was too mortified to sleep. I saw the stub of the joint in the ashtray and smoked the last few hits off of it. Then I stayed awake, cold in the living room, sad as all get-out, until at long last sleep relieved me. When I woke, I smelled coffee, but the coffee maker was cleaned and in the dish rack, and Rami was gone. I washed up in the bathroom, grabbed my things, and decided a one-night stay was long enough. I shut his door behind me, made sure it was locked, and took in the early-morning air of Akron. It was chilly, tarnished, but cleaner smelling than any other time of the day, before the tire factories filled the air with burning rubber.

I got into my beater car, gave thanks when it started, and decided to smoke a cigarette first thing. Inside my pack, there were six perfectly rolled joints. I thanked Rami out loud and smoked one. I took a long drive through the city, uncertain of any destination.

That afternoon, I met a girl with dreads at a head shop. She was part of the Rainbow Tribe, she told me, and there was always room for one more, because that's how the cosmos works. She took me to an old rundown Victorian house and told me I could live there, with them. There was a plastic pig with a makeshift police uniform in the front yard. And for the next few months, the filth in that house was turned into something far more vivid and lively with the help of weed, LSD, and lots of them.

The door was revolving constantly, because that's how the cosmos works, and one day I wouldn't remember much more than faces because none of us used real names. No one asked me about my legs, which I hid as much as possible, and the anonymity that I experienced in that ramshackle drug den is all that would make anything that happened there worthwhile. For a few brief months, under the guise of dope, I was just another teenager acting stupid, lucky to be alive.

One night, I was sitting on a ratty sofa on the porch that homeless people sometimes slept on, smoking a joint, listening to a record of Shel Silverstein reciting his poetry, when someone offered me a tab of LSD with the face of Jesus on it. "I accept Jesus Christ as my savior," I said, letting it melt on my tongue. Within an hour, I ate two more Jesuses. Soon, I was not only out of my mind, but I was in other people's minds, and then I was in the cat in the alley's mind, too.

I managed to ride a bike with some of the Rainbow Tribe to a club, where the loud music shook my body until it broke into free particles. The particles danced like a murmuration of starlings, swirling above the crowd, then piercing down into it to kiss a woman. I was dancing like I had real legs—like Pinocchio, I thought *I'm a real boy now.*

I was so free and connected and euphoric that the world could have been on fire and I'd have thanked God for allowing it. Then all of my particles swarmed above me, and everyone else turned into particulates, too—and I realized we were all made from the same matter, the same frenzied stardust of the whole universe. I felt at peace with this until suddenly all the particulates were disappearing, getting sucked into a black hole, until I was no longer conscious.

"Honey, you okay?" A man's face was hovering over me, a stranger's face, swerving back and forth. I wiped drool from my mouth, trying to remember where I was, who I was. "Honey. The club is closed. You gotta go home. You want me to call someone?"

Scared, I tried to get up quickly, and then there was searing pain. There were rings of blood soaked into my jeans around the knees, where my prosthetics connect—and I remembered everything. I hobbled out as quickly as I could, before the man called someone. The bike was still outside, and I managed to get on it and ride. The air was damp and cold, predawn. I rode for a bit, until I felt sick, out of breath, in pain. I dropped the bike and fell on my ass next to a bush to smoke a cigarette.

There was half a joint in my pack, and I was so grateful I could cry. I lit it, and then I heard a voice saying, "Smoke this—it's better." A man in shadow handed me a pipe and I hit it. I immediately felt a rush, a near explosion in my chest and head, and then I felt peaceful, high again.

I looked up at him to say thank you, but I couldn't speak. I tried, but I couldn't utter a word. And for the next several minutes which seemed to never end, he fumbled with me, tried to steal pride from me that had already been stolen, and when he was finished, he took my bike and cigarettes.

I vomited, curled up in the bush, and shook until dawn. I should have risen with the sun, but I felt a sense of death, a sense I recognized. I tried to fight it, pulled twigs away from my face so I could see what awaited me, and that's when I noticed the plastic pig across the street, and stumbled off toward its rubber snout.

The members of the Rainbow Tribe were on the porch. I wondered if they missed me. They invited me to the twenty-four-hour diner on the corner, and I thought a coffee might save me. We only ever purchased coffee at the diner. The tribe watched other diners carefully, grabbed half-eaten plates just after a table departed and before the bussers could get to it—helping to rid the world of food waste, they said. Someone set half a sunny side up egg in front of me with a corner of toast, and I was so depleted that somehow that felt like love.

I glanced up at the door and had to wipe my eyes clear to make sure I was not seeing things, but no, there was my father, walking into the diner. It was just down the road from the Goodyear tire factory. He must have worked a night shift. When I said out loud that my father was coming in, the tribe told me they'd meet me at home, and just like that, they got up, and one of them scraped my corner toast and half egg right into his mouth as he left.

My father saw me. There was nowhere for me to hide,

though I thought hard about crawling under the table. He walked over, asked if he could sit down.

"Sure," I said.

His chiseled face started to prune. He was hurting because I was hurting and that hurt me more.

"What's up?" I asked. I tried to wipe the dirt off the sleeve of the flannel shirt I was wearing when I noticed that the sleeve was ripped in half and hanging down around my wrist. I smelled like vomit, smoke, cum, and blood. There was no use hiding anything. My father was seeing it all now.

"Your mother and I," he started, his voice trembling. "We miss you so much."

"Yeah, I miss you, too," I said. I couldn't look anywhere near his eyes.

"Um," he said and stopped.

"What is it?" I asked.

He opened up his wallet, took out the only bill inside of it—a ten. "It's all I got for the rest of the week," he said. "If you won't come home, please take care of yourself. I love you so much." He said it quickly, a string of words without pauses. Then he left the diner, and I saw him wiping his eyes as he got into his truck. I put my head on the table, and the tears streamed all across my filthy face. There was no more confusion as to what love is—it's the act of the wounded extending mercy to the wounded.

"Leave the child," I imagine the woman in the red silk dress saying, because whatever she says to the miniskirt girl is in a language I don't understand, and miniskirt girl drops

Celie's hand like it's a hot potato, just as the kitchen door swings open and my fists clench and my body starts to rise.

Celie stays standing by the door as miniskirt girl goes to the beyond, and the woman in the red silk dress places her hand on my knee firmly. "We will keep you safe," she says to me. "No one else gets to park out back, and no one else has had their room cleaned so well. You asked for shelter for you and your daughter, and I am providing it."

Miniskirt girl comes out with a bowl full of ice cream, and Celie follows her back to the table eagerly. I'm left eating crow.

The bed sheets smell like bleach and vinegar, but Celie curls up in them and falls asleep almost immediately. I lie next to her, staring at a stain on the wallpaper that looks like ejaculation when I remember the prostitute who lets down her hair and kisses the feet of Jesus before washing them and anointing them with oil. Jesus is in the company of Pharisees who believe him to be a blasphemer, and his willingness to let a sinful woman engage in such an act of propriety further cements their belief.

Some historians believe that Mary Magdalene was Christ's faithful companion, wife even. Other historians refute this because they can't conceive of a woman in a leadership role who was known to travel far and wide spreading Christ's gospel of love—so instead they interpret her to be a reformed prostitute, demeaning her life, making her a sideshow of repentance to the power of the man Christ.

If I believe that a woman is less of a worthy being because she is a prostitute, then I am not extending the kind of mercy central to the gospel of Christ. If I believe that Mary Magdalene has been demoted to keep her at the mercy of powerful men, and that rings true in the heart of my life experience as well as historical experience, then I guess I can be perceived as a blasphemer, too, like Christ. Good company, some would say.

What I know is that there is very little difference between me and these women who are providing safe harbor for me and my little girl. What I know is that if women had fair access to equity, there would be fewer divorces because there would be fewer marriages. What I know is that a doctor made a mistake and wrote me off as a histrionic teenager with the flu, and according to the science, if she had treated me with compassion and not judgment, I would still have legs—I would have gone to college on a running scholarship and never have had to deal with the alienation of a wounded, young, female body. What I know is if that American lawsuit had ended poorly, and all I had had to lean on was the last ten bucks of my father's weekly salary, I may well have been a sideshow of fetishism with the backdrop of men who hoarded equity to have their sexual desires met in sad, secret rooms. What I know is that if I cannot show compassion for these women, then I should expect none for myself.

The mattress springs in the room above me are worn, and the squeak show begins. A woman upstairs has opened her legs, exposing the holy place of her love and survival, and perhaps, even pleasure. She cleanses and anoints the filth of the man so she can put food on her table. If he's kind, he'll tip her well, knowing that she is allowing him to release his own pain in a way that hurts her and is not throwing it back in his face—that's why he comes here after all, for mercy.

I get out of bed and count how much money I have in the secret compartment of my overnight bag—eight hundred euros. I will give it all to the woman in the red silk dress come morning, knowing it isn't enough to right the wrongs of history, but hoping it will be enough for her to accept my apology. Then I lie back down, my chest to Celie's back, waiting for our heartbeats to sync, and when they do, they're in sync with the mattress springs above us too. We sleep deep under another weary attempt at salvation, the desperation of wanting to know that we are worthy of any form of love that other wounded souls can offer.

VII

....

My grandmother used to tell the story of her grandfather in Greece, who, after being imprisoned for stealing a loaf of bread in a time of war, swam the Black Sea to freedom. "The whole Black Sea," she'd say. My grandmother also used to tell the story about her own father, who, after emigrating to America, was mistaken for a black man, because he was the shade of a black man, and arrested in West Virginia for driving with his much fairer-skinned bride. That same grandmother used to always refer to me, particularly in the presence of strangers, as "her adopted grandchild, not the mailman's child." I was fair-skinned and light-haired in a family of dark-haired, olive-skinned folk, and she didn't want anyone thinking that her daughter-in-law had cuckolded her son. My grandmother laughed when she told those stories, or whenever she introduced me, as if it was funny to be criminalized, shamed for simply being.

It doesn't matter where you're from, or what language you speak, judgment is inherently learned and requires consistent effort to overcome. When I began studying classical studies in college, I had a professor, Tina, who opened my eyes to Homer, Aristotle, Thucydides—to the various etymological interpretations one could make about those stories of humanity and the consequences of action. Her passion for teaching those stories, and her personal desire to contribute to the understanding of what makes a society just, not only turned me into a grecophile, but it was also a large part of the reason I asked her to accompany me to Bosnia and Herzegovina. I was afraid to ask her, and beyond delighted when she said yes.

The first time I see Greece, it's on the horizon, outside of a porthole on an overnight ferry from Italy. My heart swells with the bow wave at the sight of the blue mountains in the distance. I wake Celie, to tell her land-ho, Greece ahead. She sits upright, smiles without opening her eyes, and slowly rolls back down to sleep.

We are on a tight timeline, and though I'd hoped to get to Athens the first night so we could sleep in before going to the airport, the sun is falling and we spend the night about an hour away, near the Gulf of Corinth which the apostle Paul once traveled through on his way to give his famous speech about love being patient, love being kind. We stop there because we are supposed to—because we meet Sohel, who is working at the restaurant where we dine.

Sohel loves Athena, and he dotes on Celie all through dinner, the way everyone has on this journey—the majority of humanity still knowing how to shower a child with love in the hopes that they will one day have mostly love to pass on. After dinner, Celie plays across the street from the restaurant at a beach while I rearrange gear on a picnic table. Sohel comes across the street, bearing a bowl of ice cream for Celie. She thanks him, tucks into it like a kitten happy to be fed.

"I hope you don't mind," Sohel asks, "but I see your vehicle, and I see the Landmine Survivors Network, and I just want to know what work you do?"

"It isn't work in the traditional sense," I say. "I'm just trying to bring awareness to the plight of landmine survivors. I'm driving around the world to different places that have been affected by landmines in the aftermath of war. I'm heading to Bosnia first, the day after tomorrow."

"When I was fourteen," Sohel tells me, "I lost my best friend to a landmine in Bosnia."

My eyes widen, my heart quickens, and I feel like Sohel is a messenger from God, the gods, the universe—telling me that I'm on the right path. "Do you want to tell me what happened?" I ask.

"We were all refugees, from Bangladesh. We had a very bad dictator, and so many of us were dying for no reason at all. My parents were killed. So, one day, my best friend and I joined a group of refugees from all over, mostly Pakistan, trying to find somewhere safe to stay. We traveled for so many days and nights, mostly on foot. One night we crossed over a mountain, into Bosnia. It was around midnight when the explosion happened. Three Pakistani men, who looked out for us, died immediately, and my friend, it took him three days to die—a day for us to mourn each of the men who had watched over us. I made my friend a shelter and did what I could to care for him, but his injuries were too great. We buried them all in the mountain, and then we continued because what else could we do?"

I touch Sohel's hand. He is younger than me, though a man, but when he tells me this story it's with the heart of the child who had to leave his best friend on a mountain when they were closer to safety than they had been for years. Sohel accepts the touch, but only briefly, and says, "He would have liked it here. There is peace here. The world needs more peace."

"Is there more ice cream?" Celie says, blissfully unaware of the sorrow just spoken.

"Yes!" Sohel laughs. "More ice cream and more peace."

Before we part, I ask him how to say peace in Bengali. "*Santi*," he says. "*Santi*." Then I offer him the Sharpie, and when I ask him, he writes the word on the side of Athena— so they'll know we come in peace, I tell him.

We arrive at the Athens airport with no time to spare. We enter the main doors, and Tina is walking toward us. Even though she was my professor, she is also one of the people I feel closest to in this world, someone who saw my worth and encouraged it—someone who shared meals with me and would drop everything to help me in a crisis. I've missed her. We hug each other for a long spell. Celie hugs both of our legs the whole time as if to fasten us together, until suddenly she hears her name being shouted, pulls away, and starts running toward J as fast as her legs can take her.

Tina and I are leaving for Bosnia in the morning, while J and Celie are off to an island resort in Greece. This will be the longest time I have ever parted from my daughter, but she's four-and-a-half now—it's time to start trying out her wings, time for me to remember the strength of my own. I asked J to come spend the time with her because I decided back in England that I wanted Bosnia to be a test run, that I didn't know how to concentrate on the task at hand of listening and learning while being constantly worried that my carefree child would step off the pavement in a land still ravaged by war, or that I might have to bury her on the side of a mountain because of it.

The four of us eat dinner at a taverna in Athens, but I mostly pick at my plate. J and Celie are so tickled to be re-united that I decide I can't be selfish, but all I want to do is spend the evening alone with her, read to her, giggle with her, tell her all the things I may have forgotten to tell her in case I don't return.

Instead, I breathe in the night air and hope that I've done right by her. Instead, I check her bag five times to make sure she'll have everything she might need. Instead, I brief J on her likes and dislikes, her routines and rituals. Instead, I kiss them both goodnight and split a bottle of wine with Tina.

"Are you ready to go tomorrow?" Tina asks after the first glass is poured.

"Yes," I say, tears streaming down my face.

Tina hugs me. "She'll be okay."

"None of us know any of that," I say, full faucet on now. I cry until the wine tastes like salt. I cry until the wine bottle is emptied. I cry when my face hits the pillow and Celie's back isn't there against my chest, our hearts unable to sync.

There's a crook at the base of a mountain in Thermopylae where Tina tells me to pull off the road. We've only been driving a couple of hours. It's still early morning. "What are we doing here?" I ask.

"You haven't smiled once this morning. This should cheer you up."

We climb a few boulders before I see the steam—natural hot springs welling up in the rocky formations. There's only one older man as far as I can see. Tina yanks her pants off and steps right in, submerges her body in the healing water. I follow suit.

"Now, isn't that better?" she asks, as I step in.

"I don't know, I can't feel it yet," I say matter-of-factly since the water is only touching my prosthetic feet.

Tina ignores my joke, and says, "I know you're going to miss Celie, but I hope you're not going to be down this whole trip."

I find firm footing and let my body sink into the water up to my neck. My skin feels electric, my muscles unclench. "Miss who?" I ask, grateful for the reprieve. "At least I had her almost five years. The pope says if you give him a child for the first five years, the child will be Catholic for life. I didn't leave her in an orphanage. I didn't try to beat the will out of her. I didn't shame her for nothing. For four and a half years, I've extended as much love as I can. So, she's got a fighting chance."

I look over at Tina, for what, I don't know. Pity? But she's underwater, and when she emerges, I keep my drama to myself. She lets out a guttural sigh as the water pours over her—I envy her ability to relax, decide to try it on, as she greets the older man, one pool over from us, in Greek.

He answers in English. "It is a beautiful day. Tell me, how old do you think I am?" It sounds like the beginning of a riddle.

Tina tells him he doesn't look a day over sixty.

"I know," he says, standing up out of the water, buck naked. "Lucky for you, I am ninety-four. I've been swimming in these springs my whole life, preserves most things, but not all," he says, cupping his genitals with a feigned modesty.

Tina starts laughing. I'm not totally sure what's funny. Then, she raises her fist out of the water. Steam is coming off of it as she shouts at the man in Greek, "*Molon Labe*! *Molon Labe*!"

Then the man who is almost a century starts laughing, and repeats it three times, shaking his head while he walks away.

When it's just the two of us, Tina tells me that 2,500 years earlier, near the top of the mountain above us, the Spartan general Leonidas, with an army of around 7,000, managed to hold off and murder a good fraction of the 150,000 Persian soldiers under Xerxes for six days. They might have succeeded if it hadn't been for a local shepherd who took a bribe from the Persians and told them of a secret pass up the back of the mountain where they could sneak up on Leonidas and his men.

Leonidas got word of this before the Persians had cemented a plan and sent the majority of his troops, without haste, down the backside of the mountain to head for safety. Those that remained with Leonidas were meant to buy the fleeing group time, to fight with honor.

Xerxes, feeling smug near the bottom of the mountain, ready to hatch a plan, shouted up the mountain—*We'll kill you all soon enough. Give up your weapons. Surrender your lives.*

In an act of defiance, Leonidas shouted right back down at Xerxes—*Molon Labe!* Or, *Come and take (me)!*

At the duty-free shop on the Greek-Macedonian border, we pile up on pistachios, cigarettes, and water, then make our way to Stobi, where a colleague of Tina's from the American School in Athens is conducting an archaeological dig. When I asked Tina to go with me to Bosnia, she had only two stipulations—that we stop to see this site and again to see the reconstruction of the Mostar bridge in Bosnia and Herzegovina.

In the middle of nowhere, among low-lying mountains, we drive onto a long plateau, cordoned off in sections with orange tape. There is no one on the field, or in the makeshift building at the end of it, except a young local man and his German shepherd who remarkably both have one brown eye and one blue. The man tells us that the archaeologists are not here, that they pay him to watch the field when they are gone. Tina gives him a pack of cigarettes, and he lets us in.

In one of the sections, there is a five-foot-deep trench dug into the earth. Tina swoops under the orange tape and hops down into the trench. I follow suit while she heads down the trench and try to hide the fact that my stumps are ringing with pain after I land.

"Here's a ladder," she shouts returning, looking for me above ground.

"Too late for that," I say, biting my lip.

"Are you okay?" she asks.

"Just a flesh wound," I say, referencing the Black Knight from the Monty Python movie. "I'm invincible," I add, but it still hurts.

Tina studies the dirt wall. "Look at this," she says. She points to a striking stratum of earth—mostly rusty hues—then she singles out a long, thin stretch of solid black in the soil and wipes her finger across it. She holds it up to my nose and says, "What do you smell?"

I inhale and pull back, repulsed. I know that smell.

"You know what it is, don't you?" Tina asks me.

"Burnt flesh," I say, recalling the smell of my cauterized stumps.

Then she says, "This layer of black in the earth represents a village or a small city. It was razed by fire—could have been a result of the plague, or an invasion. The depth of this line will give the archaeologists an estimate of how long ago the city was here. It's kind of like discovering the life of a tree through the rings."

I still haven't gotten over the smell of burnt flesh.

Then Tina says, "I love my job. Isn't it amazing to think that these human lives that were fully dimensional hundreds, perhaps thousands, of years ago are now packed so tightly by time that they appear to be no more than a pretty

black line in a slice of earth? And yet the scent of human
flesh still remains—we're never really gone."

The Serbian border guard is husky and has a deep scar across
his cheek. He lumbers over to check our documents, looms
over me and Tina. Tina asked me the night before if I was
certain I had all the right documents. I told her how I'd
checked the government websites for requirements, how
I'd contacted embassies to find out all that I'd need everywhere I might go, but still he walks to his guard station and
comes back to tell us we owe permit fees. I know he is telling a whopper, but who am I to argue with the likes of him?

"Why you come to Serbia?" he asks.

"We are going to Bosnia," I say.

"Why you go to Bosnia?" he replies.

"To meet with landmine survivors."

The border guard doesn't seem to understand, so I say
narki, as if he will know the word for landmine in Greek.
When he asks Why-you-go-to-Bosnia again, I pull out
a Landmine Survivors Network pamphlet that has the
landmine symbol with the skull-and-crossbones on it.
He still looks at me, as if he doesn't comprehend. Then I
pull my pant leg up and show him my prosthetic and say,
"Landmine. Boom."

And then he guffaws. My jaw drops. Again, he asks,
"Why you go to Bosnia?"

It costs us an hour, and nearly two hundred euros to get
into Serbia. The border guard rattles our feathers, as do
the boy-soldiers we see afterward along the Kosovo border.
There's a lone boy every five miles or so, standing next to a

haystack piled similarly to a funeral mound, a pyre, bearing an automatic weapon that looks as heavy as the boy himself. I want to get through Serbia without being raped, killed, or having my truck stolen. It's silent in the cab of Athena—the gravity of the situation has come home.

Ahead we see the winged foot of Achilles—like a sign from heaven—the Goodyear logo, where my father has worked his whole life, and I feel safe, even if it's just a feeling. It's a gas station, and I pull in and fill up the tank while Tina goes to find a bathroom. Things are surely going to get better from here.

The middle-aged attendant inside tries to overcharge me by a lot of euros, and I am done being overcharged in Serbia, but when I grab a pen and paper and try to show him exchange rates and basic math, he just keeps saying that he doesn't speak English.

A huge boom comes from outside, and I imagine a boy-soldier, Tina. The attendant and I run out different doors to the cinder block building beside the front office, where Tina is standing, framed by a bathroom doorway. The door has come completely off the hinges and is lying on top of the bottom half of a little old lady, who is limbs akimbo, flat on the ground.

The man starts yelling something like "Mama" and rushes over to lift the door, and I give Tina the what-the-hell-happened look, and we start walking quickly toward the Land Rover.

"She tried to lock me in! She tried to lock me in the bathroom!" Tina repeats this several times, gesticulates with her arms as we walk. In the background, I can hear the old lady cursing at us. I'm so nervous I can't quit laughing.

Now the man is yelling at us, too, and when I glance back, I see him coming toward us with his fist shaking in the air. My rib cage feels like it's about to explode, my heart is beating so wildly. We near the back of Athena. "Get in the truck!" I shout. "Get in the damn truck!"

My hands are trembling, and I struggle to get the key into the ignition, but once I do, I depress the clutch and throw her into gear. Lucky for me, my feet don't shake when I'm nervous.

"Oh shit! He's chasing us!" Tina shouts. I look in the rearview mirror and catch a breath when I see he's still on foot. I drive as fast as the gods will allow until Athena whisks us off the battleground to safety.

When I can quit hearing something other than my heart beating in my ear, I roll the window down a crack, light a cigarette, and breathe deep. "What in the hell happened back there?" I ask Tina.

"She asked me if I had a few coins for the use of the bathroom, but I didn't have anything on me. She let me in anyway. I was going to come back to the truck and get something, but the bitch locked me in. At first, I thought the door was stuck, but then I heard her laughing. She told me I could come out when I found some money. I got a little pissed on top of panicked, and I just charged the damn door. I didn't know it would come off the hinges. I didn't know she'd be standing behind it. God, I hope I didn't break her hip."

Tina is smart and sensitive, but she is also tall and thick

and strong and from New Jersey. The old lady must have thought her an easy target, but she was wrong. "Well, if it's any consolation, her son or whoever that was—overcharged me almost fifty dollars for the gas."

"Give me a damn cigarette," Tina says.

We chain smoke half of a pack, and twenty miles later we are still full of adrenaline, still glancing in the rearview mirrors to make sure we're not being followed. Tina breaks out the pistachios, and she cracks a lot of those suckers for me while I drive, and we don't have a trash bag, so we throw the shells in the wheel wells. I hit play and shuffle on the ten-disc changer, and Tina lights us both another cigarette, and out of the speaker comes "Spirit in the Sky."

And we have the windows rolled down, and by god, we sing along.

We chant out the window the lines about sinners and friends in Jesus. We replay it and sing louder, letting the fear expel with the smoke and song. And when we have spent it all with the music, Tina grabs the map, and mutters, "These fucking people need some fucking Jesus."

The nearest city that is large enough for us to feel comfortable staying in is far enough away that we won't arrive until about an hour after sunset, and I hate that we are breaking the driving-after-dark rule on day one.

We're getting a little delirious on pistachios and adrenaline, so we tell sad stories about mothers dying and mothers unknown and lost loves and good lovers and fathers you didn't know you had. And when there's finally a pause in the conversation, Tina sets reality back firmly on the table.

"Can you imagine boys with machine guns on the sides

of country roads in Virginia? Can you fucking imagine that?"

"I don't want to fucking imagine that," I say. "Tina, do you think I'm crazy for doing this?"

"Well, when I agreed to go with you to Bosnia, some of your other professors, my colleagues, thought I was crazy. But this is a good kind of crazy. The war is over . . . it's unlikely that we are going to die going to Bosnia."

"But, we might," I say.

"Well, it's not because you didn't do your homework."

"I did," I say for myself more than Tina. "I did do my homework."

"I know you did. You always do." Tina assures me. "Do you know you're the reason I took the teaching job?"

"No. What do you mean?" I ask, because I have no idea what she's talking about.

"Celie was just a tiny baby when I interviewed at the college. I sat in on your class and listened to your translation of King Priam supplicating Achilles for the body of Hector. It was so moving. I asked the department head about you and she told me about your legs, your divorce, the baby—everything—and she said if I were to take the job, she wanted me to make sure you graduated—she felt you were special—and all I could think was that if this place was wise enough to believe in women like you, to protect and nurture them, then that's where I want to work."

A tear finds its way down my cheek, and Athena's cab falls silent again, and I find myself praying to whatever powers might hear me to deliver us safely. I'm not ready for the spirit in the sky.

The city of Niš is lit up like the giant hemisphere of an orange, glowing atom stuck to the side of the earth. We find a hotel downtown. We get a night of bad stomach issues from a nearby Serbian Chinese restaurant. We should know better, I think, than to eat at a Serbian Chinese restaurant. We have no choice but to listen to a loud, off-key band until two in the morning, one floor down and through paper walls. I lie with a pillow over my head, watching cockroaches dance in the shower.

We have to pay to get our passports back in the lobby the next morning because everyone in Serbia, I am beginning to think, is an opportunist. Tina and I are both hungover with food poisoning residue, a lack of sleep, and a previous day full of adrenaline. I embarrass her when I cuss at the front desk man.

We drive in silence again, well out of the city, by cinder block homes, a woman smacking a child on a street corner, a man with a mule in the back of his pickup. I pull over next to an abandoned building covered with graffiti, which is covered with fresh ivy. We are thirty miles from the Bosnia and Herzegovina border. I pull out the Kelly Kettle from the back of the Land Rover, and it starts to rain, but I am not dismayed. Instead, I dart under an eave—we need coffee like an engine needs gas.

I bought the Kelly Kettle in Ireland when I was twenty-one. I visited a boy who was my first kiss when I was fifteen and on a mission trip, just before I went home and lost my legs and, soon after, my piousness. He and I were supposed to go on a road trip around Ireland with another female friend, but after three days of her and me blaring

Alanis Morrisette and Beth Orton nonstop on the stereo in the rental car, having a drink or two in the evenings, and lots of raucous fun, he went running for the hills, far away from the no-longer-submissive, Christ-loving girl he'd kissed under an oak tree years earlier. I kept traveling, got a sweater and the Kelly Kettle—the official kettle of West Ireland fisherman. All you needed was a handful of twigs and a bit of paper and a way to light a fire, and you'd have boiling water in minutes, in all kinds of conditions.

I make Tina and me some instant coffee.

"I'm almost sorry I dragged you here, and we haven't even made it to Bosnia yet," I say, wondering if she would rather head for the hills with the boy from Ireland right now.

"It's not bad going through hell with you," Tina says.

A boy on a bicycle rides by in the rain.

I put out the fire, we dump the last few sips of muddy coffee, and we leave, ready to drive through Serbia for the last time.

The northern border guards in Serbia make me remove all the cargo boxes from the top of the roof rack, then they take my laptop into the main office where I sit across a desk from a woman with a tight bun who asks if I will boot up the computer. She watches as I type in my password. She watches Celie come to light on the screen.

"Who is that?" she asks.

A month ago, Celie fell asleep as we began to depart Germany, where we had an extended visit with her family on her father's side. In France, she'd come down with strep throat and a double ear infection, so I called her great-aunt in Berlin, and she took us in until Celie was fully healed. Celie fell asleep soon after we left and slept most of the day until we were just outside of Innsbruck, Austria, and the Alps were magnificent.

"Mama," Celie said, rubbing her eyes like she was both sleepy and couldn't believe what she was seeing, "I want to eat snow."

The sun was near setting for the day, so we camped by a river, and the next morning, I packed us a light lunch, and we winged it out of Innsbruck toward mountain roads and eventually started up a steep logging road until Athena's tires began spinning even with the four-wheel drive engaged. To the left of the road was a ravine with waterfalls and a rushing brook. To the right was a steep incline, the next ascent of a switchback. The road was not wide enough for me to turn around in one turn.

I put on the parking brake, put the vehicle into first, and slowly released the foot brake, praying that Athena didn't begin to spin and slide backward again. She held. I grabbed our backpack, and slowly opened the doors, afraid that she would come loose. I made Celie exit first, and told her to go up the road, above Athena, in case the truck slid backward. Then I exited, and Athena held tight.

I took the satellite phone out of the backpack and asked Celie if she remembered how to use it—we'd practiced a few nights when I needed something to entertain her. Then I gave her a number for Austrian 911 and said that Mama had to try to reverse the truck and get her facing downhill.

It's real steep, I told her, and if for some reason Athena rolls over and Mama can't use the phone, then she needed to dial the number I gave her. And she said, "Mama, you'll be fine."

First, I found a felled pine log and laid it horizontal to the edge of the ravine, about two feet from the edge. I climbed swiftly into the cab—wasting no time on worry and threw her into gear, slowly veering her backward at a hard curve until I felt the back wheels tap the thick log, and then I hit the brake, and then acid fear rose in my throat. I pulled her around easily enough after that and put her into park fifteen yards down.

"You did it, Mama!" Celie shouted, running to meet me.

We high-fived, and I told her I was sorry we couldn't drive any farther, but if we were going to find snow to eat on that mountain road then we were going to have to hike, and she was game. I had a pedometer, and we went up 4.5 kilometers, switched back and forth until the road ran out and there was nowhere to go, and there was no snow, and our bodies ached (my stumps were raw for the next three days) and Celie ran out near the edge of the end of the road and said, "Look, Mama! Look at this! We did it!" There was a deep bowl of a valley below and mountains so high and blindingly white-peaked that they seem to pierce through the sky. She'd forgotten that eating snow was the goal. Celie raised her hands in the air in triumph, and I snapped a photograph, and later that night, as we camped near the base of the mountain and Celie threw stones into the waterfall, happy as all get-out, I downloaded it from the camera onto the laptop and made it my background.

"That's my daughter," I tell the Serbian border guard.

Then the woman with the tight bun looks at me as if maybe I'm not a threat and stamps my passport and tells me to pack up my things. I walk outside to tell Tina. She's just opened the last of my heavy-duty boxes while the male guards outside stand over her. "Well?" she asks.

"Well, let's pack it all back up. We're out of here."

"Well, shit," she says.

A quarter mile later, the Bosnian border guards check our passports, thank us for coming, and when we ask them where we can exchange euros for marks, they explain that the nearest bank will be closed by the time we get there. Then, one of them takes money out of his own pocket and trades us a little—to get by, and when Tina notices that he gave us two marks too many, the man says to keep them for good luck.

We drive slowly into the small village of Bijeljina, where every single house, every building we drive past is riddled with bullet holes. Riddled to the point of killing someone long after they are dead. This is not a scene created for a film, and I have never seen anything like this outside of film—these homes covered in the art of war.

Tina and I are gobsmacked yet again. The sun is beginning to set, and we have a little more than an hour to Tuzla, where I am scheduled to meet landmine survivors through representatives of Landmine Survivors Network for the next few days. We'll be driving after dark again two days in a row, but I am too tired to care. I stop at the first gas station I see and go inside where the clerk greets me with a smile. The newspaper stand is empty. All I see is soda and candy and fake flowers. I walk toward a freezer and pull out two bright blue packages with yellow smiley faces on them and language I can't decipher. I don't care what's behind the smiley faces—I just want a treat.

I put some of the marks on the counter, take the change, and head back outside where Tina is leaning against the front bumper guard on Athena, staring at the broken houses across the street. I hand her a smiley face package and she says, "This is so sad."

We tear open the wrappers and find fudgsicles inside, maybe the best fudgsicle I have ever eaten. We watch the sky pull into long stretched fibers of purple and pink. "At least," I garble, with melting chocolatey fat in my mouth, "Bosnia has beautiful sunsets, and fudgsicles."

"*Molon labe*," Tina says, sucking the end of her stick.

And I want to say be careful what you ask for—but even Leonidas knew he was sealing his fate. Serbia has been a wake-up call. I could have spent ten years researching for this expedition, but nothing could have prepared a twenty-seven-year-old single mother from America with prosthetic legs for the reality of what is not even a war, but the aftermath of one. Bosnia, I know, is going to be more than beautiful sunsets and fudgsicles, and we still have to drive more than an hour in the dark.

I want to be more than a pretty black line in the earth. I don't want to be a girl on a missing persons milk carton or website. I don't want to be quietly buried on a mountainside. I don't want someone to chance upon the scent of my remains in an archaeological dig. I don't want to be an untold story, hard-pressed molecules buried in the dank, cold earth.

When Leonidas was finally killed in the last battle against Xerxes and his men, the Greek soldiers pushed back the Persians from the front line three times until they could secure Leonidas' body from the field and protect it from Persian desecration. They were loyal to him because he was a hero among Greeks, surely given wind by the gods, kind-hearted and noble. Leonidas is dust in the wind, too, but I'd rather they still be telling a story about me 2,500 years later like the one they do about him. I'd rather be a story than a line.

VIII

....

IN the main lobby of the Hotel Tuzla hangs a painting of nine life-sized women, standing side by side. The wall to the right of the painting is entirely glass so that the sun throws a spotlight on each woman, one by one, from morning on, until they all bask in unison for an hour or so before nightfall. The women vary in their manifestations—four are whole and nubile, two are sporadically bare-boned, three expose both abstract and graphic organs—a red box for a heart, a fibrous lung, musculature that streaks like the lights of a Vegas night. All of the women are clear, delineated with rich, black lines and splashes of vivid color—jade, pomegranate. They hold different poses—one crouches, one ponders with a fingertip to her mouth, and another looks out to the sky with her arm stretched toward it.

I stare at this painting every time I walk through the lobby—once for over an hour. Is the placement of the piece deliberate so that each muse can have her moment in the sun? I am enthralled, as if I see my own metamorphosis in

the painting, as if each hour of sunlight brings a new reve-
lation. For three days, I can barely hold a conversation that
doesn't include the painting. Tina, having heard enough,
begins referring to it as "The Art of Suffering."

Beyond the painting, through a set of double glass doors, is
a cold industrial lounge, a structure of steel beams and glass.
It is shortly after nine, our third night in Tuzla, and Tina
and I are sitting at the bar with two men. Tina hasn't felt
well all afternoon and wants to go back to the room.

I ask Tina to at least finish her drink, because I don't
want to leave the men at the bar, but I don't want to be
alone with them either.

Salko is sitting to my left. He has amber eyes and no
legs. We have a language barrier. He knows about thirty
words in English and I know about ten in Serbo-Croatian.
I turn to him and say, "How old are your daughters?"

Salko pauses, then holds up five fingers, and then eight.
He pulls a photo from his wallet and passes it to Tina and
me. Three faces smile out from the photo, all blonde and
longhaired. The man has a beautiful wife.

Tina passes the photo back to Salko by reaching across
my back. Salko turns to the man on his left. That man is
quietly sipping vodka through a coffee stirrer. He knows no
English, and he has no arms.

"Rasiê," Salko speaks to his friend, holding up the
picture for him to see. Rasiê nods his head in stag-like
approval.

The men lapse into the thick, chock-a-block fricatives of

Serbo-Croatian. I turn to Tina. "Can you make it a little longer?

"I'll try," Tina replies, pressing her thumb into her side. She adds, "It's too bad they don't let you have a translator 24/7."

Salko taps my shoulder. "You? Children?"

"I have a daughter," I say.

"None," Tina says, shaking her head.

Salko raises one eyebrow.

Rasiê pushes forward his empty glass with the two-inch stump that balls at the end of his shoulder. Someone has carefully sewn the ends of the thermal he wears, so that it fit his stumps snugly. Someone has also rolled his flannel overshirt neat and high. He orders another drink.

Salko smiles at me, then Tina, and orders another round for us all. "*Hvala*," Tina thanks him. I know both Salko and Rasiê are Muslim, but, I think to myself, like so many others during Sarajevo's four-year siege, they may have turned to alcohol for relief, or escape, or both.

A young couple walk up to the bar to pay their tab. They are less than a foot from Rasiê. The woman is smartly dressed, wearing a brimmed hat, dark hair, loose curls, red lips. While waiting for his change, her partner strokes her cheek with the backside of his fingers. They don't even notice Rasiê sitting next to them, stretching his stumps into the air and yawning.

"What time do we get started in the morning?" Tina asks me.

"The translator is meeting us in the lobby at nine."

"Maybe she should meet us outside of the lobby so that she doesn't have to endure a diatribe about the painting."

"I won't talk about the painting. I promise." And then, I think of it—this time, the woman whose flesh stops at the waist and turns skeletal, posing like an *ouvert* ballerina. "Let me tell you what I think I like most about it—" Tina interrupts me with a groan, but I continue. "I like how raw it is, how it makes no apology for the easiness of removing flesh. It makes art out of removing flesh."

"Look, Kelley, I'm glad the piece compels you. Write a thesis on it. I don't care. But last night you were approaching strangers in the lobby about it—in your pajamas."

"They weren't pajamas!" I protest.

Tina chastens me. She actually calls the painting a "muse orgy," to my great delight. Then she asks what is on the schedule for tomorrow.

"Dinner with a survivor and his family."

Salko taps my arm and motions toward my cigarettes. I push the pack toward him.

"You're not so special here, are you?" Tina says suddenly.

"What do you mean?"

"Usually you're the only one, but here you are in a world made up of amputees," she muses.

"I hadn't thought of it that way. But now that you mention it, it's rather amusing to think that between the four of us here, there are only three legs and six arms."

"That sounds like a bad bar joke," Tina says.

"Like the amputee who walks into a bar and says, 'I'd give my left leg for a stiff one,' " I say.

Tina groans and tries to leave again. "Maybe we should excuse ourselves. We're going to need some rest."

I tell Tina that I'm not feeling one hundred percent either, but I don't know if I am ever going to be in Tuzla, Bosnia and Herzegovina, again, and I need to ride it out. I don't want to miss a thing.

I finish off my drink and sit back against the stool. Salko slides the pack of cigarettes back toward Tina and me. We both take one, and Salko lights them for us. He lights himself one. They are cigarettes from the duty-free store on the Greek border. He doesn't speak a word or make a gesture as long as a drag is left on it. Then he lights another, and holds it while Rasiê smokes it, pulling it in and out of the man's mouth between smoke clouds.

"Do you like America?" I ask Salko.

He cocks his head toward me, raises his thick eyebrows, and says, "I like rock and roll."

Then he takes my hand in his large warm hand and belts out the chorus of "Let It Be." And then he laughs and says, "Good, no?" He gently puts my hand down on the bar and traces the heart-shaped scar on the back of it with the tip of his pointer finger. I don't point out that the song is British.

Earlier that morning, Tina and I are sitting in a conference room of the Hotel Tuzla with a group of landmine survivors who counsel other landmine survivors. It is a semiformal meet and greet, and there I am, suddenly in a room of at least a dozen amputees who've suffered far greater terrors than I've known. I feel small, like my gut is going to unravel. I'm about to slip off to the bathroom to do some deep breathing when the director beckons the translator to start the meeting.

Amira, the translator, welcomes me warmly in English. She is the only other woman in the room aside from Tina and me. She repeats the welcome in Serbo-Croatian and the men around the table clap lightly, which embarrasses me. Then she asks me if I can tell them a little about why I am here.

I say that I am going to try to drive around the world. I say that we have something in common, and I lift a leg above the table and tug the pant line up just above the ankle, then set it back down, then lift the other one and show them my wounds. I say that I am going to visit five Landmine Survivor Network sites worldwide, and that I hope to gather stories that might bring some attention to the needs that still remain in the regions.

Once the translator finishes, the man closest to my right begins to speak. One after the other, they all begin to introduce themselves. The translator repeats these words in nearly every introduction: *My name is x. I was a soldier.* There are a few farmers, too. And then, in a way that reminds me of the cataloguing of the ships in the second chapter of the *Iliad*, which Tina taught me in college, they tell me what they are missing: right arm, left arm, right leg, left leg, both legs, both arms, both legs and an arm, eyes.

And then when they are finished, there is an awkward silence, because this isn't a normal meeting and there is no protocol, and then Salko stands up across the table from me and says, "Hello, American woman. Show me your legs again."

And because of the way he smiles at me and pretended to play an air guitar while he spoke, I stand up, and jokingly begin to hum a burlesque tune while slowly lifting up my pant leg as if I am about to reveal a well-defined, fish-netted calf of flesh and blood. The boys love it. Then, I pop a leg off and slide it across the table to Salko.

My prosthetics aren't all that old, not even two years, but they are already beat up from my rowdy ways. Even beat up, the technology is considerably more advanced than the prosthetics I see in the room. Salko admires the duct tape on my foot shells, the knife sheath attached to the socket.

Salko speaks to Amira and Amira tells me how Salko stepped on a Bouncing Betty, how he heard it bobbing up and down almost like a water sprinkler, how he fell backward to avoid it, and how it blew both of his legs, just below the knees, clean off.

Bouncing Betty is the worst of the landmines; perhaps it is the personification of the name, but its function seems just as personal. Its job is to spew shrapnel near the waistline of a man, to maim him where it will hurt him the most without killing him. The Latin word *mine*, from which the *mine* in *landmine* is derived, refers to ore or metal. In war, the Romans would dig a hole, fill the hole with metal spikes, then disguise it. They would then try to lead their opponents into it. The original intent of the landmine was to maim rather than to kill, so that when other soldiers came to their comrade's aid, the final count of the fallen would be more significant.

Salko's wife and two daughters escaped the war before it was too late and no one could escape, and they fled to Austria. They eventually returned when they could, Amira said, slowly, quietly, and it occurs to me that Salko might have survived because of love.

I was warned not to make any concrete promises in war-torn countries—that unless you can deliver readily, it's like offering a starving child a voucher for a store that is across the globe. I look out the window where the ubiquitous marks of gunfire and mortar shelling are particularly copious on the buildings across the street. The blood was washed away long before I arrived. And how can I not think of my arrival—the hi-tech gadgets in my truck, the SAT phone just for starters—and here, in Tuzla, the windows of many homes are still covered in plastic because they cannot yet afford glass. Skeletal buildings are left unrepaired because nails and wood are too expensive. I feel like an asshole.

I speak quietly to Amira. She translates, "You gentlemen must think it is crazy for a woman with no legs to try to drive around the world."

Salko is unable to conceal his mirth. He bursts out with laughter, everyone does. Tina pats me on the back. Then Salko says, "We are all crazy! Welcome to Bosnia-Herzegovina!" The room bursts with laughter, and we spill out into the lobby where someone wants to take photos. Salko grabs me and sits me sideways on his lap, making sure our lack of legs is showing while the cameras flash us nearly blind, but not enough so that I can't see those nine women hanging there on that canvas—and their eighteen lovely legs.

I take the men outside to show them Athena. Again, photos are taken, in which some of the men are hanging from the cargo rack. Salko and I are sitting on the hood. Then, we all smoke cigarettes until Tina and I are whisked off to meet a landmine survivor who became a butcher after the war, who serves us questionable meats for lunch which lands us in the hotel room all afternoon.

At one point, trying to distract Tina from cramps that have her doubled over, I say, "I felt like an asshole today, but I think I won them over when I threw my leg across that table."

"You're not an asshole," she says, "but you won them over when you passed out two cartons of our duty-free cigarettes."

It's nearing one o'clock in the morning, and there is no Amira—no one to translate, just the four of us at the bar. We've exhausted our limited language, and Tina, too. She steadies herself, pushing back from the bar, and excuses herself for the night. "*Do videnja.*"

"*Do videnja,*" both Rasiê and Salko say.

"I'll walk you to the elevator," I say, and once we are on the other side of the double glass doors, I thank her for staying so long and ask her if she is okay and if she wants help to the room.

And she replies, "Not unless you think you should go back to the room yourself."

"What do you mean?" I ask.

"Do you think it's wise to sit up at a bar all night in Tuzla drinking with these men?"

"Tina, come on," I reply, rolling my eyes toward the painting. The women are in the dark; not even the low light in the lobby can bring them fully to life. "I'll be fine. I'll finish my drink and come back to the room."

"That wasn't necessarily a comment about you," Tina says. "You don't know these men, what they might think, what the war might have done to them."

The door to the elevator opens. "Go on, Tina. I'll be fine." She kisses me quickly on the cheek. I slip back into the lounge before the elevator door shuts.

The bartender's cigarette smoke hovers in curves. The smoke is stark against the backdrop of the night sky on the other side of the glass walls. Rasiê is face down at the bar. The bartender crushes the butt in an ashtray, then hands Salko a wool blanket that he has stored under the bar. Salko spreads it out on a wooden bench in a quiet corner. Then he and the bartender carry Rasiê to the bench and leave him there in a muted snore.

Salko is sweating. His thigh brushes against mine as he sits back down at the bar. He stares at me, a puzzled look on his face. He seems to want to explain something to me but cannot. Perhaps, I am projecting my own frustration. Perhaps I should go to the room with Tina.

"*Pivo*?" Salko asks me.

"Yes, *pivo*. *Hvala*." I'll have another beer. The bartender smirks. Salko laughs at me. I blush.

The cold beer is delicious. I feel a small, second wind.

Halfway through the beer, the bartender leaves and never returns. We simply sit, Salko and I, quietly in the bar before dawn, sipping beer and smoking cigarettes. At some point, I glance up at the ceiling. It's nearly twenty feet high. A metal-plated column runs the length. Ten feet up the column, a string of bullet holes runs horizontally, like a stream surface pocked with raindrops. I try to focus in on the black center of the holes and find myself wishing I could climb inside one of them. Who did I think I was coming to this place? Why am I staying up until near dawn with this man with whom I cannot even speak? The war is one thing, I rationalize, but amputation has a language of its own, a shared knowledge of such trauma and resiliency requires no translation.

"Bang! Bang!" Salko shouts close to my ear watching me stare at the bullet holes. I nearly fall off the bar stool. He starts laughing. I laugh, too, and pointing toward the bathroom, I excuse myself.

The water can't come out of the faucet quickly enough. I wring my hands under the cold flow, and then part them down the bridge of my nose. I look at my reflection in the small mirror over the sink. I don't recognize myself. In front of me, stands a loose apparition of who I had once been.

I wasn't born with a silver spoon. My sweet Athena, the expedition's Land Rover, and the entire trip are being paid for by a malpractice settlement. Until today, I never realized the illusion of security that comes with being an American. I've never been this close to a war and its inhabitants. And yet Salko, cut the same way I am, though with what I perceive as multiplied sufferings, seems to want me to be there as much as I want to be here.

Maybe Tina is right, maybe all I wanted was to be in a room full of amputees—maybe I want to know that I am not alone. However, the amputations that these folks have endured are beyond the severity of what I've experienced, at least that's what my mind says—a mind that doesn't fully understand yet that you can't compare suffering except in the terms of perspective. There's always someone worse off.

Humility hits me like a hangover, throbbing and thorough. I douse my face again, dry off with my shirt sleeve, and return, swaggering—a combination of the alcohol and sore stumps—back to the lounge.

Though there is still no bartender, there are two fresh beers in front of Salko and me. I look at him. He winks. A five o'clock shadow is forming on his chin. We clink beers, and I offer him a cigarette. He lights it and smokes it with his eyes fixed on mine until halfway through the cigarette, I tear myself from his gaze.

I swig the beer, and feel done in, worn out, but high. I lean forward and rest my chin to forearm, extend my other arm across the length of the bar and watch a smoke snake rise from the burning ash. I see Salko gently clench the cigarette from my hand and set it in the ashtray without bothering to extinguish it.

When I wake, my face is in the crook of my elbow, and the sky is cinereous blue. Rasiê is snoring with a low whistle, and I don't remember falling asleep. My neck pains as I pull

upright. Salko is sitting perfectly straight on his stool, looking forward, silent. He beams when he notices my movement. He gestures with his head toward the atrium doors.
When I don't respond, he takes me by the wrist and leads
me out of the lounge. We pass the painting. I pull back and
motion toward it. "Do you like it?"

Salko looks quickly, distractedly at the life-sized women
hovering above us, then pulls his eyes away hurriedly, seemingly confused. He abruptly takes my hands in his, kisses
me on the cheek and says, "Good night. God be with you."
And then he leaves.

My mind is on coffee, and whether or not I have of-
fended him by bringing up the muse orgy? Does he not like
art? Or, does his trauma linger so close in the morning air
that he can't risk relishing something as beautiful as art. As
if beauty is all too much to risk, again. After all, there are
still bullet holes in the bar where we were sitting all night,
and in the painting, the innards of women are exposed.
Are the shades of suffering represented in the painting still
too loud in Salko's mind to even be considered a thing of
beauty made with a brush? The opposite of hope is a place.

Behind the Hotel Tuzla, where I go to have a cigarette instead
of going to the room, there is a small, sparsely wooded park
dotted with the same young trees that line the streets. Glossy
with dew, stone tiles form a patio with wrought-iron tables
for two, and in the center, there is a statue of a six-foot
metallic teardrop. Behind the teardrop, there is a knoll,
where Salko has stopped and sits on the damp ground.

I watch him from a distance. His back is to me. In front

of him, the Tuzla skyline of struggling factories, salt baths, and mines is on the eastern horizon. A few funnels smoke gray against the predawn sky.

I want to walk over and join him, to take his hand in my own. I simply want to connect with him, but I am afraid of his reaction. Would it be as natural and pure as my own intention feels? I start to take a step in his direction when the sun cuts the sky, blindingly salmon, in a pencil-thin line.

Then, Salko lifts up his pant legs and removes his prosthetic legs. He sets his prosthetics to the side. He rises up onto his knees and opens his mouth and begins to pray the first *salaah* of the day. And as that man sings that holy prayer, the sun persists, and suddenly I feel as close to God and all things that a human might, like a pixel in a divine painting. I begin to weep. My fatigue is coupled with a body ache that doesn't compare to the bliss growing inside of my being. Salt cakes upon my cheeks. I hear the tremble in Salko's voice and know that I am not alone.

When Salko's prayer floats away and pink overwhelms the sky and the flesh is illuminated in its mortal light, Salko puts his legs back on and stands up, and notices me in the distance. He nods toward me, wanders away, and I never see him again.

IX

....

I met Bob through a mutual friend in England while I'd been involved in off-road training the previous year. He was ex-SAS, the British Secret Ops, and a brilliant engineer. After retirement, he'd designed two machines that worked together to perform landmine clearance. They were both operated from a remote-control site. The first one was tank-like, without a turret. It had a powerful engine and dozens of pistons that tramped the ground and detonated any potential landmines. Each piston was designed to take the full weight of any possible detonation so that if there was a detonation, they could replace just that piston, or a few, and keep working. The second machine followed the first, and it churned into the ground and inhaled the soil; then it separated the dirt from the ore, retaining all of the metallic particulates inside of it, and then it spit the now-tilled soil so that the land was ready for agriculture. Bob and I had met in a pub, and we'd hit it off so well that he'd agreed to meet me in Bosnia and give me a tour and a demonstration.

As Tina and I are preparing to set off from Tuzla, Bob
sends me an email that includes a set of GPS coordinates
and tells us to meet him there at 1500. He's succinct.

We meet Bob near Jahorina, on the outskirts of Pale
(where the 1984 Winter Olympics were held), at a pristine
chalet—the first building we have seen, Tina notes, without
the pockmarks of war. As we drive Athena II up the mountain driveway, I see Bob lightly jogging ahead of a giant
Serbian man. He opens my door, greets me with a kiss on
both cheeks, and whispers, "No politics. Only gratitude."
Then Bob walks around the Land Rover and greets Tina
in the same manner. The giant Serbian man catches up and
Bob introduces him as Borislav, and he shakes my hand so
hard that it is tender for the next three days.

We share dinner with Bob, Borislav, and his wife—some
sort of radish salad and kielbasa in a room that smells like
fresh cedar. Borislav's wife also has a huge block-body like
her husband. She wears exaggerated makeup and never says
a word. There is a young, nubile girl in a black skirt, white
blouse, and tennis shoes who serves us dinner.

Tina and I are exhausted, and after one beer with
dinner, we can barely keep our eyes open. Borislav asks me
where we will be heading after we finish touring Sarajevo.
I tell him that we are heading to Mostar. He asks me why
we want to go to Mostar. I am suddenly afraid that telling him we are going to go see the bridge would be con-
strued as political, so I keep it vague and say that we will
be sightseeing.

Borislav makes a phone call then, and when he is finished speaking in his deep Serbian tones, he scribbles a

phone number on a slip of paper, hands it to me, and says, "You call this number when you get to Mostar. Tell them Borislav sent you." Then he instructs the young girl to take us to the sauna and prepare us for bed, but we are too tired for the sauna. Our room has two small, cedar camp-style beds. The pine trees outside the window are thick, and the moon exaggerates their silhouette. It is easy to think we are safe, and we sleep that way.

The next morning, I wake before Tina and slip out to the dining room in pursuit of coffee. The young girl is there again and brings me a hot cup before I've even asked. I turn down cream and sugar, thank her, and go outside.

The mountains are chilly, as they are in springtime. The sun is bright, the mountains abundantly green. There are tulips in the lower fields, with small mountain peaks behind them, and five years earlier, just over the peaks, more than one million people were slaughtered.

A dull chime in the distance comes closer; a heifer with a cowbell around her neck eventually greets me from over a fence. I set my coffee on the ground, tear some grass from the edge of the driveway, and hold it up to the gaping, frothy mouth. The cow lets loose a kind of snort and a generous glob of saliva drenches my hand and shirt cuff. In pulling away, I realize that I have accidentally stepped off of the pavement.

An engine roars up the mountain just then, and a shot of adrenaline courses through my body. Bob rounds the bend and halts his military ambulance Land Rover twenty feet past where I am standing with the cow. The ambulance is white with a red cross on the hood, and on both sides of the vehicle, painted in red letters, is the name of his company, Landmine Disposal Systems. The truck is a behemoth, and it sticks out in the lush, idyllic countryside like a red flag. There is danger in this beauty.

"Come on, then," Bob says, bending over and pushing the passenger door open. I tell him about the cow, and he laughs and hands me a towel.

Tina is sitting on the steps of the chalet with a cup of coffee between her hands when we arrive. I feel an unexpected, enormous sense of relief to see her, the one person I know I can trust in this rabbit hole. Isn't that one of the ways in which people survive in extreme circumstances, by sniffing out their kindred in order to adapt to the chaos of war, by running with packs they know when they can?

Bob helps Tina throw her backpack into the truck, and she climbs into the back. There are control panels and monitors all up and down the interior walls of the ambulance; it serves as the remote-control base for Bob's clearance machinery.

"Good night's sleep?" Bob asks.

"A necessary sleep," I answer. And then I ask him what the deal is with Borislav.

Bob hushes me with his hand and says, "Borislav has been helpful in delivering some computers we brought back from England for the kids in the local schools."

As we near the bottom of the mountain, Bob points toward a small valley surrounded by the peaks of the highlands, coated with evergreens.

"That's downtown Pale," he says. "It's where the Serbians

prepared for the siege. And it's where they began their assault."

I can see why they would begin the siege from Pale. The only road to Sarajevo, which Tina and I drove the day before, was one with severe curves. It winds its way through a narrow, high gorge, covered in crags, perfect for snipers. The heavy bushes growing out of the cracks are easy camouflage for a man with an assault rifle.

I roll up the window.

Bob stops the ambulance in front of a small café. Inside, he orders three coffees and pastries in Serbo-Croatian. I want to ask him again about Borislav, but I decide against it. Later, after we drive through Sarajevo and are seated on a bench in the woods with a landmine field behind it, I tell Bob that I appreciate him sharing his work with us, and I ask him again about Borislav.

Bob says, "We are safe enough here. The inn where you all stayed last night is supposedly run by the man who drives Ratko Mladić from one home to another, one safe-house to another, if you will."

"Ratko Mladić, the war crimes fugitive?" I ask.

"First in command at the siege. He was also responsible for the massacre at Srebrenica, where they slaughtered eight thousand boys and men and raped the women."

"If people know that Borislav knows where Ratko is, then why haven't they arrested Ratko?" I ask.

Bob nods his head to one side, his eyes looking up to the sky, and says nothing.

"So, I spent the night with a war criminal?"

"Perhaps," Bob replies almost casually. Then, he tells me how the pencil-pushing bureaucracy of the United Nations Mine Action Service is maddeningly slow. Whether you use machines, or dogs, or mice, or humans, a company can't be approved without a 98.7 percent effective clearance rating. And the landmine clearance rating protocols are forever being updated. Even after you are given clearance, you sometimes have to wait months to clear just an acre of land.

Bob tells us that when he'd been on the scene long enough, he was approached by a Serbian man. If he cleared a lot of Serbian land first, they would let him clear a bit of Bosnian land from time to time, land that was protected by the Serbian mob. It was Bob who organized bringing those computers to students in a local Serbian school. He had braille put on the keys of a few of them for the children who'd gone blind from shrapnel. "Sometimes," Bob says, "you have to dance with the devil to do the work of the Lord."

And I say, "Bob, you're retired. Why do you do all of this when you could be enjoying a pint in the pub and a round of golf?"

"Because this is my penance."

We've left Sarajevo and Bob, and because it is all too much to simply leave behind, we pause on a gravel embankment off highway E73. Tina is preparing to make coffee in the Kelly Kettle, gathering twigs for the fire at the edge of the asphalt. I want to tell her to be careful, to watch how far into the growth her hand reaches—how little it takes to detonate a landmine. But she already knows. In Bosnia, you are warned not to leave the pavement until it becomes religion.

Twenty feet away, the Neretva river flows and gurgles. The birds are piping and the tufts along the river are verdant with the fresh life of spring. The scene is almost too idyllic, the river almost too turquoise, as if chemically persuaded. Before we left Tuzla, Amira told us that the river ran red for a year after the war.

Tina crouches at the knees, her body tilts as far away from the growth as possible while her fingers are still within reach of the twigs that she needs to bring the water to a boil. I can't focus on the map until she has what suffices, until her hand hovers safely over asphalt only. It is as strange to think of wild flowers jutting through that ravaged land as it is to think of a pocket of springtide as potentially lethal.

"How much longer?" Tina asks, sitting with her legs folded on the concrete, fiddling with the tiny flame in the base of the travel kettle.

"An hour, maybe," I say.

"Look, I know this is your journey but I'm on it with you, and for the record, I'd like to discover Mostar and the reconstruction of the bridge, which was part of our deal, without the aid of Borislav and his buddies."

I jump down off of the hood of Athena and sit next to Tina on the gravel. There is smoke, but no fire coming from the bottom of the kettle. I pull out the piece of paper on which Borislav scribbled the phone number. "It may come in handy," I say, adding it to the budding flame in the base of the kettle. The fire takes. And when the coffee is finally ready, I realize that, like so many things, the promise is often better than the thing itself.

We drive the last hour in silence, except for the low drone of news coming from the satellite radio. As I pull nearer the center of Mostar, I turn the radio down a bit. "Tina, tell me again why you've dragged me all the way to the Balkans to see an old bridge?" I attempt to joke.

"Not just old, really old," she says, ignoring my jest. "It was built in 1566 by the Ottoman Turks. It lasted over four hundred years before it was bombed in this last war."

"Don't make 'em like they used to," I reply.

Tina doesn't crack. She goes full-tilt professor. "Wait until you see it. It's impressive—a limestone arch built with voussoirs with radial links that were equal to the height of the front arch. Not a single unnecessary stone was placed, so as not to compromise the weight. It was a masterpiece."

"I love it when you talk over my head," I say. "Voussoirs, vichyssoise, *voulez-vous couches avec moi ce soir?*"

"Voussoirs," Tina continues as her student tries to goad her, "the humongous wedge-shaped stones they hand-chiseled and used to construct the arch. Hand-chiseled stones that held up the arced bridge for four hundred years."

"*Merci.* I'll see soon enough. This road should lead to the river."

I turn down an alley. A man on the corner is leaning against a wall, smoking a cigarette. He doesn't lift his head.

I stop the truck just before the alley comes to a dead end in the form of a stone wall. In an attempt to turn the radio off, I accidentally blast the volume when a voice from the

BBC announces: *Today, the United States Government has issued a statement saying that the last piece of the World Trade Center has been cleared.* I turn the radio off. I glance at Tina. She looks at me with one eyebrow raised, a wily gray strand sticking out from it. She shakes her head as if to shake the sorrow out of it.

"The bridge will have to wait. I have to piss," Tina declares, grabbing her bag, and opening the door. I watch her walk back down the alley through the rearview mirror. I admire and somewhat envy her familiar, sure-footed gait. I step out of the truck and prop the door. Unlike Tina, I have a disdain for public toilets. So, I relieve myself right there.

I walk to the back of the truck and unlock the padlock, grab my vest and the small waterproof briefcase that holds my cameras. Tina has gone to the end of the road, a city block, where the smoking man was, and turned right. I want to get a nice picture of the bridge for her before she returns. I take both the digital camera and the 35mm out of the briefcase, sliding the former into my inside vest pocket. I put the 35mm strap around my neck and walk to the wall at the end of the road.

On the other side of the three-foot wall, two hundred feet below, the clear, turquoise Neretva flows. It turns out, at the end of this alley that is now a dead end, there was once a modern bridge. Far below me, in the froth, glowing in the midafternoon sunlight, the bombed bridge wreckage lies splayed out like an industrial open-heart surgery. Concrete and steel and stone mix hard in an inverted arch that peaks in the center of the river. Cars are still hanging on to parts of the bridge, or smashed into the riverbed, as if the violent plummet happened in recent days and not five and some years earlier. The tragedy at the World Trade Center has been cleared in less than a year. A rueful sort of yelp comes out of me and gets sucked below into the din of the river's flow, the river that ran red for a year.

The restoration of the Mostar Bridge is a couple hundred yards up the river from the razed, modern bridge below. If I straddle the wall, and lean over just enough, I think I can get the shot. Upriver, where the bank widens, tall scaffolds and planks stand covered in white tarps. The large voussoirs are neatly lined along the bank, in the order they will be placed. It is impressive. I pull my prosthetic strap up and throw my leg over the wall. There is a concrete plateau about a foot wide on the other side of the wall where I rest my foot. I do not look down, but downstream. And when I bend over, a tree limb is blocking the shot.

Coming back off the wall, I start down past the tree. A small patch of grass is in the way, so I get on all fours and crawl along the top of the wall to bypass it. *Never leave the pavement.* I straddle the wall again, peer through the lens, and there are the low-lying mountains, the pale blue and pink sky, the white voussoirs and tarps on the verdant banks of the turquoise river.

I set the 35mm on the wall, reach into my pocket for the lightweight digital camera, and catch my hand on the lining of the vest as I pull it out.

The digital camera gleams in the sunlight as it bounces off of my knee and down to the wide river below. I grab after it, clutching air. Then I get dizzy really quickly. I envision myself diving after the metal box, feel a part of myself going with it—even think I hear the tiny impact of metal against stone over the sound of the river's rage.

"Fuck," I say.

Holding tightly to the wall but looking down toward the river, I am surprised to see a glimmer of silver about five feet from the water's edge. The camera is surely broken, but there's a chance that the memory card has been unharmed. The photographs on that flash card flicker through my mind—everything I have seen, all the proof I have of this war-torn yet beautiful country, is down there next to that river.

The conclusion seems easy. Legs or none, I will rappel down the concrete river wall. I did a fair share of rock-climbing in college. There is no other option. I have to get that card. I head back to Athena and dig out my recovery ropes, carabiners, whatever gear I think I might need. I secure the ropes up to the winch hook on the front of Athena. I strap myself up as well as I can without a harness and straddle the wall, gulping hard.

"What the fuck are you doing?" Tina's back.

"Did you piss a river or what?"

"No, I went to a little corner store. I bought a few things. What are you doing?"

"Well, it's a beautiful afternoon. I thought I'd rappel down this wall."

Tina looks over the edge of the wall and gasps.

"The view downriver is far more pleasant," I say.

"To think of the cars underneath that bridge . . ." she starts.

"Did that. Thought of the dead, too. Then I thought of those bastards planting landmines around the rubble so that loved ones couldn't be retrieved."

"What's with the gear, Kelley?"

"I dropped my camera."

"Down there?"

"No. I just feel like rappelling down a two-hundred-foot wall into some war ruins today."

"That's ridiculous. There's got to be another way down there."

"The bridge is out."

"You can't get down there with a bridge anyway."

"I've got to get the memory card from the camera."

"Look, there's someone down there." Tina points about five feet upriver from the crumpled remains of the modern bridge. A man is nestled among the ruins. I grab the 35mm and zoom in on him.

"I think he's shooting up," I said.

"Give me the camera," Tina says, taking the camera.

She gazes down through the lens. There's a breeze with a cold note. Tina sits the camera down on the wall, puts her foot up on the wall next to it, and starts lacing her boot.

"Well?"

"He's fishing, Kelley. He's baiting a hook. And there's a path right over there." Tina points to the right side of the alley. Sure enough, there is a path. I can't see the beginning of it, but I can see where it ends in the ruins at the base of the steep wall. I lock up Athena, and we head toward the trail.

There is a cut in the wall and natural stone stairs that descend the steep, tree-dotted cliff side. It's steep enough that I have to go on all fours at times to maintain balance.

"I wonder what this path was like before the war," I say.

"It probably had a rail," Tina replies.

"A rail would be nice."

"A cup of tea would be nice."

"I fucked up. Sorry."

"Let's just get the card, Kelley."

"What's he doing fishing in that river? Can't be a fish fit for eating in there."

"Maybe he's hungry. A king goes through the guts of a beggar."

I decide to keep quiet. I am getting sweaty and need to concentrate anyhow. At one point, I have to scoot down on my rear to avoid falling. Tina bounds ahead, limber as a goat. The path levels and I stand upright. About fifteen feet from the beginning of the largest slabs of concrete ruins at the base of the support wall, Tina comes to a halt. There's a thin, dirt path, surrounded by ankle-high, rich green grass. Weak in the knees that I still have, I catch up, and take hold of Tina's arm.

"Tina, we shouldn't go on that path." Bob told us about avoiding well-worn paths—that a hundred people could walk a path, and the hundred and first could set off the landmine buried underneath. But the images on that camera are too compelling for me. "You stay here. You've got the SAT phone, and here are the keys, and find the hospital if anything happens."

"Are you fucking crazy?"

"Tina, I've got to get that card. I'm already missing two legs."

"I'm going with you."

"Patroclus," I plead, "I could not bear the same grief as Achilles if something were to happen to you because I gave you my armor and let you fight my fight. No."

"Who thought I'd regret teaching you Homer," Tina rhetorically queries. "Shut up. Let's go."

I break off a three-foot branch from a nearby tree and begin to sweep the dirt with the tip of the stick, the way I saw displayed in a manual landmine clearance demonstration outside of Sarajevo. Birds warble. The scent of hyacinth fills the air.

Several inches at a time, I sweep the earth as if I know what I am doing. The day is windless. The sweat falling from my brow feels as if it weighs enough to set off a landmine. The dirt smells sweet until I think of decomposition, which leaves me feeling more unsteady than I already am. Tina has her hands on my waist. She is bent over my spine as I labor over the path, feeling ridiculous and trivial.

How might we look to any locals that may be watching? Like foreigners who don't face the possibility of death every day—lacking zeal, courage, in the daily face-off with darkness? How could I possibly know? Back in the US, the last piece of the World Trade Center has just been cleared, and here I am, going on six years after a war and ten years after losing my own legs to a disease, sweating profusely over a small, dirt path—all for a stupid camera.

Suddenly my leg shifts, and Tina's weight descends upon

my waist enough to make me buckle a few feet before the end of the path. My knees dig into the earth. My kneecaps throb from slamming into the hard sockets of the prostheses. My hands grasp the edge of the rough concrete within reach. Tina stumbles over me as if we are playing a game of leapfrog. The vomit comes suddenly, and I fear that in all the insane cruelties of the world, that vomit will be the instigator of my death, the force that sets off a landmine. I clamber onto the concrete slab, and lie there, ready to lick my wounds. The concrete is warm—a most welcoming piece of bombed bridge.

Tina starts hopping sure-footed from slab to slab. And I think that if Tina can do it, then so can I. Prosthetics and hopping aren't good bedfellows, but my god, I'm optimistic. Three hops in, I fall. I'm pretty good at falling. After a decade of falls, I've learned how to shift my weight to land best. I manage a successful backside flop, but I didn't plan on the rusted rebar that was protruding from the concrete block.

The haunch of my left, back love handle is pierced. The heat rises immediately, the blood pools from my body and rushes to the wound. It hurts, but I remember where I am and hold the hurt inaudible. There are cars piled up twenty feet away on the other side of this tunnel wall. I think of the hospital room in Ohio more than a decade earlier, and feel a sudden, unexpected gratitude that I lost my own legs there, and not in war.

My mom is sitting next to the window in my ICU room, blocking out the sun. I'm trying to get some advice from the pastor in the corner, but mom keeps interrupting, saying he isn't there, that he is only a mylar balloon—that I am hallucinating. My mom hardly ever leaves this room throughout the day. She sits and watches god-awful soap operas to distract herself, turns the volume up to the heavens as if she can drown out the beeping of all these machines that are keeping me alive. But I know she's paying attention because if I'm too weak to push the morphine button when the time comes ready, she pushes it before I can make a sound.

I may well be hallucinating, but the pastor in the corner advises me to pray just as clearly as the doctors told me earlier that tomorrow morning they are going to amputate my toes—wouldn't it be nice if I were hallucinating the whole damn thing, and not just the clergyman. The pastor says to find a reason for gratitude, that gratitude heals a burdened heart. So, in my head, I pray, "Holy Spirit in the sky, or in the tomb, or wherever in hell you might be, because you certainly are not here right now—let me just tell you, I love the morphine. Thank you for that, at least."

Even though I am higher than the stars, I am still in the ring with death, and the morphine doesn't erase all the pain. When I asked the doctor if I could have more, he said that I was getting 400mg over the course of a day, and that if he injected 400mg at one time into a small horse, he would kill it. I don't know what the morphine does once it enters my veins, but there is always some pain present. I think it alters the brain in a way so that I don't think about the pain too much, but that's only good for about the first six minutes. The last four minutes are hellfire and burning limbs, and I'm stuck waiting for the time to pass so I can push the button, or mom can, if I'm too afflicted. That's how we spend our days.

The other day mom brought Grandma with her to my room. Grandma sat in the corner chair looking all nervous, like I was that girl from the *Exorcist* movie. She was scared just like she had a right to be. My legs are distended, swollen three times bigger than they were three weeks ago, my extremities and face are dappled in crimson hues, and if I weren't so high one moment and focused on pain relief the next, I'd probably be scared, too.

"Say hi to the reverend, Grandma," I tell her.

My mom looks at Grandma and says in a half-whisper, "She's been talking to that balloon for the last three days."

Grandma starts wiping her eyes with an embroidered hanky.

"Grandma, are you crying?" I ask. "There's no crying in this room. Mom, tell her the rules."

My mom asks Grandma if she wants to go back to the waiting room, but Grandma ruffles up her feathers and says, "I will stay right here a while longer."

That's my grandma. "You've got to fight," I say, and then I shake my fist.

I got excited by her courage and twitched and now I have to wait the long pain out. They have these spikes sticking in the side of my feet and below my knees, fixators they are called, like some kind of scaffolding, like they're rebuilding the statue of Pallas Athena on the Acropolis. Only this intensive care unit is far from the Parthenon, and every time I move, my skin just rips, and the bones feel, well—nailed. I'm not made of marble, not painted with gold.

I think of Jesus a lot. I think of that poor man up on that cross. I think of the wind blowing up the dirt of Gethsemane, and it getting in his nose and making him sneeze, and him twitching and having to feel that long pain out, and that poor man doesn't even have a little button to push. At least he has his holy father looking out for him. Sometimes, I think I have the better deal—even when I have to wait on those last four minutes.

The sun has fallen, and mom is gone, and now I can see out the window even if it's just the city lights of Akron, orange on gray. The television is on, and I'm grateful it's not a soap opera, but David Letterman is just as annoying—I'd like to see him find humor in this ICU room. I can't reach the remote control that has fallen onto the floor, and I almost wish my mom was here just so she could fetch it, but she'd probably just turn the volume up, and all I want do is be quiet, because tomorrow morning the doctor is going to amputate my toes, and that may be just the start of it.

They've got my legs all wrapped up like a mummy, and my little toes are sticking out the top, all black and shriveled, like misplaced pieces of tar on snow. They are already dead, I'm told, and now they've got to be cut off before they kill the rest of me. I am trying to absorb that logic in a state of delirium.

I want to touch my toes one more time or bury them in sand. I'm not exactly sure how I'm going to do that since all I am at the moment is a weighted down bag of will. But I love those toes. I want to say a proper goodbye.

I try to sit up, and that's a fight to begin with because

I've got more wires running around and through me than an early desktop computer. A month ago, my coach was talking to me about scholarships for cross-country. Lord in heaven, how I wish I could jump off this bed right now and run, just run through the Metroparks, down the city sidewalks, run until my heart pounds in my chest, until the sweat breaks out all over my body and evaporates into thin air.

It's time to push the morphine button.

I make it a few inches off the pillow on the first try and fall back in stunning pain. But I like believing that line, the one about God not giving you more than you can handle. I like to run the last mile hard. I decide to rest and wait until the next button push and then I'll try again.

How can I explain what it is like to be sixteen and jacked up on morphine, the night before you are going to have your toes amputated? I'm all alone save for Letterman's voice, and the praying reverend in the corner that my mom says is a mylar balloon, and all the will I have left in this world is telling me to touch my toes.

I think of Jesus on the cross and focus on my toes at the end of the scaffolding. Suddenly the television audience bursts into laughter. I try not to take it personally. I ask the reverend to pray to God for victory over the flesh. I think of the scream that Christ let out over the hills of Gethsemane, and I gather every last particle of will and strength I have, and heave one last time until at last, I grasp several hardened toes in one hand.

I clutch onto them, but a stabbing pain rips throughout my body, and I slam back onto the pillow violently, though it feels like slow motion. I try to hit the morphine button but it's still the last four minutes. I push and push the button, trying to will it to release the poison that will set me temporarily free, to no avail. I look at my other hand, still clenched from trying to hold on to my toes, and when I open my fingers, there it is—the outer shell—the hard-black death of my pinky toe. I look up at the scaffolding and see the bone poking out from where I've ripped the blackened flesh. The room begins to spin, and I hear the reverend say the words of Jesus on the cross, "Why have you forsaken me?" The television audience breaks out into laughter again.

What do I do with the outer shell of my pinky toe in my hand? The morphine does little. Sometimes grief is vicious and unrelenting; sometimes, we make it so. There will be no putting that toe in a tomb and having it rise in three days' time. It is forsaken, but not by me. I take that piece of toe and hold it to my lips, cheeks, and chest as if death were balm, as if the toe might meld back onto me and I can pretend none of this is happening.

It's morning again, and the orderlies are wheeling me down the long hall. I slid my piece of toe under the pillow for safe keeping. Better than morphine, those moments just before you go under the knife. Mom is walking beside me, holding on to the rails of my bed. I fixate on her clenched knuckles; where skin is stretched thinnest from the skeleton, it is as white as the bone underneath.

"I got it, Mom," I tell her.

"You got what?"

"My toe," I say.

"It's going to be okay," she says. "I'll be here when you wake up."

When I wake, it feels like there are cotton balls in my mouth. Mom pushes the morphine button for me. Everything goes woozy. I glance at the reverend and reach under the pillow. There is no toe under the pillow. Where my toes were, there is now white gauze soaked with blood. It feels like an amplification of toes, like somebody has taken a hammer to each digit, and they are larger than life and throbbing, nerve endings exploding with messages of pain to toes that are now a memory. I want to curl up and hold the space where the toes are missing and cry, but I'm still locked in scaffolding and wires, and I'm the one that made the rule that there's no crying in my room. "At least I can remember them, Reverend," I say. "I guess I can be grateful for the memory of how good it feels to dip your toes in the sand."

"Are you okay?" Tina is running back toward me.

"It's just a flesh wound," I reply.

"It's already soaked through your back pocket." Tina pulls a handkerchief from her jacket pocket. "Loosen your belt," she says.

I undo the button on my jeans and pull my pants down a few inches. Tina wipes the clumps of blood and dirt from around the edge of the gash. She uses her pinky fingernail to scrape away some rust flakes from the exposed flesh in the center.

"Well if it didn't hurt before, it hurts now," I whine.

Then Tina asks me if I've had a tetanus shot—I had one

in London. She folds the handkerchief and puts it over the wound and holds it there while I secure it with the belt under the waistline of my jeans.

"I found a treasure," Tina declares while helping me to stand up. When I'm upright, she pulls a small piece of brick out of her pocket. MOSTAR is stamped on it. She gets a brick, and I'll get a scar.

I hobble past her, and head for the camera. I find it on the other side of the wreckage at the edge of the river. The camera held up better than the bridge. It had only a rough, deep dent in one corner. It does not work, but somehow it seems like it could work. The memory card seems unscathed, though I won't know until I have the laptop running.

My lower back is throbbing. I sit on a slab and watch the river go by. The water is translucent, emerald in the distance. I try to envision the scene: families fleeing the hot press of war, crossing the bridge in a car, maybe theirs, maybe one that they have stolen in desperation—a man waiting for the right moment, for the bridge to be full, wondering how many cars he can take down with the push of a button. I count parts of seventeen different cars, but there is no telling how many went unseen, hidden by the rubble, washed away. There would have been smoke and spirits rising from the water. A sad, thick morning mist.

The river ran red for a year.

"*Dobar Dan*," I hear Tina say. I look up, and the fisherman is standing next to us.

"I speak English," he says. "We all speak some English."

He is slowly reeling and tugging his line.

"Want a camera?" I ask, holding out the camera toward him, dent side up. The fisherman glances at it, then turns away, running a hand through his wiry black hair.

"What I do with broken camera? This, and luck," he says, nodding toward his fishing pole, "will feed me."

I slide the camera inside my vest pocket.

"How about a candy bar?" Tina offers, pulling one out of her own pocket. She must have bought it when she went to piss.

The man slowly sets his pole down and walks toward us. He stands next to Tina, near where I sit on the slab, and takes the candy bar from her hand. "Now this," he says with a chuckle, "will keep us alive." He tears off the wrapper and throws it on the ground, then breaks it into three pieces and shares it with me and Tina. His eyes remind me of Elizabeth Taylor, almost purple in that light. We eat the chocolate in silence, and when we are finished, he looks right at me, then pulls a flask out of a bag that lies nearby, and hands it to me.

"Oh, no thank you," I respond. "It's too early."

"Not to drink," he says.

I sit sort of dumbfounded with the flask in my hand, until he grabs it back and hands it to Tina, prodding her with a nod of his head. She walks over to me but won't catch my eye. My heart is throbbing, or maybe it's the wound. She turns me around by the shoulders, pulls my pants out from my waist enough to remove the handkerchief off of the wound where it's already started sticking, and pours the alcohol onto it. I wince from the burn.

The fisherman takes the flask and the handkerchief back

from Tina, saturates the handkerchief with the alcohol, yanks my jeans down a few inches and rubs the wet handkerchief hard into the open surface of my wound. Then he pours the flask over the wound again. There is a part of me that wishes I could will myself to pass out. The bridge, the brutal, wounded act of love, the alcohol—it all sears.

Tina just stares at me, as if there is nothing she can do. And I think of my mom, who had that same look on her face when the nurses would change my bandages in the hospital all those years ago—that sad, helpless expression of the onlooker, the same one I must be wearing throughout Bosnia.

The man adjusts my pant line and pats me on my lower back. "That's better. There is enough death in my country," he says. Then he takes a long swig from the flask.

"Thank you," I manage to say. Then I look toward Tina, pleading with my eyes for her to get us away from here. And since she can read my eyes, she suggests out loud that we need to go, and we bid the fisherman farewell.

We don't slow down for the dirt path on the way back. We tear right through it. We pack Athena up quickly, and in trying to find the way back to the E73, I accidentally drive onto a pedestrian only street. I decide to just drive through as quickly as possible, rather than back up in the crowd, but the road narrows and a dead-end sign appears. People start cursing at us, and shaking their fists, and I'm pleading internally for mercy when Tina tells me to just pull off to the side as much as I can, for just a moment. She jumps out of the truck and leaves me sitting there, with a vendor looking at me in disgust. If there are police in town, I know they'll be coming soon.

The vendor's anger has risen to the surface and he walks over to Athena and starts giving me what for, and I try to say I'm sorry while I look around to navigate just how in the hell I'm going to reverse out of this narrow corridor. Tina returns not a moment too soon, and hands the vendor a couple of marks, helps me reverse without harming any pedestrians, and gets into the cab with a smile on her face.

"What's that all about?" I ask.

She shakes some papers at me. "That was it! That was the location of the Mostar bridge. I could look right down onto the reconstruction process, and a woman gave me this information on the project! You've met both of my stipulations, now you can take me back home!"

I try to act angry, but I'm not—I'm delighted. I find a sign for the main highway, pull over and ask Tina if she can drive the main road for a little while. She looks surprised, but my body needs rest immediately, and neither of us want to spend the night in Mostar.

I wake to the sound of the engine rattling down and laughing gulls. When I open my eyes and turn my head, there is Tina, in the driver's seat. I ask her where we are.

"Dubrovnik below," she says.

Tina has parked Athena to the side, high up on a coastal road. Outside my window, the Adriatic fades into the darkening horizon. Archipelagoes glisten off the coast. The sea air is warm and wet. Seagulls screech like toddlers.

Clustered below are terracotta rooftops, movement in the streets, a kaleidoscopic stream of energy. I open the door to get a better view, but when I attempt to get out and stand up, pain rips from by backside all the way up my spine. Then I feel the wet heat of fresh blood.

Tina hands me a clean towel, and helps me onto the hood of Athena II, and then she hands me the second flask of the day—this one filled with ouzo.

We each have a swig, then she passes it back to me and leaves me on the hood. Soon, a sweet note hits the air. She's turned on music—Barber's Adagio for Strings.

Violas fill the air. A melodic arch begins to form in the music. A bridge is being built. A long flowing line like the Neretva rises. My back throbs to the tempo.

Cellos enter.

Oh, the cellos.

The gulls ride the thermals above me, floating higher and higher, in synchronicity with the strings.

Crescendo.

Fortissimo-forte.

The flask falls off of the hood at a pause, a coda that leaves me bereaved.

When Tina comes back out, I am wiping my eyes. We each take another swig. Tina tells me how Samuel Barber was inspired to write the famous piece after reading Virgil's *Georgics*, that he wanted the passages to feel like rivulets winding their way into the river.

Then Tina opens her laptop, in which she's loaded the memory card, and thumbnail images of Bosnia herd the screen.

The seaside is beautiful. I weep some more. Tina weeps, too. Then we say nothing, and then we laugh. We sit on the hood until the sun zigzags on the horizon in streaks of ruddy plum. Then we drive down the winding road, toward the sea, hoping for a warm bed and a meal, hoping for the little things that matter the most, hoping that all wounds heal, that all red rivers continue to run into each other until the hurt is washed clean out of them.

X

....

ONCE upon a time, before I knew her, Tina rode her bike from Athens to the Mani peninsula in Southern Greece— roughly a five-hundred-mile round trip. After returning from Bosnia and Herzegovina, Tina suggested that I take a month off on the rugged, isolated Mani coast before heading to visit landmine survivors on the eastern coast of Africa. It's where *Zorba the Greek* was written, she tells me. It's where the mythological entrance to Hades is found. It's where Helen and Paris stole away on their ill-fated voyage to Troy.

The Mani peninsula is rich with aged olive groves, switchback mountain roads, and rocky, hidden beaches. The Taïygetos mountain range sprawls a hundred miles down the center of the peninsula like the spiked spine of a dragon's back; it's highest peak, Profitis Ilias, is nearly eight thousand feet high. An all-terrain road goes over the top of the mountain; it is steep and requires four-wheel drive.

Celie and I have been here for a month now, surrounded

by geographical resplendence. Every day, we swim in the sea, make dinner together from scratch, and watch the sunsets. Despite the serenity surrounding us, I find that I am languishing.

I knew something was wrong as soon as Tina and I returned to Athens. When J and Celie met us at the port, and Celie came running to me, I was grateful to see her again, wrapped my arms around her as tightly as I could, but my heart felt a disconnect. It's as if the aftermath of war that I've witnessed has split me in two, and I can't bring the part I left in Bosnia to the dinner table with my daughter. I can't yet talk about it at all.

Our month is nearly up, but I'm still not ready to leave, so we decide to stay a couple of weeks in a cave with marble floors. It's owned by a French woman who we meet at a nude beach here in the Mani, and since she's heading back to France, she offers it to me until I decide in which direction I am going. A cave seems a perfect place to keep hiding.

There are bats in the main room of the cave at night, and at the edge of the cave is a ravine that cuts into the side of the mountain—a two-hundred-foot-deep slice. On waking one morning, I hear a gunshot. I jump out of bed as quietly as possible, glad that the shot hasn't waken Celie.

I see a man in the distance on the other side of the ravine. He fires off his shotgun again, pointing it straight up in the air. Twenty feet in front of him, an emaciated cow charges ahead after the shot goes off. The man shoots into the sky a third time, and the cow takes off into as much of a sprint as it can muster, until it comes to the edge of the ravine and plummets to its death.

Once, I went to Alaska while I was pregnant with Celie and I waited hours in a small boat to watch a portion of a glacier break. When it finally did break, the sound was as unforgettable as that cow plummeting down the ravine until it hit bottom. When Celie wakes, I decide that it's time to come out of the cave. Life is as scary in hiding as it is in plain view.

We head to a seaside village to see where we might camp. I'm filling my bag with fresh produce when a well-groomed collie approaches Celie. Celie is startled and grabs onto my leg. Then the man who owns the collie addresses his dog, saying, "Tartan, that is no way to meet ladies. Introduce yourself properly, please."

Tartan sits on her hind legs and raises one paw toward Celie.

"That's better. Young lady, would you like to shake my dog's hand?" Celie is charmed. So is her mother.

"And, who are you?" I ask, extending my own hand.

The man gently cups my palm and kisses the back of my hand, right on top of the heart-shaped scar. "I am Yiannis Sandwich," he says. "And, I promise that this is not Tartan's only trick, it's just the most effective one for meeting beautiful women."

"Yiannis Sandwich?" I ask, trying not to laugh in case he isn't bullshitting me.

"John Chadwick, actually. Yiannis is John in Greek, but phonetically they have no way to pronounce Chadwick. It becomes bastardized into Sand-wits—which is how they pronounce sandwich, of which they have some very fine ones on the menu over there at the café. May I buy you one for lunch?"

I say yes because I have nothing better to do. I say yes because we haven't made any real friends yet. I say yes because he makes me laugh, and laughter is the closest thing to real joy I've felt since I left Bosnia.

In front of the café is a beach, and after we order, Yiannis shows Celie how to throw a stick for Tartan. She is clapping her hands in excitement in anticipation of her first throw. When Yiannis finally hands her the stick, she squeals in a way I haven't seen since we left England. Over and over, she throws the stick down the beach. Over and over, Tartan retrieves it and drops it at her feet.

Yiannis sits down across from me and orders himself a beer. "What's your story?"

"Just passing through," I say, guardedly. "What's yours?"

"My father was British. My mother is a Hellene, lives in Athens. I was raised in England, where once I shepherded Britain's finest flocks, perhaps only smaller than the Queen's own count. Tartan there, is the best shepherding dog I've ever owned."

"Are you retired?" I ask.

"No, no. I just quit. I came here, to my deceased Aunt Voula's house, in order to drink myself to death." His face is ruddy, his hair thin, but sandy-colored, his body is almost as hairy as his dog's, and he reeks of kindness.

"Why do you want to do that?" I say, with a tinge of sadness in my voice.

"Because my wife of twenty years left me for the herdsman."

I can't help but smile, as if he's telling me one big hilarious whopper after another.

"It's no joke," he says, as if reading my thoughts. "But if we get along well, I may drink myself to death a bit more slowly."

Yiannis, Tartan, Celie, and I become a makeshift sort of family that day. We spend the next week together, exploring the Mani coast. One day, the four of us are hiking through a ravine. It's full of boulders strewn about a dried-up riverbed, not a walk in the park, but fun. Yiannis and Tartan are far enough ahead that I lose sight of them.

Tartan appears on a boulder in the distance, barking for us to catch up. Yiannis sticks his head over the boulder, too. "You're missing the good stuff, slow pokes. Come on!" I push Celie to the top of the boulder, then climb over myself. Yiannis is lying down, pointing and laughing at a random television propped on a boulder in the ravine. "This is my favorite show!" he exclaims. Celie runs to take a look at the screen, which is busted out. She starts giggling in that contagious way—so Yiannis and I start laughing, too. Yiannis is laughing so hard that he farts, and Celie's giggling escalates into delirium. I tell Tartan to keep an eye on her because I'm about to pee my pants.

I climb my way out of sight to pee, but I can't go too far

because the need to relieve myself is urgent. As soon as I disappear around a pile of rocks, I slide my pants down and pee a river in the dry bed. I lean my back against the boulder with my eyes shut, enjoying the release, and when I open them, I gasp. There are three large cow corpses, rotted down to the bones, splayed out like a massacre.

I return to the gang with the giddiness smacked out of me. It looks like the joy has worn out of them, too. We take lunches from our sacks and share a meal. Celie looks as if she is going to fall asleep standing up, and Tartan instinctively nudges the back of her leg, so that she crumples slowly into the dog's body. Tartan curls around her, and Celie lays her head into the dog's belly and falls fast asleep.

I take Yiannis to show him the bones while Celie rests. "Mercy killings," he says. "When the cows go blind and weak, the farmers scare them off the ledges because they can't bear to shoot them dead. I am almost ready for that fate, myself," he says.

When I tell Yiannis that I am planning to head to Africa soon, his face crumples, as if the fate he speaks of in the ravine is closer than he actually wants it to be. We are two souls steeped in sorrows that we can only speak of superficially. Though he teases romance, there is none—we are simply two people willing to distract each other with an almost forced joy, hoping that we can fake it until we feel the real thing, but I feel as if I must remove myself from this equation and toss myself back into the unknown. The more comfortable Celie and I become in the Mani, the harder it is going to be for me to go.

The fates have different plans. The same day I book ferry tickets to Crete, and then Egypt, I receive an email from an off-roading buddy who is also a Marine Corps attaché. His email tells me to avoid northeast Africa until further notice. He tells me that there are reports of terrorists fleeing the Middle East and regrouping in northeastern Africa. The invasion of Afghanistan has been going on for about a year, following the 9/11 attacks in the United States. It's a week before the news he delivers makes American headlines.

Yiannis and I celebrate my extended stay at a taverna on the beach that evening. Celie is playing fetch with Tartan when a blond boy, not much taller than she is, asks if he can have a try. They take turns throwing the stick to Tartan.

The boy's name is Thimo, short for Efthimos, Greek for *good soul*, his parents tell us. They join Yiannis and me for a glass of wine, to watch the sun go down another day. Yogi and Dagmar are German expats. They live in the next village up the mountain on ten acres, where they harvest organic olives and love on rescued animals. Yogi is a retired psychiatrist and Dagmar is an artist. They are calm and kind, and we take to each other as quickly as our children do. When I tell them about my predicament, they tell me of a home I can stay in just up the hill from where they live.

Up the hill from Yogi and Dagmar, where Celie and I settle into a home, there is a spring that trickles down a rocky incline in the center of the village. Our first week in the house, an elder woman in the village dies, and the local women clean and dress her body, the priest prays over her, and they keep her in the center of the village, next to the spring, while the women take turns wailing lamentations for a whole day and night. I hear them through my window, the chants of mourning, and I quietly sing my own.

When autumn arrives, I enroll Celie in kindergarten in a one-room schoolhouse with a woodstove, and I decide to spend the days processing the sorrow, filling journals with the things I witnessed in Bosnia. The war in the world won't go on forever, I think, and I must be prepared to one day finish what I've started.

The day Celie starts kindergarten, she is full of pride and wants to walk alone down the small corridor from our house through the village to the main road, where a van that serves as a school bus will pick her up. I wake long enough to make her breakfast, put more wood in the woodstove, and then happily tuck myself back into bed grateful for a reprieve from motherhood. Just as the blankets are getting toasty, I hear the opening of the door, and her small voice.

"Mama, there are dead cats everywhere."

"What do you mean, Celie?" I ask.

"Mama, I mean there are dead cats everywhere," she says more loudly, this time with hand gestures.

Sure enough, there are seven dead cats in the small distance she has to walk from our house to the main road. In the other direction, down the corridor toward the center of the village where the largest number of cats could routinely be found begging and waiting for scraps, I see at least that many more.

The same old women who wailed the lamentations for the deceased have cooked up a batch of ground meat and laced it with arsenic. All of the cats hemorrhaged slowly from the inside throughout the night. Feral cats are a multitudinous nuisance in the region. I have one that clawed through the screen door in our kitchen. The naivete washes out from me—this village is no different from any other human village. It picks and chooses who gets sent off with honor, who lives, and who dies.

The days become habitual. Some days, I help Yogi and Dagmar build stone walls, harvest olives. On others, I sweep the floors of our house, gather firewood, wash laundry in the sink and hang it out to dry. I gather greens from the mountain in the mornings for dinner. We eat figs and lemons and harvest olives from the trees in our yards. We find joy in our simple toils.

We spend days by the sea, and in the mountains. We eat slow breakfasts and long dinners with Greeks, Germans, and Brits, a parade of characters that we are now calling friends. We sit on hillsides, clinking glasses as the sun begins to set. We burn bonfires on the beach after school, and the children make shelters out of palm fronds. We eat baked potatoes cooked over open fires. We spend nights at the taverna where there is almost always a bouzouki player, and on occasion, a dance. On weekends, we visit nearby shipwrecks, sleep in the ruins of castles, observe where the ancestors have left their marks.

Celie learns her ABCs in Greek, and her numbers, and how to ask sweetly for ice cream. Before we know it, we've been through three seasons, and we are both as healthy and happy as we've ever been.

One day, returning from a sundry gathering trip to Kalamata, the nearest big city two hours to the north, I round the high road overlooking the Mani coastline, see our village in the distance, and pull to the side. My heart quickens. For the first time in my life, I realize that I have found a place that I do not want to leave, a place I would like to call home, a place where the balance of goodness seems to tip the scale, if only slightly. And suddenly, I fear I'm like Odysseus' men—I've eaten the lotus, and I may never return.

The expedition grows farther from my mind with each passing day, until one morning, I receive an email from Poppy. I'd emailed her several months earlier to tell her that the expedition would be delayed due to the war in Afghanistan—that I'd be in touch when I was ready to cross the Sahara. I'm not ready for her words when they appear on the screen.

Are we ready to cross the Sahara yet? I'm itching for an adventure!

And without sitting on it, I respond, as if I'm trying to resist the lotus subconsciously, and I invite her to come to Greece, suggesting that instead of a follow-up story in the desert, we can do a story about off-roading in the Taïygetos mountain range—we can go on adventure in my new backyard. This gives me more time in Greece, I tell myself, but reminds me also that I will one day have to leave.

Yiannis and I have been spending more and more time apart the longer I remain in Greece as it becomes clear his mission of drinking himself to death is not in jest, and I miss him. So, I invite him to come with me to the Kalamata airport to pick up Poppy and spend an afternoon off-roading. It will give him something to look forward to, I think. It will give me a buffer with Poppy, too.

We drop Celie off at school in the morning before we take to the road. Yiannis reeks of alcohol and Tartan smells of smoke when they climb in Athena. I crack the window while Tartan licks Celie's face, delighted to see her.

"Can I take Tartan to school with me?" Celie asks.

"No, sweetheart," I tell her. "You're going home with Thimo after school, and I'll pick you up later this evening when I get home."

"Tartan can stay with her," Yiannis says, and then I know he's probably still drunk from the night before. Yiannis is never without Tartan. I shoot him a concerned look. "Tartan will wait for her in the school yard. She'll keep Celie safe. It's for the best," he says.

"Yiannis—" I start to intervene, but he's already stashing the leash and a bag of food into Celie's backpack, and as happy as she is about it, my heart begins to break. Yiannis is beginning to distance himself from his closest companion.

I stop and get him breakfast before we go, to sop up some of the alcohol. And I'm relieved when he falls asleep halfway into the two-hour drive. I start to wonder if Poppy won't be a buffer for Yiannis, instead of the other way around.

Yiannis has better color in his face when he wakes up, but he regrets having left Tartan. "Why did you let me do that?" he asks.

"You were pretty insistent," I say.

"I'm a fucking moron, girl. A fucking moron."

"Yiannis, we are all fucking morons," I tell him.

That lightens his mood a bit, and in order to keep his mood steady, I tell him all about Poppy without skipping a detail while I'm parked outside the airport waiting for her flight to land.

"Oh no," he says. "You brought me along as the third wheel, didn't you? You brought me along, so the lesbian doesn't hit on you, didn't you? It would be much more fun if you two hooked up, and I could watch. Shit, this isn't going to be any fun at all."

Just then, I see Poppy coming out of the airport. She knows to look for Athena, and I know what she looks like, but I had no idea that she'd be decked out in one of her Lara Croft get-ups—brown, tight pleather short-shorts, a mint pleather tank, a belt with gear, badass combat boots. Her hair has extensions and is pulled back tightly into the long signature braided ponytail. Her face is caked with contoured makeup.

"Well, shit," I say, as she walks toward the truck.

"Well, shit," Yiannis says. "I take it all back—this is going to be so much fucking fun!"

As she gets close to the vehicle, I open the door to greet her.

"Wait, wait, wait!" she tells me. I watch in the rearview mirror as she opens her suitcase and retrieves two handguns. One she places in a belt holster, and the other in a holster on her calf. "Okay, now, come out!"

I roll out of the truck and behold the sight.

"Ta-da. What do you think? The guns are fake, but security made me put them in the baggage claim. I wanted to
surprise you with the whole get-up!"

I am stunned, overwhelmed, my mouth is agape.

Yiannis is so absolutely tickled that I think he's going to
pee in my truck.

We aren't fifteen minutes from the airport, when Yiannis
cracks open a flask. Poppy says she doesn't drink much, but
what the heck. I drive the switchbacks sober, while the two
of them go back and forth on all things England.

About thirty minutes from the village, I take a dirt road
that I am pretty sure will get us to the four-wheel-drive
part of the Taïygetos mountain range. Most likely, I'm
taking the deviation as a symbol of my desire to be somewhere else, like back in the village with Celie and Tartan,
rather than with these two, who now have a buzz at noon.

"You're on a dirt road now," Yiannis says. "Take a swig,
will you?"

"I will because I'm weak," I say.

Yiannis takes a swig first before handing it to me, then
pours it upside down. "Oh, shit. It's all gone," he says.

I feel both relieved and pissed off, and then he laughs,
and pulls a fresh bottle of whiskey out from his sack.

By two o'clock in the afternoon, I'm buzzed. Lara Croft
and Yiannis Sandwich are toast. And I can't find the right
road, but I know we are close. I think it's just above a sec-
tion of olive groves, and when I see some tire tracks in the
grass, I decide to cut through and try my luck. It's slow
going, mostly because the tire tracks have stopped, and

I'm weaving between trees, and Poppy and Yiannis need to stop and pee, and have another drink, and laze about, and look out at the sea, and when I notice that evening is coming upon us, I call the excursion off.

"We're going to have to go to the top of the mountain another day, folks," I announce. "I have to get home tonight in three pieces."

Yiannis gets the joke at the same time as he's taking a swig and he inhales the bourbon down the wrong pipe and starts laugh-choking so hard that he can't catch his breath. His face turns plum red and Poppy starts slapping his back real hard, and then he falls to the ground, clutching his heart.

"Not now, not here, Yiannis," I shout, straddling him, trying to remember CPR. I pull his hands away from his chest and put my face close to his. "Open your eyes, you bastard," I beg him angrily.

His eyes don't open, but his lips purse in a grin, and then he says, "How about a little kiss first? And you could say please."

I smack him in the chest and roll off. My buzz has been replaced by adrenaline, and I just want to get home. We're all back in the cab, and the sun is masked by a mountain peak. I've got the high beams on the roof rack lit up, but it's still difficult to see weaving through the trees.

Yiannis is sitting between me and Poppy on the bucket seat, and they're both trying not to laugh. Yiannis lets out a snicker and Poppy punches him in the arm, which knocks him into my arm, the one with the hand on the gear shift.

The clutch goes into neutral and the truck jolts. I throw it back into gear, and step on the gas, while telling them both to behave when I hear the crack. We all feel the crack. I put Athena in reverse, and I can see that I have taken out a humongous branch from an old, gorgeous olive tree, and my stomach flip-flops.

Two days ago, while walking among my neighbor's grove, Yogi tells me that olive trees take up to thirty years to bear proper fruit, that you don't plant an olive tree for yourself, but for your grandchildren. I make a mental note to find out who these olive trees belong to, to pay them restitution.

When we return to the village, I realize that a biblical sort of restitution has already been paid—an eye for an eye—one of the spotlights from my roof rack is missing.

Come morning, I make breakfast for Poppy and Celie, then we head to the beach. Poppy and Celie stack rocks at the water's edge while I swim. The weather has just a hint of winter coming in it, but the sun is still warm enough to shed clothes. We go to a tourist village for lunch, where Poppy rents a motorbike so she can explore a bit on her own. That evening, we meet Yogi and Dagmar and other friends at the taverna. Poppy regales us all with Lara Croft and off-roading stories.

Tartan wanders down the corridor and slides under the table, where Celie drops him some potatoes. And sure enough, Yiannis comes ambling into the scene, too, and he's wasted. He is slurring something no one can make out; then he plops into an empty chair next to Poppy, who is noticeably displeased to be interrupted in the middle of a story.

Poppy tries to finish her story, but Yiannis is echoing her, hand gestures and all, when the restaurant owner walks out onto the patio and begins to play bouzouki and sing. Fresh carafes of wine and baklava are delivered to the table. Everyone partakes. The music subdues Yiannis. He slumps in his chair and flops his head from side to side. The children get up from the table and begin to dance. It should be a lovely scene, but the chaos settles in my gut like sour wine.

I excuse myself and walk Yiannis to his Aunt Voula's house. We stroll down the corridor arm in heavy arm, and I plead with him, which is futile, to not drink himself to death, to stick around, be my friend, believe that he will find love again one day.

"Even if I do," he slurs, "I won't be able to trust it."

I tuck him in on the sofa; he doesn't want to go to bed. And as I'm leaving, he asks me to hand him the bottle of vodka in the kitchen, but instead I shut the door behind me.

It's near midnight before I tuck Celie into our bed. I lay an extra blanket on top of the futon in the living room where Poppy is sleeping since she was chilly the night before. Poppy is out on the terrace, under the lemon tree, looking out at the moon's reflection on the Mediterranean, drinking a shot of ouzo.

When I join her, she offers me a shot, and though we've both had plenty to drink and I'm not a fan of ouzo, I take one to calm my nerves, and then I pour another round for us both.

And Poppy says, "In case something happens between us, there is something I need to tell you."

I take an extended breath, realizing stimulation overload is not ending anytime soon. "Nothing's going to happen between us, Poppy. This is a work trip, a working relationship. But if there's something you need to tell me, then feel free."

She looks at me as if she doesn't believe me, then begins to tell me how the woman she'd loved went on a three-month assignment to Japan, and that when she returned, she found Poppy.

"I don't understand," I say. "Weren't you Poppy when she left?" I ask, wondering if Poppy is drunk, like Yiannis, speaking in complicated metaphors.

"Well yes, I was Poppy before she left, at least in private. I mean, I've always been Poppy, and she loved me—we had so much fun together when I'd get all dressed up—and we had *the* best sex—so I thought I'd surprise her while she was gone and bring Poppy full circle."

"I still don't understand," I say, wishing I hadn't asked in the first place.

"I had a sex change. There, I've said it. The body I was born into didn't reflect who I am, and so, I had the operation, to make me feel whole."

An uncomfortable silence follows. It is a lot for me to swallow, and I don't know how to respond. I feel my muscles tightening and sweat pooling on my forehead.

"Please, say something," Poppy breaks the silence.

"Were you in that long-term relationship with the body of a man, and then you had surgery while she was gone, without her knowing?"

"Oh, she knew, I mean she knew all along that I was Poppy in my heart. She knew I was taking the hormones; she knew that my life in public, as a man, was torture. She just wasn't ready for me to make the full change, but I'd waited on her to be ready for nearly a decade, and I had to do what was right for me. I—" she paused, her voice cracking. "I just didn't think she would leave me once I fully blossomed."

My eyes were on the stars. It was a lot to comprehend.

"Poppy, I'm sorry. I'm sure it was difficult for both of you. It's a difficult situation."

We both sit there on the terrace in silence. The wind is the only thing making sound and even though it's gentle, it feels like too much. I tell Poppy that I need a moment to comprehend everything, that I need to walk off the alcohol, too. I tell her I won't be long.

Then Poppy starts crying. She takes my hand and pleads with me not to go. This always happens, she says, that as soon as she feels a connection with someone and shares her situation, they run away. As sad as that makes me feel, it also makes me want to walk faster. "I'm coming back," I say. "I just need a little time."

"Well, can I walk with you?" she asks.

"I need to go on my own," I say, though it pains me to say it, because it reminds me of people I've had affection for who couldn't handle my incomplete body, who had to walk away from the fear of my wounds. And yet, I get up and walk into the moonlight, leaving her alone on the terrace under the lemon tree.

I walk to Yiannis' house because I don't know where else to go, and I feel the need to talk to someone, and he's the only person I know who doesn't mind waking up at any hour. He never locks the door, so I walk right in. He's watching television with the vodka bottle in his hand. "What's up, Buttercup? Come for the midnight special?" he greets me.

I tell him everything, and he just laughs like the Cheshire cat. He laughs so hard that he rolls off the sofa and his face turns that plum shade again. "Yiannis, this isn't funny. I don't know what to do," I beg him foolishly. He's flailing his arms in a feigned act of hilarity when he knocks over the vodka bottle. And when he starts licking up the liquid off the stone floor, I know I'm as good as alone.

I am walking in the dark down a tiny path toward home and I'm afraid. Sure, we've enjoyed some lighthearted flirtation since we met, but I never thought Poppy was seriously interested in me in the biblical sense until she got off that plane all dolled up. I certainly didn't mean to give her the wrong idea—I was simply thrilled to have a female friend who loved off-roading as much as I do.

I don't care that she's had a sex change as long as she's happy, but it's a new concept to me. Plus, I've spent enough time in surgeon's offices to have seen all the ways in which women enhance their bodies into some kind of image they believe is deemed acceptable, and given everything I've been through, I simply struggle to understand how anyone can risk their life with anesthesia and a knife if it isn't a life-saving situation. But maybe, for Poppy, that's exactly what it was.

Maybe I'm also afraid of remembering the desperation that came with a time when I still struggled to accept myself, the body with which I was left, and how I allowed myself to be degraded by going to the dark places of stranger's flesh, pretending it was love, the places of primal need, the places that sometimes come before we truly accept ourselves.

I enter the house as quietly as I can—Celie is snoring in one room, and Poppy in the other. I look in on Poppy, curled up on the futon, and I gently lay the blanket over top of her.

"Why did you bring me here?" Poppy asks.

"I felt bad that we aren't crossing the Sahara. You'd said you'd already cleared some time from work. I thought off-roading in the Taïygetos mountains would be a decent substitution."

"Strictly work, eh?" she nudges me.

"Yes, and friendship, of course," I say.

"I don't believe you," she says.

"Let's get some sleep," I say.

I leave her, and crawl into my bed, curl up with Celie, sync our hearts, and stare out at the moon and wonder how best to love the whole universe to the moon and back.

The next morning, Celie and I slip out early before Poppy is awake. We walk down the hill to Yogi and Dagmar's because I think Yogi, being a former psychiatrist, will know how to help me handle this. Yogi is working on a stone wall, so I offer to help, while Celie runs off to the house to find Thimo. I tell him everything. He sits on the wall, and takes it all in, and says, "There are a lot of variables here, best to move slowly. Let's go back to the house and have breakfast."

As we are heading toward the house, Poppy pulls up on the motorbike.

"Good morning," she says.

"Good morning," Yogi and I both return the greeting, even though she only seems to be addressing me.

"You couldn't even be bothered to leave a note and tell me where to find you?" she snaps, and then I know she is only addressing me.

"I didn't realize I was obligated to let you know every minute of my day," I snap back.

"Well, I'm going to head down to the café for breakfast," she lowers her tone. "Would you like to join me?"

"Enjoy your breakfast. I'll catch up with you later," I say, as my gut fills with the weight of something like guilt.

Dagmar and I set the breakfast table while Yogi sits on the terrace with the children and a gaggle of rescue animals. I slice a fresh loaf of bread, a tomato, salami, and some cheese. Dagmar boils eggs and fills a huge ceramic pitcher with water. There are a lot of potters in the region, but I've not seen a pitcher quite like this—the curves are sensual, almost like the figure of a woman. It's glazed in a blue like the turquoise in the sea, and it has golden veins all over it.

At breakfast, Yogi tells me about a sexology institute in Germany in the early 1900s. He tells me about Magnus Hirschfeld, who founded the institute and coined the term *transsexualism*. The institute was visited by tens of thousands each year while it was open and was a treasure trove for scientific research—a safe haven for those who lived their lives in secret anguish, and a place for reformers to be educated on how to make the ambiguous nature of these lives acceptable in a world where only princes and princesses were given story lines. Yogi tells me how the Nazis burnt the whole place down in the precursor to WWII, the early holocaust he called it, the purging of the gays.

He offers to go to the house and talk with Poppy. He says some space is good, and though I'm moved by the history I've just learned, and though it makes me think of my cousin in San Francisco, and the night in Eden I shared with the woman who identified as French-Asian, I don't feel ready to take on Poppy's pain. I can barely handle my own.

I spend the rest of the day at Yogi and Dagmar's house, and when evening approaches, we begin to make dinner. I know I should contact Poppy, but I'd like to avoid conflict a bit longer, so I decide I'll go home after supper; I'll ask Yogi how to handle the situation best, put Celie to bed, and sit with Poppy on the terrace again.

I carry bowls of food outside to a stone patio. Thimo and Celie are there lighting the candles on the dinner table. I sit at the table, and I can see Yogi kissing Dagmar's neck in the kitchen. When we are all sitting at the table, speaking our gratitude for the food and each other, I hear the motorbike approaching. Poppy comes to a sudden halt and the back fender flares, kicking up a dust cloud that floats just beyond the dinner table. I stand up and go to greet her.

"No dinner invite for me?" Poppy asks.

"It's not my home," I say.

"Yes, you have a guest at your home, and you're being a terrible hostess."

I stand there, just looking at her. I don't think she'd expect me to entertain her if we were crossing the Sahara, and I'm unsure of what we've crossed over now.

"So, come on then. Celie, come on—I got you some sweets, and I've bought us dinner."

Celie doesn't move but I can see Yogi gently rising from the table. "Poppy," I say, "that's very kind, but we'll be back home in a bit. Celie can have her sweets then. Thank you."

Yogi walks into the space that Poppy and I are holding, although we've been well within earshot of the dinner table the entire time. Poppy looks at him as if she's sizing him up, then her face crumples slightly, then she raises her voice and says firmly, "Tell her, Yogi. Tell her to come home with me now."

Yogi looks at me and nods his head, motioning me to return to the table. He takes the motorbike by the handles and begins to push it around to the front of the house. Poppy follows him. Dagmar passes the salad, tells the children to eat. Celie and Thimo both look unsure about the situation but become easily distracted when Thimo throws an olive toward one of the rescue dogs. I take a couple of bites, but I feel suspended by the tension, and I can't help but think that Poppy was subconsciously begging Yogi to tell someone other than me to come home to her, the woman she loved, the woman who left her during what had to be one of the most frightening periods of her life. Then, the motorbike starts up and sputters into the distance, and

Yogi returns to the table. Before I can ask him what I ought to do, he says, "You and Celie will stay with us tonight. We'll let things cool off for a bit—but not our supper. Let's eat."

The sleepover lasts the rest of the week and so does the lack of communication between me and Poppy. Yogi has gone to check on her a few times, and soon she is going to need a ride back to Kalamata, to the airport. At dinner one night, Yogi asks me how I feel about the space, if it's been enough for me to feel comfortable taking Poppy to the airport.

"I don't know," I say.

"Raw wounds rarely heal each other," Yogi says. "Why don't you buy her a bus ticket back, and I'll deliver it."

"Yogi, will you tell her that I'm sorry for whatever part I had in this, for whatever confusion I may have caused."

"I'll do my best," he says.

Then I fill his glass with juice from the turquoise pitcher, changing the subject because it hurts too much and I don't know what else to say. "I love this piece. Is it locally made?"

"No," he says. "I inherited it—most likely from relatives who were Nazi supporters."

"What?" I ask, setting it down as quickly as possible, as if all of the sudden its history has rendered it untouchable.

"Have you ever heard of *kintsugi*?" he asks. I shake my head no.

"It's an ancient Japanese practice. When a family heirloom, like this vessel here, falls or breaks, the Japanese do not just throw it away. Instead, they repair it, and they fill the cracks with a precious metal, like silver or gold—because they believe that even when something is broken it still has purpose—that if you take the time to put it back together piece by piece, it has greater value in that purpose—it has a history.

"Most of us German expats here in the Mani are living on land stolen from the Greeks by our predecessors. Some of our predecessors invaded and occupied this land and tortured some of these families, my neighbors, only a generation ago. What good does it do to resurface those broken pieces when we were ignorant of the history as we grew up here, made friends? Do we punish our children, the next generation, for not yet knowing any of it at all, just for growing and loving the land, and their neighbors who are now their friends? Do we turn our backs on the broken pieces, or do we rebuild one another by taking the time to fill in the cracks with knowledge and understanding, by trying to prevent further breakage, by making what is broken more useful in purpose with time and care?"

I feel like I'm on an acid trip, as if every time I turn my head there's something unexpected behind unending curtains. I sit back in my chair and remember learning that the houses on the Greek isles were painted white and blue during WWII as an act of defiance against the German occupation—because the Germans wouldn't allow the Greek flags to be flown—so the Greeks painted their homes the colors of the flag instead. When tourists buy those idyllic postcards of the homes on a Greek isle, they're buying an image of pain, and using it to send an expression of love to someone far away. One day, I think, I'll send Poppy such a postcard.

When Poppy has left, I return to the house and open all the windows, let a new wind cleanse the pain. There are roses on the kitchen table, and a drawing, in which Celie and Poppy and I are all holding hands. We are on the beach, standing near the water between rocky outcrops. We are all wearing bikinis. I have pins for legs. Poppy has an extra-large bosom. Celie has a sun hat on since she sunburns easily. Above each of our heads is a caption cloud. Poppy has a motorbike in her cloud. I have a Land Rover in mine. Celie is thinking of an ice cream cone. And under all of this, she wrote, "The Way Things Could Have Been." I feel so unsettled that I cry.

Later, I show the drawing to Yogi. He slowly nods his head and looks out to the sea. The wind roars and the water churns and it takes some time before he says, "Your body tells me that a lot of people were invested enough in your worth to take the time to put you back together. In time, you'll fill all these cracks with gold. In time, you'll be able to pour water into the mouth of someone else who is thirsty, but you can't quench someone else's thirst when you're leaking water as you pour. You also can't blame Poppy for being attracted to someone else who is working so hard to heal. Without injury, there is often no compassion.

"After all, it's the wounds that bind us. It's the being heard that puts us back together. When we value ourselves, then we can value others—when we have purpose, we shine."

XI

....

KARNIVALI is the Greek Mardi Gras, a festival that found its roots in Ancient Greece, a full-tilt Dionysian fete the weekend before Lent. Celie and I go with Yogi and Dagmar and some friends to a parade on the other side of the Mani peninsula, by the Gythion harbor. There are ornate floats reminiscent of Venetian extravagance—dragons, drag queens, clowns on stilts. I've dressed in drag myself, with an eyeliner mustache and beard, my hair slicked back under a fedora, a suitcoat and tie. Celie is wearing a pink tutu, everything pink. She has a sparkly crown and a magic wand with a glittery star at the end of it. She's painted her cheeks crudely with my lipstick.

I buy Thimo and Celie balloons from a vendor. They are the largest two balloons he has to sell—they are bunny heads. Celie takes the red one and Thimo picks the blue. I tie the balloon strings onto their wrists, so they don't lose them, but it also helps me not to lose the kids. The red and blue bunny heads bob high above the crowds.

It's a kaleidoscope of chaos and then the fireworks begin. Celie is gnawing on a cone of cotton candy that is bigger than her head. Suddenly, a huge man in drag comes by on a float, wearing a horned helmet, and singing into a microphone. The show's almost over. The fat lady is singing. I glance back, and I see the red bunny head bobbing a few feet ahead. I weave around the crowd, there's a child dressed like Saddam Hussein, and when he passes me, I see Celie, her cotton candy has fallen to the ground, and she's bending over, picking off the good pieces as fast as she can before they melt into the slimy streets.

I swoop her up, and she wails for the cotton candy. She is drunk on sugar, past her bedtime, spent. I head to the harbor, toward Yogi's van. The fireworks finale is beginning. We'll all be leaving soon. I watch the reflection of the fireworks in the harbor while Celie fake-cries on my shoulder, smearing it with sugar and lipstick. At five and some, she's almost too heavy for me to hold. I set her down, not wanting her to fall asleep until we're on our way home. She cries for me to pick her back up. And then, the perfect distraction, "Look, Celie," I say. "Here comes the blue bunny head balloon!" She remembers her own balloon and waves her arm up and down so the red bunny head greets the blue bunny head.

Thimo is staggering, he's had his fill of carnival, too. Dagmar opens the van door, and I scoop Thimo in first, tucking the blue bunny head in behind him. And then I go to scoop up Celie, but my finger catches her wrist and loosens the tie, and before I can set her down, we watch the red bunny head balloon float out amongst the lights reflected on the harbor, far away, until it's so small we can no longer differentiate it from a tiny red star.

And then, the child wails.

The kind of wail that every parent dreads hearing. The sugar-infused, boozy, rocked-out, angst-filled, high-pitched, full-lunged, nothing-is-going-to-make-it-better-until-it-all-comes-out wail. I hold her in the van while she thrashes against me, slams her sticky hands against the window, chokes on her tears so there's a moment of silence, and then her engine roars again. "It will come back," I say, desperate enough to tell her a lie if it will soothe her, but my lie makes her angrier and she wails with more force. She wails halfway through the forty-minute trip home, and everyone's good time is ruined. Even after she settles into my chest in a fitful sleep, no one in the van says a word about fun, fearful that she'll wake again.

I fall asleep ten minutes before we get back to Yogi and Dagmar's, and I wake when Dagmar slides the door of the van open. "Bring her inside, and lie her on Thimo's bed," Dagmar says. "Then go up to the tavern with the others and have a good time. We'll be here in the morning, well-rested."

"Are you sure?" I ask her.

"I insist," she says.

The tavern is different from the taverna—it's more like a bar, less family-oriented, though kids are allowed. I've only been in here once, on a quiet night, when the bartender, who everyone in the village calls the Doctor, got drunk and sent everyone home in an unprovoked, angry fit. But tonight, it's all revelry. Outside the door, Tartan is leashed to a bench, slumped on the ground. She raises one eye toward me, whimpers, and then burrows her head into her paws.

Inside, I see Daniel at the bar, a German expat, a carpenter, who I often see walking the beach, though I've never spoken to him. I roll up next to him to order a drink and ask him if he saw the parade.

"No," he replies, without looking at me. I've never seen him close up before. He is ruggedly handsome, thick from top to bottom, with a large jaw that takes up the whole of his face when he speaks.

"I'm Kelley," I say, extending my hand.

This time, he looks at me, and I notice he's a tad cross-eyed. "I know."

Suddenly, he lifts his hand from the bar and starts for my face. I pull back, startled by the movement. He pauses until I calm, then he smears his thumb across my upper lip.

"What was that for?" I ask.

"To make sure you're really Kelley, and not some male relative." I forgot about my mustache.

The Doctor comes over and I order a glass of wine. "Lightweight," he says. Then I notice Yiannis at the other end of the bar. His head is on the bar, cocked to the side. He waves at me with two fingers. The opposite of lightweight, I think. I wave back. He blows me a kiss, then sips his drink and stares aimlessly at the liquor shelf behind the bar. There's a mannequin leg with a fishnet leaning up against the shelf, glass bottles glimmering behind it as if it's Las Vegas and that leg is going to start kicking hijinks at any moment. Yiannis' eyes close.

I ask Daniel if he'd like to get his ass beat by a woman on the pool table.

"No, but I'll play a boy," he says.

"You'd like that, would you? Is half of a mustache okay? What shall we play for?"

"*Wir spielen für veilleicht*." *We'll play for perhaps*, he says.

Daniel racks the balls on the table. I stroke the pool sticks, trying to find one the right weight. I like the way he holds his tongue on his upper lip while shooting a ball into a pocket. All this revelry has me looking through a narrow lens, as if no one else is in the tavern, as if Daniel and I exist alone in this concrete-floored Eden with cinder block walls. I notice nothing else until a woman I know from the village grabs my hips and begins grinding into me as I lean over the table to take a shot.

Daniel stands back and watches as more women come up behind me—sirens with bells and whistles. I drop the stick on the table and let myself be sucked into the wave. They gyrate all around me. It's a fleshy blur—an elbow, a breast, a teasing bite on my neck. The painting in the Hotel Tuzla flashes through my mind.

Daniel's thick hand grabs my arm and pulls me out from the eddy. He sweeps me up under my armpits and sits me on top of the pool table. I clutch my knees to keep my legs on. He whispers into my ear. "Watch this."

The Doctor is racking up tons of drinks onto a silver tray at the bar. He is standing on a step ladder, pouring liquor like a waterfall into the shot glasses. It's splashing all over a man's head at the bar. The man is passed out, but it isn't Yiannis.

"That's the Father."

"The Doctor's father?" I ask Daniel.

"No, the father-father. The priest. The Doctor hates the Father. This is an old feud."

"Why does he hate him?"

"Because the Father is entitled to free services in the village, and some he takes advantage of more than others, especially the Doctor."

The Father has fallen asleep, passed out cold, in the lion's den.

"Daniel," I whisper into his ear, pausing on a note of saccharine wafting up from his neck. "Is the bartender really a doctor?"

"No. Long ago, he was called Costas. He wanted to become a doctor. He went to Germany to study medicine, but instead he became a heroin addict. His whole family went to Germany to bring him back alive. He's been running the tavern ever since—some twenty years. He's a little off, but nobody minds."

The Doctor is picking up the tray now. He has white, spiky hair that stands up all over his head. His blue eyes are wild and darting all over as he walks through the tavern passing out shot glasses. He brings the tray toward Daniel and me. He holds it up like a silver sea full of treasures. The concoction is syrupy, red. I down it.

"Easy," Daniel says. "There will be many more." And he is right. The Doctor refills the tray over and over, making his way around the tavern, fueling a bonfire of indulgence.

The Doctor turns up *Rembettika* then, a Greek opioid-infused music inspired by resistance to the junta, and he begins to dance and juggle empty liquor bottles, throwing them high into the air. As the tempo of the music elevates, so does the Doctor's performance. A woman's voice begins to wail from the speakers, and as it does, the Doctor steps back, flips one of the bottles gently into the air, where it bounces off of the sleeping Father's back and crashes onto the floor. Shards of glass shoot out toward the ankles of revelers. I am standing on the pool table now, taking in the scene. Bottle after bottle, the Doctor bounces them off of the priest until a sea of broken glass covers the floor. When the last bottle breaks, the Doctor jumps into the air and kicks his feet together with a victorious smile that reveals a mouth half full of stained teeth.

Then the Doctor beckons a group of men, including Daniel. He announces that it's time to close and divides the men into two groups. One group carries the Father out of the tavern and the other carries Yiannis. I'm starting to wonder if Yiannis and the Father have been drugged, because they do not wake. I round out the door behind the men and Tartan is barking, then whimpering, then barking again. I pet her on the head, then I follow the crowd to where they lay the drunks out on the stairs of the church across the street.

The Doctor stands over the Father as if he is Achilles fuming over Hector's corpse. He is ravenous and weary. No man dares to get close to the Doctor and the drunks. The Doctor arranges the Father so that his smock is raised up over his waist. Then he places Yiannis' head gently onto the crotch of the Father and he leaves them there, four hours before the first church bells will ring.

In the dark behind the church, I'm wondering if I should wait for the Doctor to leave, or if I should unleash Tartan but I worry that someone will hurt her. Suddenly Daniel swoops me up over his shoulder, and carries me to the edge of the village, to the path that leads to his house.

Daniel opens a bottle of wine, and motions toward a ladder which leads to a loft, where he sets me down on a bed and asks me to take my clothes off. I am still wearing a tie. We drink the wine straight from the bottle and run our hands all over each other's bodies, kiss and press, and make love, slowly at first, then with more force. I sit on top of him and he holds on to my hips as if they are no heavier than a strainer and he is shaking water out of boiled pasta. He thrusts my body against his, until we both shudder simultaneously—and I fall onto him, a sweaty cheek against a sweaty chest, and we ride the tremors out.

"I could get used to this," he finally says.

I could, too, I think. I curl up next to Daniel until my body succumbs to sleep.

A growing rumble wakes me. The sky is twilight blue, the rumble grows louder, the sky grows darker. A thunderstorm, I think, but then the sky starts to go black. I roll off the bed, startled, forgetting where I am for a moment. Then I crawl out, naked, onto Daniel's balcony, and watch as the largest fleet of Harriers I have ever seen darkens the whole sky. It feels as if the house is going to crumble. They are a murder of monstrous crows, cawing death. I go cold, unable to move until the fleet moves over the sea and disappears into the horizon, an expansive shadow following behind them on the surface of the water.

I crawl back into bed, and Daniel says, "Your countrymen are plundering the earth again. Just like you plundered me."

"We plundered each other," I say, curling up around his head, my breast leaning against his shoulder. He nuzzles his face into it, gnawing with his eyes shut.

"Make love, not war," he says, and slowly and sleepily, we do.

We spend the afternoon near each other, watching Celie and the other children fly kites on the cliffs over the village. Two days later, Daniel comes down with the flu. A week after that, I come down with it, too. A few days, later, it hits Celie.

And in that down time, I learn through the village, where there are no secrets kept forever, that Daniel has a girlfriend who lives in Athens, a Greek girl he's been dating for many years. And when everyone is finally well enough for me to see him again, I discover that I am pregnant.

One morning after I drop Celie off at school, I see Daniel walking on the beach, and I sit on a rock ahead of him. When he joins me on the rock, I smell him, and I want to curl up and rest my head on his shoulder, but I've learned too much, and I'm scared, and rightfully so, because when I tell him I'm pregnant, he accuses me of trying to trap him. He offers to pay for an abortion, and when I tell him that I'd like to have another baby, he cuts me off and tells me he wants nothing to do with any of this. "You damn Americans," he says.

I'm devastated. I don't know him well. I may not like him if I did, but we made magical love on a wild, god-infused night, and couldn't we give it a try for the sake of a life, or if not, couldn't we at least be kind and support-ive? Mostly, I'm devastated because I was foolish enough to hope that he'd be happy, too, that I could have a family in this land I've grown to think of as home.

I take a deep breath, inhaling the sea air. I will not beg. Instead, I curse at him, tell him that this will come back to him, and all he says in return is, "Perhaps."

Wir spielen für veilleicht. Don't we all play for perhaps?

I'm so distraught when I return to the village that I head to the *kafeneio* to distract myself, which is an unofficial man's club, with mostly old clientele. These guys are funny. They like to make jokes about Viagra and the village widow with Parkinson's, and how together, with her shaking, it is no work at all.

Yiannis is sipping coffee at a corner table, so I sit down with him. And just as I am being asked what I want to drink, George Bush comes on the fuzzy television in the corner, announcing that the United States has just declared war on Iraq. When Bush finishes speaking, the men in the kafeneio break out in a cacophony. Someone shouts above the crowd, "What do you think of all this, Amerikanida?"

I freeze. I am pregnant, the father of the baby just left me in the cold, I come in here for distraction, and they want to know what I think of another war. I remember the Harriers. I want to take a shower and curl up with my daughter and a book. I want to vomit. I want to be anywhere but in the kafeneio. "I think we've had enough war," I say.

"Don't worry, Amerikanida. It's only business, and maybe some of the profit will spill over into Greece." Then the men in the kafeneio raise a toast, and the cacophony begins again.

I get up to leave, and Yiannis grabs my arm, asks me to stay a little longer, but his eyes are bloodshot, near vacant, and I pull away and walk out the door. I walk down the corridor toward our house when the nausea hits me solidly. I lean against a stone wall and puke, and then I cry until suddenly a sharp pain takes over my ear. It's the Parkinson's widow, she's pinching my ear and shaking it. She maintains her pinch so that my head cocks to one side. Then she lets go, cups my cheek with her hand, and asks, "Has someone died?"

"No," I say, wincing.

"Then don't let them see you cry," she says, and waddles her way toward the village center. I wish that I could run.

Yiannis says he'll stop drinking and help me take care of the baby when it's time. I don't put much stock in the promise, but I don't have a lot of options. I'm not ready for the scrutiny of the village, to be the foreign single mom who gets pregnant on a one-night stand while dressed as a man with half of a mustache, so we make a pact that when I start to show, we'll go away until the baby is born, and then we'll come back to the Mani and buy a stone house, and while the days away, raising Celie and the baby on lemons and olives and the simple things in life. It's a pipe dream I still have the money to buy. Money can't buy happiness, but it does buy temporary escape routes.

On the day that I struggle to button my jeans for the first time, Yogi and Dagmar invite Celie and me for a picnic on the beach. They know that I am pregnant because Dagmar was with me when I took the test. We pick up the kids from school, head to the beach, and send Thimo and Celie to gather sticks for fire. Yogi is digging a hole for the fire when he asks me how I'm feeling.

"Scared," I say.

"You've been awfully quiet lately," he says. "Are you thinking about running?"

"I can't run if I want to, Yogi. I have no legs."

"You're already running," he says with a frown. The children have gathered enough wood for the fire, and Yogi lights it while Dagmar sets a tray full of potatoes wrapped in aluminum foil in the sand next to him.

"We've grown to care so much about you," Dagmar says. "We hope you'll stay."

"I'm not going anywhere," I insist, "although I do have to go to Athens this week to meet a gynecologist."

"It doesn't have to be here," Yogi says, "but it might do you good to stay in one place long enough to form your own history, to learn to live with the people around you and let them learn to live with you, fill those cracks with gold, no?"

My back arches in defense. Yogi stops pushing, and I head to the water to swim and clear my mind. I walk out into the water and Celie splashes me. She takes me by the hand and tries to climb up. I sink down in the water and hold her there, weightless. She kisses me on the lips, tells me she loves me to the moon. The whole universe, I tell her, then I swim beyond her to where the water is over her head, and I float. The sun is bright, so I shut my eyes and let the undulations take me. I smooth my hand over my burgeoning belly, and I think about the beginning of this little life.

My little life—the one that began in abandonment from a birth mother, the one that ran from beatings throughout childhood, the one that literally ran as fast it could until its legs were cut to the quick, the one that got up again and ran on peg legs, ran from every prince who offered empty promises, ran until a daughter came along and tried to anchor it, then simply picked up the anchor and kept running, running to find a place to call home. Yogi is right, I'm afraid of staying put—I'm afraid of the pain that comes with love, the mercy it can bestow only with time and commitment.

Thimo is shouting. I hear him through the water. I right myself and see him pointing beyond me. There's a blob in the water, and it's red and shining in the sun. I swim as fast as I can to shore, toward Celie and Thimo. Dagmar and Yogi are running from the fire toward the water's edge.

The blob slowly floats toward the shore, but it's still too far away to identify. We ponder whether it's litter, or something a shark has killed, some unfortunate prey. There's no action around it, no predator nibbling at whatever remains, and everyone but Thimo heads back to the fire for nourishment. We're unwrapping potatoes when Thimo starts shouting again, running toward us with the mystery in his hand. He plops down in the sand next to the fire, pulling seaweed off of what we now see is some sort of plastic. He slowly unfolds the mass, and there it is—the red bunny head balloon. It came back, after all.

I stop for gas half an hour from the village on my way to Athens. Just as I hang up the gas hose and head back toward the cab, wondering when I'll get back to the village and how all of this pain will unfold, a man comes out of the gas station, shouting, "I've been looking for you! Wait! Please wait!"

The last thing I need is to pile up another oddity, another episode of strangeness, and I want to drive off, but I watch the man head to a pickup truck and retrieve something from the back of it. When he's within a few feet of me, I see it—the light from Athena's roof rack, and I immediately feel shame.

"I'm so sorry," I say. "I meant to come find you, to apologize for the olive tree I ran into, can I please pay you for the damage?"

"No, no, no," he says. "The tree needed pruned. I'm just so glad to have found you so I can return this."

I climb into Athena, humbled, and I can't shake the feeling that the universe has just handed my daughter and me our coats, on the way out a door that's about to shut.

XII

....

CELIE and I are lying under the stars on a beach an hour from Athens. Our hearts are not in sync. She is sleeping next to me, on a blanket on top of the sand, nestled in, content with what the world has had to offer her thus far. I'm up on one elbow, restless, trying to look past the heavenly bodies for an answer that I know I will not find there.

I stopped here to look for Sohel, the young man I met before I went to Bosnia, the young man who buried his best friend in the mountains there. I came here because I thought it might console me to talk to him now about the atrocities of war I've witnessed, that we might somehow bring each other the comfort of being together and saying nothing when there's nothing that can be said that doesn't break you more. But I did not go to the restaurant where he worked, I didn't try to find him at all. It isn't his job to tell me how to cope with the heavy weight of the world's woes when he's already granted me the kindness of allowing me to witness his ability to heal from them.

Instead, I set up camp on the beach and let Celie swim, and we cooked some artichokes and potatoes over a small fire, and now I'm lying here with all sorts of emotional fires trying to purge themselves from inside, trying to shoot forth from my mouth all the way to the immortal stars above so the light can keep radiating, so that we can continue to find our way. Every time I toss or turn, another blistering thought surges, and on top of it all is a new life forming inside of me, another heartbeat with which to sync.

I suppose it's an age-old question, one that Celie will probably ask herself one day—is this world a good enough place in which to bring another life? A life to which I will again have to delicately convey the balance of forces—light and dark, yin and yang. A life to which I will one day have to say, to my own child, that I do not believe that in a universe borne from wild explosions, there is ever a chance for some utopian idea—but from those blasts, those sometimes decimating eruptions, there emerges the lush gardens of earthly delights, the sand and seas into which we sink our weary bodies, the fruits we pluck from trees, the winds that carry us, the holiness of human union, the breath of life it brings forth.

And yet, right now, it's hard for me not to think of riptides that drown, berries that poison, winds that tear down, and people who are needlessly cruel.

Tonight, under these stars, I feel the weight of the kids in the nightclub in Tuzla, children who survived the war, smoking and drinking and carousing in a sorrowful haze. When I asked one of them what it was like there during the war, he blew a plume of smoke in my face and when it cleared, he declared that they'd all seen the dead there, the corpses of their loved ones strewn along the roads where they once played ball games. And when I asked him what it was like to survive the war, he nodded toward my legs and said, "You ought to know. You're here where the music is aren't you?"

Tonight, I see the children sitting three stories up on concrete slabs, their legs hanging over the ledges where walls were bombed out, the shoes on their feet two sizes too big. The beaming smiles on their faces as they wave to me, their lives still brimming with the delights of discovery.

Tonight, I think of the drunk man I encountered in the rubble underneath the National Library of Sarajevo. The library was in the process of being reconstructed but the man underneath had gone jaundiced, let his anchor drop before he could rise again.

The sign on the front of the library doors read:

ON THIS PLACE SERBIAN CRIMINALS
IN THE NIGHT OF 25TH–26TH AUGUST, 1992, SET ON FIRE
NATIONAL AND
UNIVERSITY'S LIBRARY
OF BOSNIA AND HERZEGOVINA
OVER 2 MILLIONS OF BOOKS, PERIODICALS
AND DOCUMENTS VANISHED IN THE FLAME.
DO NOT FORGET,
REMEMBER AND WARN!

Tonight, I remember the man who lost a leg and a foot on the war field, how immediately after the explosion rendered him freshly crippled, he heard another boom, a Bouncing Betty taking down his comrade. He told me how he army-crawled over to his friend with appendages newly missing, and somehow he hoisted what was left of his mate onto his back, then slogged to the safety of makeshift barracks—how they both survived.

I will not forget the picture in his office—the shed from which he now conducts landmine clearance efforts. In the photo, he and his wife are standing beside Paul McCartney and his then wife Heather Mills. Heather Mills is a model who lost her leg after a police motorcycle crashed into her as she was crossing a London street. After she healed, she took up landmine clearance as a passion and promised this man some help. A year and more passed before he received a phone call from someone representing Ms. Mills and said that she was delighted they would be hosting a dinner and fundraiser in the City of Angels for landmine clearance, and that they wanted the man to be the guest of honor and would provide him with two plane tickets and a hotel. He accepted the offer, and his comrades pooled together enough money to buy him and his wife a suit and a nice dress since they did not own, nor could they afford, such fineries. Word was that lots of celebrities attended, including Oprah, and the event was huge and made lots of money and cost far more to put on than it raised. The man gave an impassioned speech, and everyone felt good. Later, back in Bosnia with his suit and his wife's nice dress hanging in plastic in a closet, useless, he would hear that the fundraiser made somewhere near $750,000 for landmine clearance, but it had already been more than a few years, and he hadn't seen any of the money. He simply received the framed picture in the mail with a thank you card.

Tonight, and possibly forever, I will not forget his downward glance at me, while he said, "You all mean well enough."

Tonight, emblazoned on my mind like the branding of a horse is Anna, an artist who lost all of her limbs to an antitank mine. Anna and her husband lived in the surrounding mountains of Sarajevo, where the longest siege in the modern history of war took place for 1,425 days, from the spring of 1992 until the late winter of 1996. She was Muslim, her husband a Serbian, and as the war and propaganda continued to build prior to the siege, he felt it was necessary to sign up for the Serbian army, it was involuntary after all, and he concluded that it might be the best way to keep their peace.

When Anna's husband left soon afterward for ten days of training, he had no idea that the Serbian troops would later raid his wife's garden and surround the house with landmines.

Anna said that her husband was in a tank outside of the house the day it happened. Perhaps he had been told that they would both be executed if he made a move in any way. Anna woke and spotted him through the window. She also spotted other soldiers stealing food from her garden. Angry, she ran out of the house with only a robe, shouting at her husband, marching along the yard toward the road. She thought she heard him shout back, but she wasn't sure because it all blended in with the explosion. She had stepped on the anti-tank mine. Time stopped, as it does when an eruption occurs, a line is drawn between the before and the after.

Anna's husband was found later, two miles down the road, lying atop a pile of leaves, with a single bullet to his head. A professor from Sarajevo who was friends with the artist and her husband would later say that he'd received a call that day from the husband to hurry to the house with medics to save his wife.

Anna chose not to use prosthetics; it was too much work she'd said. By the time she got her arms on with no legs, and her legs on with fake arms, she could have half the house cleaned, she'd said.

When I met Anna, she was two tiers up her stone-walled terraced garden, planting. She had one leg to the knee and one just above it, and the same with her arms, one with an elbow and one just above it. She did her own fluid version of an army crawl. She had a rope in her mouth; it was attached to a small wooden wagon filled with seeds. She dug a hole with her elbow. She inched the wagon closer to her, by pulling the rope a bit at a time with her mouth. When the wagon was close enough, she nudged it even closer with her chin, took a few seeds in her mouth, spit them in the hole and covered them with dirt using her elbow stump again.

I think of this as hope.

Not long after the day I spent with her on her terrace, Anna was raped at her home. Inevitably, her belly began to burgeon. Perhaps she could not swallow the thought of giving birth to the child of an anonymous man who has raped her. So, while I am in Greece, clinging to the hope I find in her perseverance, she crawls to the kitchen and drinks enough rat poison under the sink.

I think of this as despair, when the scars are too wide for the map of your body, when the sea and the fruits and the winds of Eden aren't enough to maintain the steadiness of your breath, when the agony is so severe that to fold back into stardust is freedom. Some scars burn down the whole landscape of love and loss. And still, they need to be honored. They need to be remembered as a warning, so that we may learn to walk more gently, with or without legs, on this earth that already harbors savage uncertainty.

I slowly shift my body away from Celie's. I cover her with another blanket so she won't feel the absence of my warmth. I've let my mind wander, or my mind has had no choice but to wander because my vessel is cracked and seeping—either way, I know that sleep will not find me anytime soon tonight, on this beach, under these stars, immersed in these scars.

I unzip the mosquito net surrounding us. The amblers have left for the night, so I crawl to the edge of the water and lie down in the gently lapping tide and let the water wash over what is left of my legs. I can sit here and list a catalogue of afflictions that I've witnessed, but the only thing I can offer the wounded is the opportunity to tell their story. Money might buy them things, rebuild their infrastructure—but only the wounded can look back and fill their cracks with gold, no matter how the cracks got there. And I now realize that part of the reason the rawness of their stories pains me so, the truth they've shared with me because of the absence of my legs—proof that I've paid my dues at the table of suffering—is because I haven't yet looked back on my own afflictions, the wounds not only visible, but invisible, and if I'm going to lie here and look back at it now in this seemingly safe space, then I'll do it with as much tenderness as the earth holds—the way a wound should be handled, with grace.

Tonight, I remember the tunnel from which I burst forth, an orb of stardust formed from the gravity of a union whose heat gave me the breath of life. There is only abstraction here—I have no facts to go on, no story of my birth. All I know is that a society who hadn't looked back on their scars enough to learn to walk gently forced a young woman to relinquish her child. I do not know if the woman who gave birth to me ever held me, or if she just heard me scream as a stranger lifted me up and away after I was wrenched out of her womb.

Almost a year later, another woman purchased me from an orphanage, a woman filled with anger and shame for all the ways that society points futile blame toward a human for being a human. This woman became my mom, and her inability to utter her truths, and her belief in the shame with which society branded her, made it so difficult to raise a child aware of her own inherent freedom on this earth that this woman took her rightful pent-up rage out wrongfully on me.

I have two mothers, and although they may not have intended to do so, they have both left me scarred.

I am four the first time I recall being backhanded in the face by my mom. It is my birthday, and my grandma buys me a plastic kiddie pool from Kmart, where she works. We fill up the pool with the hose and I play in it all afternoon under an oak tree, lying down flat on my back so my ears are submerged, waiting for the waning leaves to fall from the branches and helicopter down. I try to catch them as they spin, study their veins one last time before they hit the earth and begin to dissipate. Near dusk, my mom says it's quitting time. But it's still my birthday and there's still sun in the sky I tell her, so she lifts up the lip of the pool with me in it. Out onto the ground we pour, the water, the leaves, and me.

As soon as she goes back inside, I drag my gift right over to the hose and start filling it again. She sees me from the window, and turns the water off from inside, from a place I don't yet know about, because the hose just dries up, but I've already scored a few inches, just not enough to put my ears down into it the way I like to, so I go into the garage and find two big red plastic jugs full of liquid, and add them to the pool. The liquid smells funny, but in a pleasing way, and I curl down into the pool in a fetal position, half my face submerged, letting the spiraling leaves surprise me as they tickle my body.

Mom yanks me out of the pool by an arm without warning, grabs at my slick limbs until I'm upright, then backhands me across the face so hard I fall right back to the ground. Grandma swoops me up right after, smells the gasoline on my breath, and runs inside to call an ambulance. While I lie in the hospital being treated for vapors in my lungs, all I think about is whirling leaves.

I am six-almost-seven, in first grade, and my teacher, Valentine, has brought in the wallpaper for our book covers. All day long, we write and draw. I write that day about Kmart, where my grandmother started working to make her "own money."

Sometimes my grandmother takes me and my cousins to play miniature golf or to an amusement park, and there is always a gift shop with a myriad of junk you can buy with your name on it. One day, my cousins all get license plates with their names on them and I feel left out because my name isn't there. To make things worse, there are two variations of my name available, just not *my* name. I could purchase a license plate with K-E-L-L-Y, or even K-E-L-L-I-E, but not Kelley with an E-Y. My name is the surname of my maternal great-grandmother, the daughter of Irish immigrants born in Morgantown, West Virginia. I like the stoic monochrome photo of Grandma Kelley in the hallway, the hard determination that chisels her face, and I don't want a license plate that has someone else's name on it, so I go home with a rope bracelet and salt candy instead.

In my book, I draw actions on the top of the page, which is blank, and on the bottom half, where there are line charts so that you can perfect your handwriting, so it is as ornate as Valentine's, I write about the blue light special at Kmart, where, after the license plate fiasco, my grandmother purchased a small turquoise canvas bag and white velvet letters, went home and got the iron out, and applied those letters to the bag, and they read K-E-L-L-E-Y.

I write about how much I love my grandmother and the

quarter carousel ride outside of Kmart, but that the noise and whirl of blue light specials kind of frighten me even though Grandma can sometimes afford to bring me a cheap token home when the blue light, like a cop's car, starts flashing and wailing from somewhere in the store denoting heavily discounted items we could probably live without.

I don't know then that those cheap tokens—that turquoise canvas bag and white velvet letters—are tokens of resiliency, hope. I used to not bother telling people when they misspelled my name, and sometimes I still don't, but when you begin learning that loss is loss is loss, sometimes you like to hold on to everything you're able to, even just an extra *E*.

I'm sad when my grandparents get divorced but thrilled when Grandma comes to live with us—my mom doesn't touch me for the couple of years Grandma is part of our home. I never saw Grandpa as anything but cool, with his garden full of string beans and his ferret named Elvis. Grandpa was a coal miner in West Virginia before he got the black lung and they moved to Akron, Ohio, where he took up truck driving, but together my grandparents had a band and performed a sassy love act with songs like Johnny Russell's "Rednecks, White Socks and Blue-Ribbon Beer" in smoky bars and rec halls from Cleveland to Charleston. I loved when they harmonized to the old hymns the most, my grandma and her perfect pitch, the yearning of her lilt and twang, and my grandpa playing the guitar like a god who'd sold his soul. When he'd practice in his den, I'd sit by the fireplace and listen, and when he went up to the kitchen to get himself another beer, I'd light the longest cigarette butt I could find from the ashtray and inhale it with fevered curiosity and uncertain desire.

Much later, I will learn that off the stage, Grandpa sometimes beat Grandma. When they weren't singing together, and he wasn't off having a fling, he terrorized her. And if my mom, just a girl, stepped in between them, she'd get pulverized, too. Eventually, if Grandma wasn't half-assed scrapping supper together, she'd be in bed swallowing valium like candy while my mom took care of her younger sister and the household. But when my grandma left my grandpa after thirty-seven years of that, she became a new woman or, perhaps, her old self.

I'm five when she moves in with us, and if my parents aren't around, she sometimes stands on the sofa while vacuuming the floor, holding the vacuum chord as if it's attached to a microphone, shaking her hips while singing "Cow Cow Boogie," and then she drops the chord and takes my hand, and we dance and swing until we're winded. She's as wild and wonderful as the lands from which she came, and she loves and stokes every bit of fire in me now that she's set herself free. And then, she meets a man who wouldn't harm a flea and moves away.

Grandma's been gone about a week when I bring the finished book about Kmart home. My mom is lying on the sofa watching television, and I walk in and high-heartedly hand it to her, proud of my creation.

"I have something for you to read, too," she says and hands me a small booklet. "Go upstairs and read it, then we'll talk."

I plop on my bed with the booklet, happily thinking this is possibly a new start to a better relationship with my mom—a book exchange, something we've never done before. The booklet is illustrated for the times—on one page there is a woman with a coifed afro wearing bell-bottoms. She is holding the hand of a young boy and they are standing on the lower stairs that lead to a small porch. Before them, at the front door, is a middle-class white sub-urban couple. Their arms are both around each other and extended. In the text, I learn that the boy is an *adoptee* and is about to spend some time with his possibly new parents. The text clearly states that this is a visit, that there will be an evaluation to see if they all get along. How frighten-ing is that—to be evaluated on your worthiness of accep-tance into a loving family? How much are any of us worth? I finish the booklet, which promises that the adoptee is on his way to a loving family that he deserves.

I close the booklet and bite my lip to stop the hot tears that I feel welling up around my eyeballs. It has not yet oc-curred to me that I bear no physical resemblance to my family. There will be no better relationship with my mom, and now it seems there will be no more relationship at all, which makes me sad because she's not all violent outbursts—sometimes she teaches me how to sew or plays a board game with me, and she always makes my Halloween costumes, even though I don't always get to pick them. Like the year before, when she made me dress up as Martha Washington, and I didn't even want to leave the house to get candy be-cause of the mole she put on my face with her eyeliner.

I grab the turquoise canvas bag and fill it with a Ticonderoga #2 and a sharpener, a small notepad—the kind my grandma buys to write down recipes, card game scores, and grocery lists—and my favorite T-shirt, pink with an iron-on of a kitten in a basket, in a field dotted with yellow flowers, a sparkly rainbow above. Then I go downstairs, sit on the bottom stair, and wait.

When her television show ends in the next room, my mom hoists herself up off the sofa—I can tell by the squeak of the sofa springs. She walks toward the kitchen with a glass in her hand and glances over at me. My turquoise bag is on my lap, my arms clenched around it.

"Did you finish the book?" she asks.

"Yes," I say, without looking at her. "I'm ready to go."

"What do you mean?" she says, then breaks out into nervous laughter. When she calms down, she adds, "No, we are not giving you up. We adopted you. We aren't giving up on you." Then she pats me on the knee, a touch from which I instinctively flinch since I can't recall any physical touch from her that doesn't hurt, and she takes her glass to the kitchen. There is no further discussion.

A pressure builds in my chest, like a firework is about to go off in my brain, and suddenly it dawns on me that this woman is not my mom, and for some reason, the woman who is my mom has given me up, and that the name on my turquoise bag might not be my name at all.

Looking back, I think that's the exact moment I am handed the baton of societal shame and open my hand to receive it. Those thoughts are so painful that I dissociate in order to survive. I make up stories in my head in which my biological mother is always a heroic victim, still looking for me—that one day she might save me.

I haven't yet experienced much life, or the amassing of hardships that come with time. I'm limited to childish logic, like in fairy tales where children are only surrendered by dire necessity, accident, or evildoing. I'm not yet able to see Grandpa beating Grandma, the toll it takes on my mom, and therefore me; all I can see is the quarter carousel ride in front of Kmart, and I know that if I sit on it and put one of my grandma's coins in the slot, the music will start and I will drift away, even if I just go around in circles.

The beatings my mother gives me are consistent, but not regular, just often enough to reinforce my growing sense of being unworthy of unconditional love—the kind I hear about in Sunday school, the kind I receive from my grandma, who I barely ever see anymore. My mother beats me without warning mostly, when I have no idea what I've done wrong or how to correct it. She hits me in a quick rage, with a stick or a belt or a hand, and it's over in no time, without explanation, and I get up and walk away and pretend it doesn't hurt because even though I have begun to believe something is wrong with me, the defiant fire of nature still burns hotter.

But some incidents are harder to forget. Like once when I was eight, and we are all watching *A Charlie Brown Christmas* on the television, and our tree is lit in the corner with presents underneath, and I feel this great, if misguided, joy that everyone in the world might be snuggled around a fireplace, as we are, rooting for Charlie's flimsy tree while snow blankets the outside world with peace.

I say or do something during a commercial break that sets her off, and she drags me by the hair and puts me outside on the porch and locks the door. It is December in Akron, Ohio, and I have on pajamas. First, I bang on the door. Then, I scream, then cry, and then I watch my hot breath turn into smoke and decide to run away, but I slip on the ice on the top of the brick stairs and bust my two front teeth on the bottom one. And then nobody gets to watch the end of the show because we have to go to the emergency room instead.

When my mom goes off, my dad always seems to retreat to his garage or goes to the store, as if there is nothing he can do to douse her rage. When my mom is in calm periods, he teaches me preventative measures—he coaches my softball team and keeps me away for long practices. And when he sees how fast I can dash around the diamond, my father teaches me how to run. I am nine when he begins to encourage me to take up track and field, cross-country, any community race he sees advertised in the paper. Perhaps, it is the only way he knows to save me, and I take the lesson to heart.

At thirteen, my mom and I argue because I'm half an hour late and she can smell cigarette smoke on me. She says that sometimes her father comes to her in nightmares, and when she wakes, she can smell the smoke of his cigarettes. Her anger quickly escalates since I've learned to talk back. When I shout at her—*You're not my mom!*—it sets her off like a bonfire. When she begins to chase me, I dart easily through rooms, but then I make the mistake of jetting upstairs instead of outside. She catches me by the heel. I wiggle free and reach my bedroom. She pushes the door in before I can shut it. We circle the bed, predator and prey, until I cross the bed and grab a pillow. She catches my leg. She's found a wire hanger and beats me from the waist down long enough for blood to streak the sheets. My arms are mostly spared because I've managed to get the pillow and use it to cover my head. When she exhausts herself, she heaves up off of me, heads toward the door, and tells me to go to bed.

In gym class the next day, I'm wearing the one-piece shorts uniform required, and I'm pulled aside by the gym teacher, who asks if I got in a fight with a mountain lion. When my eyes well up and I go silent, I'm sent to the guidance counselor's office. And when the guidance counselor finally pulls the truth out of me and tells me that he's going to be making some phone calls, including to my parents, I beg him to forget everything. I plead with him to understand that this is all my fault, but it's too late.

I'm terrified, waiting for my parents and social services to arrive. I'm even more terrified when a police officer shows up. I simply stare at a poster in the guidance counselor's office on which lemons cascade from the upper left part of a sky, descending into a metal press with a hand crank, where a liquid rainbow comes out the other side and fills a glass with shades of blue, green, and gold, and the letters below it read *If life gives you lemons, make lemonade.*

Social services comes for a home visit, and mom has the house cleaner than I've ever seen it, and she's baked a cake, which she sometimes does, and despite the long list of incidents that have required minor hospitalization and the years of physical scars she's left on my legs and backside, I lie and say it's the only time I can remember my mother hitting me, and the investigation is closed, and according to the official report, the whole thing is "an isolated incident of extreme discipline. The child has behavioral issues stemming from adoption."

I start running harder then, and longer, and farther away each time.

One day, at sixteen, I meet and fall deeply in love for the first time with a kind young man who never takes advantage of me, a young man who is studying journalism in a college two hours away, who knows how to use words to tell me the things about me that are to be valued—my heart, my head, the things my hands create—and I begin to believe him.

One night, after six months of weekends together and handwritten letters and all the lush greenery that first love offers, I spend the night alone with him in a college dorm room, and we come so close to having intercourse that we are locking toes, and his cock is throbbing against my abdomen, and I tell him it is okay, that I love him more than anyone and that I only want to be with him, and then he rolls off me, caresses my cheek over and over, and tells me that he loves me, too, and doesn't want to be with anyone else either, and that is why we were going to do it right and get married first.

A week after that, I participate in a training program at Ohio University for the best high school runners in the state, and Wilma Rudolph is the keynote speaker, and she paces me and talks with me for a whole mile, and I am suddenly convinced that I am worth the great and simple things life has to offer, and two days later, I fall ill, and several weeks after that, my legs begin to be amputated, and I never run or lock toes with anyone ever again.

I lie to my parents the day I fall ill, say I'm going to a youth group program with a friend that won't be over until late, when really I've just convinced the friend to drive me two hours to see my boyfriend so I can drop off a basket of goodies I've prepared for him since he is taking exams, and then we'll drive right back to Akron. I start feeling ill just before we get to the college, and though I find the strength to deliver the goods, my boyfriend sees how sick I am and offers to take me to a doctor, but I'm more afraid of my mother than illness, so my friend drives me back to Akron, and by the time we get there I'm so sick that I'm crumpled up in the wheel well of the car. I'm taken to a hospital with a 104-degree fever and sent home with Tylenol, but not a blood test, which may have been able to indicate that I've acquired a bacterium known as meningococcemia, and I'm starting to go septic.

My father carries me to my bedroom that evening, and during the night, I vomit in a bucket next to my bed, and I whimper until my mom comes to my room and empties it. Some hours later, predawn, I feel like I am going to die in a way I've never felt before, as if everything inside of me is literally on fire. The toxins have invaded my blood stream and are beginning to burst through the vessel walls, and blood is pooling under my flesh even though I can't see it because the lights are off and the sun hasn't yet risen.

Sometime later, I defecate all over the bed, liquid diarrhea—it comes without warning—so I call for my mom again, and she comes in and yells at me, accuses me, like the doctor at the first hospital, of being overly dramatic by not getting myself to the toilet, and instead of changing the sheets and cleaning me, she tosses me a towel and says to cover it up until morning.

When morning comes, my grandmother enters my bedroom. My mom has called her to ask for help cleaning me up. She pulls back the sheet, and sees the blood pooling under the skin, my eyes getting ready to hang up a vacancy sign. She screams at my mother to call 911, then screams at her again, saying, "How could you not know how sick this child is?"

At the next hospital, my mom will realize how sick I am when I begin to seize in the emergency room, when a spinal tap reveals a diagnosis, when my kidneys begin failing and my brain begins to swell, and my lungs collapse, and I die for fourteen seconds, but instead of dying, I find myself in Vietnam.

I was born at the tail end of Vietnam, and when I was a child, the war was personified. In overhearing the conversations of adults, I came to understand that the war was responsible for men's drunkenness, for their murderous acts, for the leaving of wives. I felt sorry for everyone. I didn't understand why war couldn't be made a better person. Trauma ripples, and the war affected everyone I knew.

So while the doctors are defibrillating me over and over, and my body is leaping off the bed with each shock, I'm in the jungle, the heat is sinewy, the tangled broad-leafed vines are lush and stunning, the noises the birds make fill my heart with something glad, until I notice a soldier lying in the thick, motioning me to be quiet with a finger against his mouth. Then comes gunfire in the distance; it begins to gain ground. I contemplate curling up against a tree to wait it out, but to the west, I see sunlight, and I know it's the jungle's edge, and I know I have only a moment to decide whether to run or to freeze, and if there's one thing I know how to do well, it's to run, so I do.

And then I'm back in the ICU, and my mother is there, and we spend nearly a century of days together in the hospital after the disease runs its initial course, and the doctors have nothing left to do but prune me like a rotting tree, spending well over a dozen surgeries cutting off my toes, then half the feet, then up and up until the knees, debriding parts of my arms in a desperate attempt to save what is left of me.

Mom calls me foolish when I tell my boyfriend, who drives two hours each way every day for weeks, to never come back again. And maybe I am less afraid of the boy I love seeing my body fall apart than I am that he might see that maybe my mother is right, that I'm not worth the stardust from which I was made, that I'm not worth being put back together again.

One thing is certain, even though my father can't come in the hospital room without crying, he'll never leave me—my father who was spared the draft due to a heart murmur, my father who kept a scrapbook of all my race reports from the newspaper, my father who taught me how to run for my life.

Sometimes, I see myself as a little girl, walking through Akron, running away from my mother, and hopping over drunken vets on the roadside. I spent the night with a girl from school once. Her dad lost his leg in the war. She cooked his dinner every night, and he had her washing the socks he wore on his stump by hand in the sink. He just sat in his chair, drinking beers, staring blankly at the television. The whole thing made me sad. I asked her that night what happened to her dad to make him that way. "The war," she said, then we painted our toes with nail polish by flashlight.

I think of all this, my childhood, and when it hurts, I hop into my father's pickup truck and we head toward the field to play ball. Then somehow, we are out of the truck and flying. He's holding my hand as we glide over the lakes, heading for the stars. The higher we get, the harder it is to see the drunken vets, girl children washing stump socks in the sink, my mother as a girl getting beaten over and over until she quits believing in the beauty of her own being, until the pain outweighs her joy and festers in her, until she explodes on whatever is near her to remind her of the pain she cannot face—all the angry muck. I look back at all this, but I cannot stay. Instead, I float on, and the stars above and the lakes below glisten, and the wind blows through my hair, and my hand fits perfectly in my father's.

The last time my mother beats me, I have been discharged from the hospital. I am seventeen, and I weigh eighty-six pounds, and I'm living in a makeshift bedroom on the first floor of my childhood home, recovering. I can't say the word *stump* any more than I can look at my own, but I am supposed to be rubbing them with a pumice stone several times a day, so they can begin to callus, so I can prepare them for prosthetics. A week before the prosthetic appointment, my mother asks every day if I've rubbed my stumps, and every time the word comes out of her mouth, I wince and say yes, even though it's a lie. And when the appointment comes and goes, and the prosthetist can't fit me because my stumps aren't ready, my mother says they'll be ready in a week. And when we get back to the house, I can see the anger in her building, the anger I thought had been subdued by the wastelands of this illness.

She enters into my space with the pumice stone in one hand, and she slaps me across the face with the other. Her voice fills every cavity of the room and my heart as she tells me I'm not the only one who has suffered, that she's given up everything, that I have to do my part, too, and then she straddles my waist with her ass in my face, rips off the cotton covers protecting my stumps and rubs them with the fury of Hecuba, rubs them raw until they are sitting in a pool of blood.

I yell right back. I tell her I hate her.

And she says I can hate her all I want, but that I'm going to *walk* out of there hating her.

But I can't hate her because hating her only hurts me,

and if I let myself hold on to that hate, I might hurt someone else. So instead, I learn to walk again, and I run far away, even though I can no longer run, and stay in touch from a safe distance, over the telephone lines.

As if she can feel all of this pain I'm letting the sea wash away, Celie lets out a moan in her sleep. I crawl back to where my daughter is sleeping, unzip the mosquito net, and lay my weary body down next to hers. She whimpers but doesn't wake. Better a nightmare, I think, then the hardships that often come with waking. I nuzzle my nose into her hair and take in the blessing of her essence, her pure, sweet self, and wish that someone could have loved my mom as a child the way I have chosen to love this one next to me, the way I will love the one inside of me when it arrives.

By the time I am pregnant with Celie, my mother's strength has waned. Celie is my mom's first grandchild and makes her melt like butter, and I am in a state of constant surprise by the tenderness with which she handles my daughter. I am wary of letting her spend time alone with Celie, but the two of them bring each other such joy that I'd feel foolish questioning the mysteries of alchemy.

J and I have recently split up, but not cleanly, and I'm at my parent's house for the first time as a single mom. Celie is around six months old. It's evening, and we're watching a television show, and my mother gets angry and sends me upstairs when I start to nurse my daughter in the living room. So, I go up to my childhood bedroom, and J calls, and Celie is attached to my breast, and J and I are still so full of love and regret that I start weeping, and the tears are falling all over our daughter's cheek to the point that she is getting the heartache caught in her throat, and she begins to cry, struggles to latch back onto the nipple between sobs, so I gently hush her, stroke her hair, and then my mom appears in the bedroom door, which frightens me the way it used to when I was a child. And as Celie feverishly begins to latch back on to my breast, my mother swoops her off the bed, away from me, and it feels as if my nipple has been ripped off. I calmly ask her to give me back my baby, but she refuses. She tells me that when I'm finished with J, I can have my daughter back, and then she goes downstairs. I tell J I'll call him back. I go to the bathroom and run a washcloth under cold water and hold it to my bruised breast, and I tell myself that I will not let my mother shame me anymore, that I'm a grown woman now and I've fought too hard to take back my worthiness. I will not let her dictate my life, my own experience of motherhood.

When I go downstairs, my mother is sitting on the floor in front of the television. A cartoon is on, and Celie has a popsicle in her mouth. I say firmly that I've calmed down, and need to finish nursing my daughter, put her to bed; then I walk over to pick her up. Celie reaches her arms up to me and I swoop my hands up under her armpits, feeling grateful that this is going smoothly, but then just as I start to stand upright, my mom starts pulling my daughter back down by the legs, and for a moment, Celie is suspended there like she's in some sort of medieval rack, stuck in a tug-of-war between my mom and me, and it horrifies me.

It's only moments that we stay that way, my daughter

suspended between sea and stars, but it feels like eternity, and rather than physically harm my daughter, I let her go. I sit down a few feet away, and try to convince my mother to let Celie go, but she has quit speaking to me, and Celie just keeps looking back and forth between me and the cartoon, and just as I'm thinking that I may need to do something drastic, even though I don't know what it might be, my father enters the room and tells my mother in a voice I've never heard from him that she has to give me my daughter back. My mother shoots him a glare that could kill a lesser man, and he knows he's going to pay for it later, but he takes Celie from my mom's arms, hands me her precious body, and tells me to go upstairs—he tells me, once more, to run.

A couple of months later, I'm back home with Celie in Virginia, and I'm beside myself with grief. Nothing will soothe Celie, not toys, mushed bananas, or the breast. We have exhausted each other, so I pack her up in the car, turn up some classical music, and drive. It takes thirteen miles for her to fall asleep.

I pull off at the side of a country road in the Blue Ridge Mountains. It's a late summer day, and a solitary crow takes perch on the fencepost outside of the car window. I begin to cry so hard that I have to muffle the sounds to keep them from waking my daughter, but I can't contain them, so I step out of the car and walk away from it. The haughty crow watches me as I begin to sob.

I am angry. I'm angry about the men who've taken advantage of me. I'm angry that my relationship with J has ended, that I placed too much of my self-worth in our relationship. I'm angry that I was abandoned at birth and beaten bloody through childhood. I'm angry that my legs were cut off, that I almost died. I'm angry that every step I take brings me pain.

I am full of postpartum depression and loneliness, and I'm not sure I know how to raise a child by myself. I am not sure I am physically able. I am not sure I am worthy of the perfect gift she is. She is my only blood relative and she looks like her father, and she is the only thing that brings me joy, and right now all she does is suck the marrow from my bones and shit and spit up on me. And I have little marrow left, I think. I can't do this, I think. Someone out there is better qualified to give her undying love.

The crow flies away, leaves the fencepost bare. And I think that the handle on her car seat will fit perfectly over the post. I think it is just after midday and surely someone will find her before dark. They will not be able to turn away from her undeniable beauty and the light in her eyes. My legs buckle, and I fall backward into the fence and let myself envision her on the fencepost for the afternoon. I see myself placing a blanket over her for shade, tucking a note between her perfect arm and belly, praying, even though I no longer believe in the same kind of prayer that I learned in the church, that God will look over her and deliver her to some Promised Land. Then I dry heave saliva all over the field grass while a grasshopper jumps across my rubber foot.

Celie begins to mewl in the back seat. I struggle to get up from the fence, and before I can get to her, the cry has become more urgent, sadder. By the time I unbuckle her and pull her from the car seat, she is sobbing, as if she's been dreaming my thoughts. Her face is flushed. I take her in my arms and sit in the tall grass. I open my blouse and offer her a breast. It is engorged and spilling over with milk, and she is so upset that she struggles to latch on. When she does, she gulps the milk so hard it sounds like she is drowning. I am wiping tears from her eyes as fast as my own are falling all over her cheeks. We sit there for half an hour. She feverishly sucks both of my breasts until they are emptied. I am empty. She is full, and snoring.

On the drive back home, I think of my mother, and my daughter, and me. I will never know how excruciating it would have been to leave my daughter on that fencepost, because I didn't do it. I begin to feel so sorry for the woman who gave birth to me for having left me on some metaphorical fencepost that I can barely breathe to think of her pain. I begin to feel heartbroken for my mom losing child after child, never knowing this bond that I feel with my daughter.

When I lay Celie down that night, I will think of her tears earlier that day—she almost certainly felt my despair—we are so enmeshed by genetics, choice, and time that right now, we are as much one as we are the other. At the side of the road, when I cried on her face as she suckled, and warbled out the words *I love you I love you I love you* over and over again, I was also saying, *I love me, I love me, I love me.* In loving someone else, we learn to love ourselves. In losing someone else, we learn to lose ourselves. In the gaining, there is always the loss.

I've grown cold spitting all these fires up and out of me. I remove my damp clothes and crawl under the blanket with Celie. I've wept enough throughout the night, looking back through all these tunnels on this map, that I could swear I've added another inch to the sea.

I want to tell my mom now—after all the beatings have been served, all the anger and gravity that she bore down on my body—Who's to tell a star not to be a star, a sea a sea, the wind the wind? I want to tell her that I am not covering over the scars she gave me with concrete as if they never happened; instead I am filling them with gold—that I'm honoring the pain passed on through the generations, that I am calling it out, that I am remembering, that I am sending out warning. And I want to tell my father that I can't run forever, that sometimes I need to stay still and reflect on what has broken me so I can repair this vessel, so I can make it golden, so it can serve others well.

Celie's breath is sweet and yeasty. My chest is to her back, and I feel our hearts going back into sync. I cradle my womb with my hand, to comfort the new heartbeat growing inside. I stare out at the sea just as the sun slices through the horizon, pierces right through the darkness, makes everything clear.

XIII

....

AT the gynecologist's office in Athens, I hear the heartbeat and it stays in my head like a song that gets stuck. Celie hears it, too, only hours after I first tell her that I have a baby inside of me, and she takes the new information in stride, telling everyone we encounter that she is going to be a big sister.

Yiannis and Tartan are waiting by Athena when we come outside, and Yiannis has a bouquet of flowers in his hands. "It's a boy," I tell him, and his countenance beams with the thought of a new life that he has had no part in creating. The whole scene feels surreal, like we are mismatched paper dolls, leftover from a forgotten childhood. We continue with our game of make-believe.

On a whim, we drive to a port and pick out an island at random. We ferry to the island and rent a house on the beach. We lie in the sun and eat good food, and sleep, a lot. Celie finds endless sticks for Tartan. I could pretend that we are on an extended vacation forever, except that my belly keeps growing, and the larger it grows, the more empty vodka bottles I find hidden around the house, and I know that something is going to give eventually, and one morning, when I wake up in a small pool of blood, it does.

The blood has slowed a bit, but when I call the gynecologist he tells me to get on the first ferry back to Athens. I call Tina, too, because she happens to be teaching at the American School in Athens, and I ask her if she will go with me to the hospital when I arrive. And then, I call my mom and dad. My mom cries when I tell her I am pregnant, and she cries even harder when I tell her that I'm bleeding and on my way to the hospital. I tell her that I'm sorry that I've been so distant, that I'm halfway around the world, and she says to me, "I'm sorry I've given you so much grief about it. Truth is, I've been jealous of the way you've always had the strength to follow your heart." She fades out, and I hear her sobbing. My father takes the receiver. I tell him the situation, and he is silent for the longest time, and then he says, "Is it too late for an abortion?"

My heart stops beating for a minute. I don't ask him to repeat what he's said because I don't want him to say it again. I don't know what the laws in Greece are, but it's too late in the United States, and even though I think he's trying to set me free, it also feels as if he is freeing himself from me and his whole history—as if he wished he'd made a different choice when he was a young man. And even though I'm frightened of the answer, I ask the question anyway, "Why, Pops? Why are you saying that?"

And he says, "Don't you remember how close you came to death when you had Celie? I've almost lost you twice in this life, and I'm afraid of the third strike. I love you so much."

And the game of charades is finally over. I am worthy of this love.

Tina meets us in the hotel, where I've booked a room with a balcony overlooking the Parthenon. I'm hopping out of the shower when she arrives. Celie and Yiannis are watching cartoons and eating room service. Tartan is sleeping on the balcony. I sweep Celie into my arms and tell her that I have to go check on the baby, and I won't be long. "I love you to the moon, Mama," she says, with her eyes fixed on the television. I glance past her and see the Parthenon, and think of Athena, the expedition that won't be happening, the baby that might not either.

"The whole universe," I say.

I remember the cherry of a cigarette glowing brightly as the taxi driver flicks the ashes out the window, how fiery it is against the night sky. I remember Tina yelling at a nurse in Greek. I remember a nurse saying she can't find a heartbeat—intense spasms, a nurse tapping my arm to locate a vein for an IV. I remember telling the nurse that the baby is coming, and her saying that he's not. The nurse checking between my legs, and her face going pale. The doctor running to the table and catching him with one glove on. A wrinkled, blue baby boy, who does not cry.

I trace his protruding spine, fix my eye on each bone, so as not to forget them. I rub my nose into his matted hair. I touch each finger and toe, his nose, his eyelids, his lips.

I think of the fact that he is the second blood kin I know, aside from Celie, and I love him. My son is premature, and stillborn.

I hold him, while the olive groves in the village stretch out inside my mind. It's slightly overcast, a gray band across hazy blue, the trees swaying underneath the sky all the way out to the sea. And the sea, every day of it—the greatest of all mother's waters—even it is prone to bursting out in murderous ways. And then the trees, how they grow and twist and take the beatings that come, how they eventually produce that perfect, hearty fruit, the oil that is worth more than gold.

When we step out of the hospital, it's a sunny day in Athens, like nothing ever happened. Tina insists that we take a few days and go to a hidden cove of which she knows and rest, but first I have to go to the pharmacy and pick up a prescription to slow the bleeding, and I want to get it by myself. I tell Tina that I'll meet her back at the hotel.

"Are you sure you'll be okay?" she asks.

"Going to a pharmacy? Tina, did we not make it through Serbia alive?" I want to be alone, so that it might be easier to play a mind game with myself, one in which it is just another day. Other than severe fatigue, I feel fine, good and numb— the adrenals are kicking out all the right juices. I trot down through the Athenian suburb, and I think of Bosnian mothers trotting through the streets of Sarajevo, avoiding snipers, sweeping up the bodies of their children, witnessing the mass executions of their children, or of the children that watch these mothers while they are being raped.

Schoolchildren are crossing the sidewalk. There's an old man missing the pinky on his left hand carving a backgammon board. There are men carrying a large glass pane across the street in which I see my reflection and have to look away.

The pharmacy is air-conditioned, and I start shivering within moments because I'm wet with sweat. I hand the pharmacist the paper and he glances down at it, then looks at me with what I perceive to be pity while a cigarette dangles from his bottom lip. He motions me to take a chair, and before I sit down, he is beside me, gently taking my arm, and laying a towel down in the chair before I sit. My pants are soaked with blood.

He hands the paper to an assistant and stays by my side. He has gray hair, slicked back with pomade, and he smells like lemons. He is kind. I won't speak to him. Tears fall down my cheeks, and he kneels beside me, with his arm around my waist.

When the assistant returns with the medicine, I start for my wallet, but the pharmacist put his hand on mine, and pats it, saying, "I'm sorry, doll. I'm sorry. You don't owe me anything." He calls me a taxi, and when it arrives, he sets the towel down on the seat, and helps me inside.

"Where are you staying?" he asks, and I speak only the hotel name.

"God be with you," he says, cupping my cheek with his hand. Then he hands the fare to the taxi driver.

I must be in shock because it doesn't bother me one bit to walk through the lobby of the hotel with my pants soaked in blood. Tina helps me into the shower, and into fresh clothes, and we eat in full view of the Parthenon. Celie comes out and lays her head in my lap. I stroke her hair, but I try not to look at her because I don't want to cry. "Tomorrow, we're going on an adventure," I tell her.

"I'll pack my things," she says.

That night before we fall asleep, she curls her back up to my chest, syncs our heartbeats. "Mama, is the baby okay?"

"No, sweetheart," I say. "The baby is gone."

Tears fall down my cheek and cascade onto hers. We lay there quietly, looking out at the Parthenon with a full moon behind it. After a time, Celie reaches for my hand, and pulls it around her belly. "Mama," she says, "remember when Daddy accidentally threw my blanket away?"

"Yes, I do."

"And remember when you said I could squeeze your hand whenever I missed BlanK-it?"

"Yes, I do."

"Mama, when you miss the baby, you can squeeze me." And, I do.

The sun is hovering over the cliff's edge, as if waiting for us before it disappears for the night to come. We are all somber. Tina walks into the water at the cove until it is knee-deep and plops herself down to cool off. Celie stays happily near the edge, throwing a stick to Tartan, and Yiannis leans against a tree in the shade.

I'm numb and lost in a sea of thoughts. I walk to the water's edge and slip off my pants, and legs. I scoot out on my rear until the water is deep enough to swim, and then I swim like a frog out into the blue. My stumps ache in the cool water. Farther and farther I swim out into the liquid world. On the shoreline is a reality in which I have just lost a child, so I keep swimming into the expanse.

Abruptly, the waves are no longer gentle. Neither are they rough, but they are too much for me while I am still so weak. A small wave smacks me in the face, and I choke for air. The water fills my nose, and I start below the surface.

Under the water, everything slows. I drift down and run my hands over my still-swollen stomach. I open my eyes, and the darkness is blinding. My lungs feel as if they are about to explode. I drift and drift, and the light at the surface grows dim. I begin to wave my arms frantically, paddling toward the sky. I remember Celie and fear seizes my heart. I rush to the surface, soaking up the air.

I am angry, irrational. Poseidon, I think, you can't have him yet. Frantic, I splash through the waters looking for my son's body, but instead I find sapphire swirls, a numbing wind, an aqueous prison, a sinking sun.

He is gone.

Floating on one's back in the sea and looking up at the sky is like the place just before death. You're grounded in one world, which is holding you up at the surface, ready to launch you into the dizzying hereafter. The cool air on your face and breasts is welcome.

When I died at sixteen, I was hovering, floating just like this, but instead of a sky above me, I saw the jungles of Vietnam below—every plant and vine seemed to have a divine purpose. I wanted to stay and explore the resplendence—it felt as if there were mysteries of healing there, save for the soldiers, the war of my childhood, the war of the season, always a war. I run for the light, but this time is different. This is emotional death, and now I have to consider whether or not to let my body accompany my broken heart. I drift in the undulations while some ethereal limb, a part of me, floats off into the realm of the unknown. And because in life, the two are connected, my body feels the loss, as severe as any amputation. Some ancient cry bursts out from me, so deep and loud that I frighten myself. If any of the gods will hear me, I think, I don't want to run toward the light this time. I'm tired of running.

And then, Yiannis' arm is around my chest, and he carries me ashore, and Tina wraps me in a towel, kisses me gently on the forehead, and Celie places herself firmly in the hollow where the baby had been—they all treat the wound with grace. That night, after they all tuck me in, I lie there in the dark, thinking of how we must give what we can when we are able and be willing to take what we need when we are not. This is how the wounded heal each other. If we give less than we are able or take more than we need, wounds fester, then kill.

Days of sleep and sorrow follow. And it is there, in a little pine bed by the sea, that I grant mercy to those wounded who have wounded me and pray that I am extending the same. In that bed, I think of the pain the woman who bore me must have endured upon leaving me behind. I think of the mother who raised me, and I do not replay the hard and cruel moments of her love. I remember the simple story of the day that she chose me to be her daughter—how when she first came to see if we were compatible, she said I was wearing a pink, lace dress. My fine, blonde hair was combed neatly to the side. I kept pulling my socks off, and she said she wanted me immediately. She cried when they had to leave me behind. A week later she received the phone call that the paperwork went through and that she and my father could come and pick me up at their earliest convenience.

They came immediately, with the whole of my extended family back at my parent's house waiting to meet me. At the agency, they hurriedly signed papers, and when a woman finally brought me out, I had a runny nose, a full diaper and a dirty onesie. My parents stopped at a department store and bought me a honey-colored dress and patent, white-leather shoes, and lace socks, which I pulled off.

I think of the fact that for nearly one hundred days while I lay fighting for life and limb, my mother almost never left my side. I cannot imagine her suffering. I cannot imagine the extra suffering I put her through with my hard, unapologetic ways. Raw wounds rarely heal one another, but we loved each other with what we had.

Every child has their own spirit, divine purpose—to try and tame that natural instinct will only bring sorrow. When you are a mother, you do what you are able with the tools that you have. You do what you have to do with a dead infant in your arms. You do what you have to do with a dying, unruly teenage daughter. You do what you have to do when your child is ready to fly. You do not stop loving them, you just let them go.

One evening, there's a riotous card game going on in the living room. The laughter is infectious, and it's interfering with my pity. I shout from the little pine bed, and when Tina comes in to check on me, she stubs her toe on the bed post.

"Fuck, fuck, fuck," she shouts over and over, hopping about on one foot, wincing in pain.

And then I lose it. I cannot remember the last time I laughed. I laugh as hard as all my cries in one. Celie comes running into the bedroom and stands in a sun spoke that's pouring in from the balcony, glowing like a cherub.

Between spasms of laughing, I ask Celie to get Tina some ice. When the throbbing subsides, Tina sits on the bed, holds up her foot, and says, "At last, we've turned the corner, even if it's at my expense. I have to be back in Athens soon to teach. What are you going to do?"

I take her hand. "I can't go back to the village now," I say.

"You don't have to go back there," she replies.

"But we have belongings there, and our friends."

"You can always come back," Tina says. "Why don't you go back to America and finish up your degree? I'm supposed to make sure you do that, after all."

The war in the Middle East is nowhere near ending. The wars never seem to end. Expedition Athena is no longer safe. And though I do not want to leave Greece, it will break my heart and pride to return to that village, so a few days later, I book the last room left on a passage back to New York from England on the QE2's final transatlantic voyage.

The wind is warm, a low, loud roar. This ship bobs and plows her way through ancient territory. I thought I'd heard the captain announce earlier that tonight we would be passing the latitude and longitude where the *Titanic* sank, although the actual spot was something akin to one hundred nautical miles north. Someone said that it was customary for the crew and passengers to throw flowers, whirling down in the dark, at the hour that it finally sank. I can't remember the facts at all because I've been mildly drunk since embarkation.

The bartender is nice. They call him Gin. He is Lithuanian, and his real name is Gïnter. He says that the umlaut gives a lot of folks fits, particularly drunken Brits, and Gin seems to fit his occupation just fine. I've be-friended a Canadian couple at the bar. He's a banker. She changes clothes, a lot. They always save me and Celie a seat. One night after dinner, we go to the club deck, and Donovan Leitch is there—the Scottish troubadour who sings "Mellow Yellow." I remembered the chorus. Donovan Leitch's hair is dyed a mellow yellow, and he looks to be tucked a little tight. He makes me so sad, whispering past glories into my ear on the dance floor and smelling like cheap cologne, that I start crying while we dance, and have to excuse myself.

I'm sitting on the floor of a starboard balcony from which I thought we were going to drop flowers. There's nothing here but wind and stars and the ship and me. A deckhand approaches and I ask him for a lighter. He's the only human I've seen in the last hour. He crouches down close to me to light my cigarette in the breeze. "Thanks," I say when the cherry lights up. "Did I miss the *Titanic*?"

The man tilts his neck back, looking perplexed, as if

he hasn't heard me right. Then he chuckles. "What's your poison, madam?"

"My poison?"

"What are you drinking?"

"Whatever it takes."

"We passed *Titanic* yesterday—this time. Flowers and everything. You missed it." He chuckles again.

I turn my face away from him. My face is now against the rail, and I've one arm flopped over the side. I probably look more drunk than I am, and then I start crying, again. I begin to wonder if I am ever going to stop.

The deckhand must have felt bad because he crouched down again and said, "Madam, you ain't missed everything. You're looking straight at Halifax, though you cannot see it. Of course, you cannot see it in the day neither. It's too far away. But!" he says, handing me the lighter for keeps. "It is there, right where it's always been. You see?" He walks away, whistling against the wind, and I wonder what his poison might be. Nonetheless, I'll take it—unseen hope from a deckhand. I'll take hope wherever I can find it.

I think about those folks on the *Titanic*, how many of them leapt into their final destination, the cold horror of their coming rest. I think about the folks I met in Bosnia, and those that I could not. I think about the dead of wars. I think of my now dead son. How tempting it is to join them all, how easily my body could flop over this slick, wet rail and be swallowed by the bellowing waves.

The bow wave from this majestic old ship is magnificent and unceasing. I light another cigarette. I could smoke a whole pack, one after the other, I care so little for the body's demise. The expedition failed. I got pregnant and lost a son. And I headed west from Athens and never looked back, never returned to the village that I loved, never even said goodbye. The ability to start anew is a crucial part of survival. It was ingrained in me at birth. I'm a woman without legs, and I'm really good at running.

I could use sleep now, but not against this railing. I've missed the *Titanic*, and I can cautiously say, at this moment, that I'm not quite ready to join its passengers. I sneak back to the room to check on Celie. She wakes when the door opens.

"Mama?" she says, wiping her eyes.

"Come on, baby girl, come with me outside and look at the stars from the middle of the sea." She rolls her sleepy body off the bed and runs into my arms. She gasps for air when the wind hits her on the balcony of the ship. I sit on the deck, and she curls her body into the hollow place, fills it with her goldenness. The stars are heavenly, each one burning the wick at full brilliance. Can you imagine telling a star how it should burn? The wind fills our sails as Celie points out the constellations, as our hearts sync into one with the whole universe. She talks and talks and talks, the joy of this moment palpable through her body, and I can only understand fragments of her elation because the wind is roaring by, then suddenly, she goes limp, and before long, she is snoring against my breast. Even the bliss is exhausting.

I hold my daughter tightly all night, here between wind and water, underneath this constant sky in which a mother and her baby girl are playing the lyre, where instead of being punished, they have chosen to shine. I can still smell my tiny son, and the pain of this loss anchors me back down from the heavens into the depths of the water below, and to all the lost bodies at the bottom of it. It's a moment of cold emptiness and searing intimacy, but how could I ever recognize the beauty of these blazing stars without knowing the way it feels to lose the breath of life, to anchor back toward dust.

Would I do it all again? Would I travel the map of this life with all of its tragic tunnels, the weighty losses and aching scars? In this moment, with the sky above and the sea below, this ship plows on. And this precious child in my arms, with all the love and hope she is—she helps me to heal this vessel, reminds me to handle hers gently, to keep it whole for as long as I'm possibly able. The light of the child makes us all shine brighter.

Yes, I would do it all again—countless times, to the moon and back, the whole universe.

ACKNOWLEDGMENTS

....

Twenty years ago, shortly after I returned from the journey detailed in this book, the poet Eric Trethewey sat with me at a bar one long afternoon and listened to me tell a good portion of this wild tale. As he was getting ready to leave, he grabbed me by the shoulders and said, "You must write this story." So, because of him, a big hole was dug, which I might have filled more quickly had I not birthed him a son and spent the last eleven years of his life loving his difficult ass. He got his thanks in life, and yet, I wish he could hold this book in his hands, just once.

First, the hole was filled with a collection of short stories on top of which I placed plastic flowers. The flowers faded; the dirt was tilled. Then, I poured a novel in the hole and packed it in tight until a kind agent said they would not represent it, but that I should know it was too unbelievable for fiction. It collapsed like a sinkhole. Finally, I filled the hollow with a memoir, and put a large part of me to rest with it.

Then a daisy chain sprouted, starting with Wynn Cooper

who agreed to edit the first iteration, and that led to
Madison Smartt Bell, my agent at Ayesha Pande Literary,
and finally to Sarah Munroe and the rest of the team at
WVU Press who looked at the raw ground, took a soil
sample, and decided it might be worth the risk to see what
grew. I am ever thankful for their guidance in turning a
burial site into fertile ground.

My parents are now dead, but they graced me with their
willingness to talk about painful things near the ends of
their lives and gave me permission to tell our collective
story. I was able to read sections of this book to my father
before he died—it brought us ever closer in his last days. I
wish both of my parents could have held this book in their
hands just once, too.

I'm grateful for my children, who've allowed me to
be open about my life, and therefore, theirs, too, in a
humble effort to provide them with a more fruitful garden.
Hopefully, the book will sell well enough to pay for their
therapy, in whatever form that takes.

Cheers to my tribe of women who always tell me straight,
who have gathered with me at the garden no matter the
season, no matter the state of things—Tina, my compadre
in the metaphorical trenches of this book and life, Lydia,
Trudy, Mickey, and Carmie—Sisters, you make the winters
bearable and the summers full glory!

And to my dear one, Fitzy—thank you for all the water
and dusting and steadfast care—no one can coax a wither-
ing plant back to life and beauty better than you.